HEMINGWAY'S FIRST WAR

in memory of

ALAN DOUGALD McKILLOP
1892-1974
the better teacher

MICHAEL S. REYNOLDS

HEMINGWAY'S FIRST WAR

The Making of *A Farewell to Arms*

BASIL BLACKWELL

Copyright © Princeton University Press 1976

First published in the UK 1987
First published in the USA in paperback 1987

Basil Blackwell Ltd
108 Cowley Road, Oxford, OX4 1JF, UK

Basil Blackwell Inc.
432 Park Avenue South, Suite 1503
New York, NY10016, USA

British Library Cataloguing in Publication Data

Reynolds, Michael S.
  Hemingway's first war: the making of
  A farewell to arms.
  1. Hemingway, Ernest. Farewell to arms $10
  I. Title
  813'.52   PS3515.E37F3   OCLC
  ISBN 0-631-15826-X   16276188

Library of Congress Cataloging in Publication Data

Reynolds, Michael S., 1937–
  Hemingway's first war.
  Reprint. Originally published: Princeton, N.J.:
Princeton University Press, c.1976.
  Bibliography: p.
  Includes index.
  1. Hemingway, Ernest, 1899–1961. A farewell to arms.
  2. World War, 1914–1918—Literature and the war.
  I. Title.
  [PS3515.E37E358 1987]   813'.52   87-20855
  ISBN 0-631-15826-X (pbk.)

Printed in Great Britain by Billing & Sons Ltd, Worcester

CONTENTS

L I S T O F
I L L U S T R A T I O N S

L I S T O F M A P S

ACKNOWLEDGMENTS

This book began as a question, first asked fifteen years ago. Sitting at my library carrel, I reached out of curiosity across the aisle to a collection of scrap books on World War One. The volume I chanced to pick covered the year 1917. It was nothing more than a grade-school tablet into which some careful hand had clipped and pasted news stories of the Great War. There, spread over several pages, was the running account of the Italian disaster at Caporetto. I wondered, as I read it, how closely Hemingway's description of the retreat matched the historical event.

As with all good questions, every answer produced more questions, which led me from Raleigh to St. Petersburg, Washington, Princeton, New York, and Cambridge. Every dead end raised new problems, new questions. Friends who knew of my research finally stopped asking how it was going for fear I would tell them in endless detail. My questions had become an obsession; pursuit was happiness. As in all quests, chance and good fortune have played a major role. There have been many electric moments that would seem sentimental or curious in the retelling. Finally, I have had to admit I can pursue it no further. There are still questions unanswered; it will always be so. Perhaps no good book is ever finished.

In my pursuit I have accumulated debts of kindness that cannot be repaid, only acknowledged. I am deeply indebted to Mary Hemingway, who has kept her trust intact and who has so graciously allowed me to quote from the manuscript material, which is the heart of this book. I am also grateful to Charles Scribner's Sons for permission to quote from *A Farewell to Arms* and from the Perkins-Hemingway correspondence.

I am particularly grateful to Princeton University Press for its faith in publishing this book and particularly to Mrs. Arthur Sherwood and Ms. Miriam Brokaw, whose editorial experience and understanding have made pleasant what might have been painful.

Over the several years of this book's progress, I have received counsel, aid, and direction from several people, without whose encouragement I might have stopped short. I wish to thank: the School of Liberal Arts at North Carolina State University and its Department of English for support in research and typing; Arlin Turner, who forced me to become a scholar; Bernard Duffey, who made me think; Louis Budd, who tempered my zeal; and Richard Walser, who never gave me bad advice.

Whatever this book's merits, their basis is primary data, without which all would be speculation. For their assistance I must thank: the Library of Congress, photography and map divisions; Mrs. Lillian Kidwell and the Red Cross National Archives; the manuscript divisions of the Firestone Library at Princeton and the Houghton Library at Harvard; Mrs. Agnes Stanfield, who was there and remembered; the John F. Kennedy Library and Jo August, who is a scholar's librarian; and the interlibrary loan division of the D. H. Hill Library, NCSU, for tracking down my strange requests.

For reasons that they know, my special thanks to Susan Lomax, Lydia Bronte, Cecilia Wan, and Kathryn Hardee.

For years of patience, even when I lost mine, I thank my wife, Ann, whose questions, criticism, and insights are very much a part of this book. For reading all five drafts without losing interest and for understanding my compulsion, she fulfills the poet's definition:

> A gode womman is mannys blys,
> There her love right and stedfast ys.

There remain two people whose contribution cannot be easily measured:

Raymond Douglas Reynolds, my father, who taught me the language of maps and the love of research. If I have been persistent in my obsession, I learned it from a master.

Carlos Baker, whose aid, generosity, criticism, concern, and encouragement have made this a far better book than it would have been. No matter how the game changes, he has defined by example the standard of excellence.

MICHAEL S. REYNOLDS

North Carolina State University
Raleigh, N.C.
June, 1975

SECTION ONE

1928-1930: The Writer at Work

Going Back

So we walked along through the street where I saw my very good friend killed, . . . and it all seemed a very sad business. I had tried to recreate something for my wife and had failed utterly. The past was as dead as a busted victrola record. Chasing yesterdays is a bum show—and if you have to prove it go back to your old front.—Ernest Hemingway "A Veteran Visits Old Front" (*TDS*, July 22, 1922)

When Frederic Henry, hero of Hemingway's *A Farewell to Arms*, lived in the house "that looked across the river and the plain to the mountains," it was the late summer of 1915. Italy had just entered the European War, and Ernest Hemingway had just turned sixteen in upper Michigan. In the spring of 1918, Catherine Barkley died in childbirth in Lausanne, Switzerland; in April, 1918, Ernest Hemingway drew his last pay check from the *Kansas City Star* and left for his own war experience in northern Italy.[1]

When he reached Italy in 1918 for his shortlived tour as a Red Cross ambulance driver, the Italian front bore no resemblance to the front at which Frederic had served for two years as an ambulance driver in the Italian army (Map 1). In June, 1918, American Red Cross Ambulance Section Four, to which Hemingway was assigned, was stationed at Schio in the Dolomite foothills. Although there was a major Austrian offensive in June, there was little action at Schio. Hemingway drove Section Four ambulances

[1] Carlos Baker, *Ernest Hemingway: A Life Story* (New York: Scribner's, 1969), pp. 20-38.

3

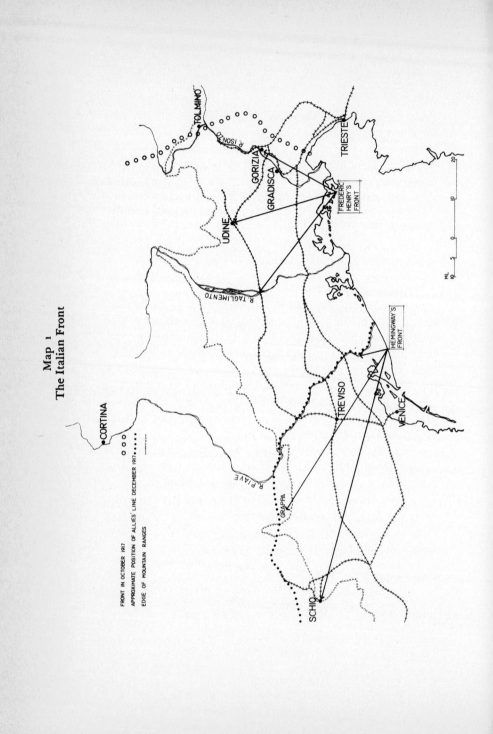

Map 1
The Italian Front

CORTINA

FRONT IN OCTOBER 1917
APPROXIMATE POSITION OF ALLIES' LINE DECEMBER 1917
EDGE OF MOUNTAIN RANGES

TOLMINO
R. ISONZO
GORIZIA
GRADISCA
TRIESTE
UDINE
FREDERIC HENRY'S FRONT
R. TAGLIAMENTO
HEMINGWAY'S FRONT
TREVISO
VENICE
R. PIAVE
GRAPPA
SCHIO

ML 10 5 0 10 20

for only three weeks. In July he asked to be transferred to the canteen operation along the more active Piave river front. At Fossalta di Piave, on July 8, 1918, he was blown up by an Austrian trench mortar. He had been in the war zone for about one month, and he was not to return to it actively in that war.[2]

Carlos Baker has remarked that Hemingway was acutely conscious of *place*, and that he was painfully accurate in his geographic descriptions.[3] Mary Hemingway has described the careful checking of street names and distances that Hemingway put into *A Moveable Feast*.[4] Hemingway himself said that his concern was for "the way it was," which he loosely defined as "the people, the places, and how the weather was." Against this concern it is difficult to balance his lack of firsthand knowledge of the Italian front of 1915-1917. He had not seen the Tagliamento river when he wrote *A Farewell to Arms*; he had not walked the Venetian plain between Codroipo and Latisana. It was not until 1948 that he saw Udine.[5] He may never have seen Gorizia, the Isonzo river, Plava, or the Bainsizza plateau; he certainly had not seen them when he wrote the novel. His return trip to Fossalta di Piave in 1922 and his skiing trip at Cortina d'Ampezzo in 1923 did not take him to the terrain of the novel. His 1927 trip to Italy with Guy Hickok did not cover the war zone of 1915-1917.[6] Not only had Hemingway not experienced the military engagements in which Frederic Henry takes part, but he had not seen the terrain of Books One and Three of *A Farewell to Arms*. Yet the geography is perfectly accurate and done with the clarity that made its author famous for his descriptions of place.

Because the Caporetto section (Book Three) is so power-

[2] *Ibid.*, pp. 41-56.
[3] Carlos Baker, *Hemingway: The Writer as Artist*, 4th ed. (Princeton: Princeton University Press, 1972), p. 49.
[4] Philip Young, *Ernest Hemingway: A Reconsideration* (New York: Harcourt Brace, 1966), p. 290.
[5] Carlos Baker, "Hemingway's Italia," *NYTBR* (Jan. 23, 1966), p. 2.
[6] Baker, *A Life Story*, p. 184.

fully written, most critics have confined their remarks about military descriptions to this portion of the book, being content to make generalizations about the remainder of the military activity in the novel. Book Three has been widely recognized for its narrative excellence, and early reviewers like Malcolm Cowley, Percy Hutchinson, and H. S. Canby responded to Hemingway's power in this section.[7] Canby called the description of the retreat a "masterly piece of *reporting*" [my emphasis].[8] Yet none of these men had served on the Italian front and should not be expected to notice minor inaccuracies if they existed.

Later critics, more knowledgeable about Hemingway's biography, knew that he had not participated in the retreat; but they also knew that he had covered the Greek retreat in the Greco-Turkish War (1922) as a journalist. It was an easy assumption that Hemingway had transposed his Greek experience to the Friulian plain of northern Italy: steady rain, muddy roads, stumbling refugees. What this assumption fails to account for is the considerable amount of specific detail in Book Three of *A Farewell to Arms* that has nothing to do with muddy roads or refugees.

One would expect European readers to be more critical. Yet one French reviewer wrote: "The one aspect of the last war which has least interested writers is the defeat. . . . There has been need for an American witness on the Alpine front who could reveal to us, in its abject horror, the Italian rout near Caporetto: . . . If Hemingway has not dedicated all his book to this debacle, . . . one can believe that he had to obey autobiographical motives."[9]

Italian critics, some of whom took part in the Caporetto retreat, were unable to find any fault with Hemingway's

[7] Malcolm Cowley, "Not Yet Demobilized," *NYHTBR* (Oct. 6, 1929). p. 6; Percy Hutchinson, "Love and War in the Pages of Mr. Hemingway," *NYTBR* (Sept. 29, 1929), p. 5; Henry S. Canby "Chronicle and Comment," *Bookman*, 70 (Feb., 1930), p. 644.
[8] Canby, p. 644.
[9] Denis Marion, "L'Adieu aux Armes," *Nouvelle Revue Francaise*, 41 (Oct., 1933), p. 632.

history or geography. The Italian fascist government under Mussolini found the account of Caporetto so painful, and presumably so accurate, that *A Farewell to Arms* was banned in Italy until after World War Two. In 1930 one Italian reviewer saw the novel as unvarnished autobiography: "[The novel] narrates autobiographically his experience as an officer on the Italian front after he, although a foreigner, enlisted in our army as a volunteer, more through the desire to do like everyone else (he was already in Italy as an architecture student) than through ideological dedication; and then of his flight as a deserter after Caporetto . . . every page of the books resembles a sheet torn from a notebook. . . . One hears the eulogy of the Duke of Aosta pronounced in words so banal and nasty as to move anyone who remembers the Duke and those years at all well to protest. . . . *the time is objectively precise, with references to dates and 'historical' episodes,* but it has no color, no duration . . . diary composition comes to mind . . . rather too scrupulous and unified." [My emphasis][10]

Twenty-five years later another Italian critic, reading the book more sympathetically and more nostalgically, was no less convinced of the historic and geographic accuracy: "Four-fifths of the work unfolds in Northern Italy, in Milan and above all among the hills, mountains and plains of the Veneto which are particularly dear to my heart. *Every landscape evoked in the now famous novel, every place cited, is familiar to me. . . . The novel . . . evokes the climate of the first two years of the war until the disaster of Caporetto with extraordinary vivacity. . . . All that his protagonist narrates has an undeniable sound of authenticity. . . .* After the intoxication of the days in May *(which he does not mention but in which he* [Hemingway] *certainly must have taken part to be led to enlist and leave for the front during his stay in Italy)* he found himself in a country in

10 Umberto Morra, "*A Farewell to Arms* di Ernest Hemingway," *Solaria*, 2 (1930), rpt. in *Antologia di Solaria*, ed. Enzo Siciliano (Milan: Editore Lerici, 1958), pp. 377-380.

which the war was not felt but only submitted to as a ca-
lamitous circumstance . . . *this actually was . . . the climate
of Italy between the summer of 1915 and the autumn
of 1917. The picture painted by Hemingway is exact. . . .
one who wishes to know what the defeat was like in the
minds of officers and soldiers of the Second Army after Caporetto can read* A FAREWELL TO ARMS. Perhaps in no other
book are the tragic days relived with such intensity. . . .
Only one who truly loves the country, who has suffered
there and lived there intensely can describe the Venetian
countryside, or speak of the disaster of Caporetto as Ernest
Hemingway has done." [My emphasis][11]

In 1954 Alberto Rossi, who had collaborated on several
translations of Hemingway novels into Italian, reviewed
Charles Fenton's *The Apprenticeship of Ernest Hemingway*.
Rossi reminded his Italian readers that Hemingway's considerable talents are above all "his ability to present a situation as actually lived with a few well-chosen touches; one
tends instinctively to identify the character who narrates
with the author himself, and thus to attribute to the author
the intention of affirming, as authentic and experienced by
him, all the details of his own story." But Rossi had great
difficulty in believing that Hemingway had not taken part
in the retreat from Caporetto: "That the work was in effect
one of imagination and not of history, however evident this
seems, was not an affirmation which could satisfy everyone's
curiosity." He was perplexed by the accuracy he could not
account for biographically: "It is no less evident that for
certain parts of that novel his imagination was not working
on data of direct experience; and among these is the impressive evocation of the retreat."[12]

Even after Malcolm Cowley, in the introduction to the

[11] Giacomo Antonini, *"Addio alle Armi* Venticinque Anni Dopo,"
La Fiera Letteraria, 9, no. 1 (March 21, 1954), pp. 1-2.
[12] Alberto Rossi, "Ernest Hemingway e la guerra italiana," *La Nuova
Stampa*, Anno x, num. 261 (Nov. 2, 1954), p. 3.

Portable Hemingway, pointed out that the author had not taken part in the Caporetto retreat, American critics failed to question Hemingway's accuracy. The main stream of Hemingway criticism has followed either Carlos Baker into romantic and biographic criticism or Philip Young into psychological analyses, all of which were encouraged by the virile public image Hemingway cultivated. One need only to read through the massive bibliography of Hemingway criticism to see how limited most second- and third-generation criticism has become and how debilitating it has been for the novels.[13]

As early as 1922, Hemingway had begun to formulate a method of dealing with reality. In a feature story for the *Toronto Daily Star,* "A Veteran Visits Old Front," he told how depressing it was to return to the scene of battles he had taken part in, for the country was so changed that it ruined the memory. It would have been better to have visited a battle site he had not known: "Go to someone else's front if you want to. *There your imagination will help you out and you may be able to picture the things that happened*" [my emphasis].[14] This same idea appears in the deleted coda to "Big Two-Hearted River" (c. 1924):

> *The only writing that was any good was what you made up, what you imagined. . . .* You had to digest life and then create your own people. . . . Nick in the stories was never himself. He had made him up. Of course he'd never seen an Indian woman having a baby. That was what made it good. [My emphasis][15]

In a 1935 *Esquire* article Hemingway gave a somewhat fuller statement on the point:

[13] Audre Hanneman, *Ernest Hemingway: A Comprehensive Bibliography* (Princeton: Princeton University Press, 1967).

[14] Ernest Hemingway, "A Veteran Visits Old Front," *Toronto Daily Star* (July 22, 1922), p. 7.

[15] Quoted in Baker, *A Life Story,* pp. 131-132.

Good writing is true writing. If a man is making a story up it will be true in proportion to the amount of knowledge of life he has and how *conscientious* he is; so that when he makes something up it is as it truly would be. . . . Imagination is the one thing beside honesty that a good writer must have, the more he learns from experience the more truly he can imagine. *If he gets so he can imagine truly enough people will think that the things he relates all really happened and that he is just reporting.* [My emphasis][16]

In 1948, when he wrote his own introduction for an illustrated edition of *A Farewell to Arms*, Hemingway made no pretense of having experienced the historical events of the novel firsthand:

I remember living in the book and making up what happened in it every day. Making the country and the people and the things that happened I was happier than I had ever been. . . . Finding you were able to make something up; to create truly enough so that it made you happy to read it.[17]

And in 1958, when he was interviewed by the *Paris Review*, Hemingway restated his position with the same simplicity he had used in 1922:

Q: Have you ever described any type of situation of which you had no personal knowledge?
A: That is a strange question. . . . A writer, if he is any

---

16 Ernest Hemingway, "Monologue to the Maestro: A High Seas Letter," originally published in *Esquire*, 4 (October, 1935), 21, 174a, 174b; rpt. in *By-Line: Ernest Hemingway*, ed. William White (New York: Scribner's, 1967), p. 215.

17 Hemingway, "Introduction," *A Farewell to Arms*, illustrated ed. (New York: Scribner's, 1948), pp. vii-viii.

good does not describe. *He invents or makes out of*
his knowledge personal and impersonal.
[My emphasis][18]

Over a thirty-six-year span, Hemingway's attitude toward
his profession remained constant on the point of "making
it up." Yet no one ever took him very seriously, for he had
been typed as an autobiographic writer when he published
The Sun Also Rises. His statements about invented action
on the basis of knowledge "personal and impersonal" appeared either simple-minded or some sort of ruse. They
were neither.

In his terse disciplinary sketches written in 1922-1923,
Hemingway had already developed an objective style that
treated the experience of others as his own. Of the eighteen
sketches, called "chapters," collected in the 1924 edition of
in our time, eight were based on second-hand information.
Two of the sketches were based on the war experiences of
his British friend, Captain E. E. Dorman-Smith, at the fighting around Mons. Another (Chapter 16) described the gor-
ing and death of the matador Maera. At the time Hemingway had never seen a bullfight, and Maera was very much
alive. Hemingway based his description on conversations
with Mike Strater and Gertrude Stein. Chapter 6, which
describes the inglorious execution of the deposed Greek
cabinet ministers, was based on a newspaper clipping. The
ninth chapter, which describes the shooting of the cigar-
store bandits, was based on a story in the *Kansas City Star*
from Nov. 19, 1917. The hanging of Sam Cardinella (Chapter 17) probably came from either police-station or city-
room gossip from the Kansas City days. The description of
the King of Greece in his garden (Chapter 18) was based
on information related to Hemingway by an acquaintance

[18] George Plimpton, "The Art of Fiction, xxi: Ernest Hemingway,"
Paris Review, 5 (Spring, 1958), p. 85.

who had an informal interview with the king.[19] From the beginning Hemingway felt free to use second-hand sources.

After Hemingway showered Stephen Crane with praise in his introduction to *Men at War*, critics began to note thematic and structural similarities between *The Red Badge of Courage* and *A Farewell to Arms*. What was carefully ignored by the critics was the reason why Hemingway said he admired Crane's novel:

> Crane wrote [*The Red Badge of Courage*] before he had ever seen any war. But he had read contemporary accounts, had heard the old soldiers, they were not so old then, talk, and above all he had seen Matthew Brady's wonderful photographs. Creating his story out of this material he wrote that great boy's dream of war that was to be truer to how war is than any war the boy who wrote it would ever live to see. It is one of the finest books in our literature and I include it entire because it is all as much of one piece as a great poem is.[20]

Hemingway's praise is neither for Crane's structure nor for his theme; the praise is for the technique and the verity. In 1928, when he was writing his first war novel, Hemingway already knew about Crane's research method in *The Red Badge of Courage*. While working on the *Transatlantic Review* in 1924, Hemingway served as a sub-editor under Ford Madox Ford. Ford had known Crane during the Brede Manor days in England, and later Ford both wrote and lectured on the young American writer. One of the things that Ford knew about Crane, and that was not

19 See Baker, *Writer as Artist*, p. 12; Baker, *A Life Story*, pp. 108-110; M. S. Reynolds, "Two Hemingway Sources for 'In Our Time,'" *Studies in Short Fiction*, 9 (Winter, 1972), pp. 81-84.

20 Ernest Hemingway ed., *Men at War* (New York: Crown Publishers, 1942), p. xvii.

public knowledge, was the way in which Crane had re-searched his war novel. During Hemingway's association with Ford in 1924, he must have heard the anecdote, prob-ably more than once. Crane's research methods that Hem-ingway chose to praise—reading histories, talking to vet-erans, and looking at pictures—were the same methods that Hemingway used on *A Farewell to Arms*.

As early as 1922, Hemingway had already done sufficient historical reading to pose as an expert on a war in which he had served only briefly and that he later admitted he did not understand. When he wrote his *Toronto Daily Star* fea-ture, "A Veteran Visits Old Front" (July, 1922), he created the flat tone of the seasoned campaigner, alluding to many more events than he had experienced:

I remember . . . looking out the window down at the road where the arc light was making a dim light through the rain. It was the same road that the battalions marched along through the white dust in 1916. They were the Brigata Ancona, the Brigata Como, the Brigata Tuscana and ten others brought down from the Carso, to check the Austrian offensive that was breaking through the mountain wall of the Trentino and beginning to spill down the valleys that led to the Venetian and Lombardy plains. They were good troops in those days and they marched through the dust of early summer, broke the offensive along the Gallo-Asiago-Canove line, and died in the mountain gullies, in the pine woods on the Trentino slopes, hunting cover on the desolate rocks and pitched out in the soft-melting early summer snow of the Pasubio.

It was the same old road that some of the same brigades marched along through the dust in June 1918, being rushed to the Piave to stop another offensive.

Their best men were dead on the rocky Carso in the
fighting around Goritzia,[21] on Mount San Gabrielle, on
Grappa, and in all the places where men died that
nobody ever heard about.

When he wrote those words Hemingway had never seen
the Carso, Gorizia, or Mount San Gabrielle. When the road
turned dust at Schio in 1916, he was preparing for his
senior year in high school. The journalist must always be
the expert, and he had already developed a keen sense of
the insider's information. He had learned that hard facts
create an immediate sense of authenticity. Those were not
just soldiers on any road—they were specific brigades who
died at specific places. In order to write this article, Hemingway had done extensive reading on the art of war, which
he continued throughout his life. He may not have known
in 1922 how much he would need that reading in 1928 when
he came to write *A Farewell to Arms*, but in the manuscript
of the novel, historical facts, dates, places, and events roll
from the writer's pencil with facility and accuracy.

In that 1922 visit to Schio, Hemingway realized a truth
that he passed on to his readers and that he remembered
when he tried to make fictional sense of his own war
experience:

Don't go back to visit the old front. If you have
pictures in your head of something that happened in
the night in the mud at Paschendaele, or of the first
wave working up the slope of Vimy, do not try and
go back and verify them. It is no good. The front is
different from the way it used to be. . . . Go to someone
else's front if you want to. There your imagination will

21 There is an Italian spelling for the town: *Gorizia*; and an Austrian
spelling: *Goritzia*. In 1922, Hemingway used the Austrian spelling. In
the first draft and holograph revisions of the AFTA manuscript, he
used the Austrian spelling throughout. The change to the Italian
spelling occurred in the typescript. By the time the novel was serialized in *Scribner's Magazine* the spelling was *Gorizia*.

help you out and you may be able to picture the things
that happened. . . . The past was as dead as a busted
victrola record. Chasing yesterdays is a bum show—
and if you have to prove it go back to your old front.[22]

If he functions in the realist/naturalist tradition, a writer
is always chasing yesterdays. In writing *A Farewell to
Arms*, however, Hemingway went back to someone else's
front and recreated the experience from books, maps, and
firsthand sources. It is his only novel set on terrain with
which he did not have personal experience; in it, his imagination, aided by military histories, has recreated the
Austro-Italian front of 1915-1917 more vividly than any
other writer.

Hemingway, the public man, may have been just as much
of a romantic as some readers would see him, and many of
his plots may have smelled of the museums, as Gertrude
Stein thought. But as an artist, Hemingway was able to approach his material in those early years with an objectivity
that never allowed personal experience or friendships to
interfere with his fiction. Like most twentieth-century in-
novators, he found himself his own best subject, but to mistake his art for his biography is to mistake illusion for
reality. In *Green Hills of Africa* no reader can believe that
the dialogue is a reportorial account of what was actually
said, or that there is no artistry in Hemingway's arrangement
of the action. Even in *A Moveable Feast*, Hemingway warns
the reader: "If the reader prefers, this book may be regarded
as fiction. But there is always some chance that such a book
of fiction may throw some light on what has been written
as fact."[23]

To read any of Hemingway's fiction as biography is always dangerous, but to read *A Farewell to Arms* in this

[22] Hemingway. "A Veteran Visits Old Front," *TDS* (July 22, 1922).
p. 7.
[23] Hemingway. Preface. *A Moveable Feast* (New York: Scribner's.
1964).

manner is to misread the book. Hemingway himself was particularly anxious, during those early years, for Scribner's to keep biographical statements about him out of print. In letters to his editor, Max Perkins, he urged that the critics and readers be allowed to make up their own lies (Feb. 14, 1927). He belittled his own war experiences, telling Perkins that the medals had been given to him simply because he was an American attached to the Italian army. One medal, he insisted, was awarded for action on Monte Maggiore when he was three hundred kilometers away in a hospital at the time. He did not want anyone to think him a faker, a liar, or a fool (Feb. 19, 1929). Perkins agreed to correct misinformation that Scribner's had unknowingly given out to the media and to restrain the publicity department in the future, remarking that usually authors were so intent on such publicity that it had not occurred to him that Hemingway might be sensitive on the point.

Like most of his central characters, Hemingway in 1928-1929 preferred to exist in the present tense, with as little reference to the past as possible, particularly his private past. Later, when biographical critics like Fenton and Young began to probe into his private life, Hemingway resented it bitterly. In a letter to Carlos Baker, he said that biographies of living writers were destructive in several ways. Because all writers wrote out of their own experience, the premature biographer was nothing more than a spoiler, ruining experiences that the writer might have turned into fiction. All writers, he insisted, write about living people; that is, they use them for the base upon which they build their fictional characters. Biographical critics were forcing him to create characters no longer credible because he had become so conscious of covering up the original.[24]

Readers have always wanted to see the heroes as projections of their author, and critics have generally promoted

[24] Hemingway letter to Carlos Baker. June 11, 1953.

the parallel. Hemingway, however, in the Twenties never encouraged the parallelism. He admitted to using real prototypes for characters, like Cohn in *The Sun Also Rises*, but he felt that most of the characters he used did not read books.[25] Unfortunately, *The Sun Also Rises* was read as a thinly veiled who's who of Paris and Pamplona, and Hemingway was never able to convince his critics afterwards that he did not do this all the time or that his central character was not himself. In 1926, he told Scott Fitzgerald that in spite of what he and Zelda always thought, "Cat in the Rain" was not a story about Hemingway and Hadley. He explained that the two characters were a Havard graduate and his wife whom he had met in Genoa.[26]

To read *A Farewell to Arms* as biography is to believe that Hemingway learned nothing from *The Torrents of Spring* and *The Sun Also Rises*, where the use of real people had caused him considerable difficulty. In the correspondence with Maxwell Perkins during the galley-proof stage of *The Sun Also Rises*, Perkins asked him to make numerous small changes to avoid libel suits. After much bargaining, Hemingway obscured references to Glenway Wescott, Hilaire Belloc, Joseph Hergesheimer, and Henry James. In *The Sun Also Rises* there is still a passing remark about "Henry's bicycle," which in the manuscript referred to Henry James's apocryphal groin injury similar to the one of Jake Barnes. Perkins advised Hemingway: "As for Henry James, you know how we feel about it. . . . this town and Boston are full of people who knew him and who cannot regard him as you do, i.e. as an historical character. There are four right in this office who were his friends. . . . Then as to the fact of a groin injury, I have inquired into it and it is at most, extremely doubtful. Van Wyck Brooks who questioned everyone who knew James, does not believe it, nor anyone here. There are a variety of rumors, and many ob-

25 *Ibid.*
26 Hemingway letter to Scott Fitzgerald, Feb., 1926.

vious lies, but no certainty."[27] Hemingway removed James's name, finally admitting that it was a mistake to put real people in a book. He vowed not to make the same mistake again. That same year, 1926, John Dos Passos criticized Hemingway's use of actual people and names in his writing. Hemingway agreed with Dos Passos. He explained that in *Torrents of Spring* he was satirizing that type of writing, but concluded that it was still a bad thing to do.[28]

When Hemingway began the holograph manuscript of *A Farewell to Arms* in the spring of 1928, he consciously avoided actual names and people wherever he could. He could not altogether eliminate prominent names in an historical novel, but people like King Emmanuel and the Duke of Aosta are mentioned only in passing and are kept well offstage. The central characters were based on real people, but they were not meant to be those people. Hemingway used people he knew as models much as a painter will use a model. Frederic Henry is not Ernest Hemingway at the Italian front, for Frederic is no nineteen-year-old novice. Catherine Barkley may possess some of the physical features of a nurse in Milan but she also resembles several other women Hemingway had known.

Guy Hickok, who read the novel in manuscript, recognized something of Hemingway's second wife, Pauline, in the character of Catherine: "How is Pauline as a blonde? She talks a lot like Catherine as a brunette. Hennaed-up she would be Catherine if you could stretch her up height-wise a few inches."[29]

Scott Fitzgerald, however, was determined to see Ernest doing the same sort of novel he had done in *The Sun Also Rises*: "You are seeing him Frederic in a sophisticated way as now you see yourself then but you're still seeing her as you did in 1917 through a 19-year-old's eyes—in consequence unless you make her a bit fatuous occasionally the

27 Perkins letter to Hemingway, July 20, 1926.
28 Hemingway to Dos Passos, Feb. 16, 1927.
29 Guy Hickok to Hemingway, July 26, 1929.

contrast jars—either the writer is a simple fellow or she is Elenora Duse disguised as a Red Cross nurse. In one moment you expect her to prophesy the second battle of the Marne—as you probably did then."[30]

Apparently Hemingway had discussed the plot of the novel with Fitzgerald before he began writing it, but he did not let the older author criticize the manuscript as he had done with *The Sun Also Rises*. Fitzgerald did not see the war novel until it was in typescript. Yet it is interesting to note that Fitzgerald assumes that Hemingway was in Italy in 1917 and that the experience of the book is largely autobiographical. Although Hemingway did not correct Fitzgerald's assumption, neither did he encourage anyone to read the novel as autobiography. The best part of the novel, he later told Perkins, was invented.

[30] Scott Fitzgerald to Hemingway, undated, 1929.

The Writing of the Novel

Each day I read the book through from the beginning to the point where I went on writing and each day I stopped when I was still going good and when I knew what would happen next. . . . finding you were able to make something up; to create truly enough so that it made you happy to read it; and to do this every day you worked was something that gave me a greater pleasure than any I had ever known. Beside it nothing else mattered.—Ernest Hemingway, 1948 (Introduction to *A Farwell to Arms*)

On March 17, 1928, Hemingway wrote his editor at Scribner's, telling him that he was at work on two manuscripts. Forty thousand words were completed on a "modern Tom Jones" novel, but he was not sure that he knew enough to finish it. The second manuscript had begun as a short story but was going better than he had expected.[1] By April 21, he had set aside the "Tom Jones" novel indefinitely; the short story had grown to several thousand words.[2] Still untitled, the "short story" expanded over the next four months until it became *A Farewell to Arms*.

On April 26, with 108 pages of manuscript in rough draft, Hemingway had hopes of finishing the novel before the end of June. The completed first draft ran to 650 manuscript pages, apparently much longer than Hemingway anticipated in April. Evidence indicates that he was not working from a plot outline and that in April he did not have the

[1] Hemingway to Perkins, March 17, 1928.
[2] Hemingway to Perkins, April 21, 1928.

final version of the novel in mind. Twenty years later, he remembered "living in the book and making up what happened in it every day."[3] The first 45 pages of the published novel were in draft at the end of April; Frederic Henry had just been blown up at Plava. From that point through Frederic's recuperative summer in Milan, Hemingway was on very sure ground, working out of firsthand experience. If the novel was to be finished in two months, Hemingway must have envisioned a shorter and certainly different version of the story.

On the basis of the first 108 pages of draft, it is interesting to speculate how a shorter version of the novel might have developed. Hemingway had carefully set Frederic's wounding in the spring offensive of 1917. His own experience on the Italian front was in the summer of 1918. To use the 1917 setting with the historical accuracy that he demanded, he had to do a considerable amount of research. The only structural reason for the 1917 setting was the Italian disaster at Caporetto and the humiliating retreat that followed. During the Twenties, Hemingway had become fascinated with Caporetto, and he must have intended to use the retreat when he began the "story." Internal evidence supports this theory. Frederic Henry serves in the Italian Second Army, which was the only unit that experienced widespread desertions during the retreat. The bridge crossing at Codroipo on the Tagliamento river was the only place that executions of Italian officers took place, and it was at Codroipo that the Italian Second Army crossed the river.

On MS-149 there is evidence that Hemingway may have intended to cover Frederic's summer in the Milan hospital with a narrative bridge, which would have considerably shortened the story. First he wrote: "I did not return to the war for three months." Dissatisfied with that beginning for Chapter Ten, he began again:

[3] Ernest Hemingway, introduction to *A Farewell to Arms* (New York: Scribner's, 1948, illustrated edition), vii.

There are only three people of any importance in this story although

      all whom were   at the time
my life was full of people and/~~they were all~~ important/

        over three months
and I did not see any of the three for ~~nearly four~~ months. During

this time I was at hospitals, first at Dormans [sic, Cormans],

         the field hospital at the front
then at Mestre and finally in Milan. I saw them all three before I left/

and all three of them wrote me.

          MS-149

Although he rejected this false start, this passage indicates that Hemingway had only a general idea of where the novel was going. The three people are obviously Rinaldi, the priest, and Catherine Barkley. Frederic had been wounded during the Plava bombardment on May 12, 1917. "Over three months" later would have put him back at the front at the end of August. By leaving Catherine at the front, Hemingway could have synopsized the three-month recuperation. Frederic would have returned in time to participate in the September fighting on the Bainsizza Plateau that culminated in the Caporetto breakthrough in late October. If the story was to end tragically, Frederic could plausibly have been executed at the Codroipo bridge. Such a foreshortened version of the novel would have run well under 300 manuscript pages, and it could have been finished by the June deadline that Hemingway had projected.

Such a solution would have cut Hemingway off from the experience he knew best: the Milan hospital, where he himself had spent the summer of 1918. At first glance, one could not agree that the author intended to leave out this experience. However, to use his own experience in Milan posed serious historical problems. First, there was the stage problem of moving Catherine from Gorizia to Milan. Hemingway knew that the flow of nurses was from Milan to the front. During his summer in the Milan hospital, the nurse he loved was twice sent to field hospitals to fill a shortage. When he revised the first draft, he added three sentences to Rinaldi's visit to Frederic at the field hospital:

The English you go to see every night at their hospital?
She is going to Milan too. She goes with another to be
at the American hospital. They had not got nurses yet
from America. I talked today with the head of their riparto. They have too many women here at the front. They send some back.

MS-180

The sentences in emphasis were added to support an awkward piece of stage managing that Hemingway knew to be historically inaccurate.

The second problem posed by Frederic's Milan summer was even more serious. The United States had not entered the war until April, 1917; there were no advance troops in Italy that summer. In May, 1917, there was no American hospital in Milan. It would not be there for another year. In July, 1918, when Hemingway entered the Red Cross hospital, he was the first wounded soldier to do so. The only hospital in Milan used for military purposes in 1917 was Hospital Maggiore, where Hemingway had undergone physical therapy as an out-patient and that he had used in the short story "In Another Country" (1927). To have moved both Frederic and Catherine into Hospital Maggiore would have put an added strain on his accuracy. He did not know the routine of the hospital, or the layout of its rooms.

These considerations of historical accuracy probably influenced Hemingway's initial desire to circumvent Frederic's summer in Milan, but such a solution cut him off from rich material. On his third beginning to Chapter Ten, he made the decision to play a little loose with history by moving the Red Cross hospital of 1918 back to 1917 as an American hospital. This decision put Hemingway back on familiar ground. Frederic's recovery lasted from mid-May until the third week in October—five months rather than the three or four Hemingway intended in his first start on Chapter Ten. If this analysis is approximately correct, Catherine's pregnancy was either not part of his original story, or it did not figure prominently in it.

For the next six weeks Hemingway worked on Book Two of the novel—the section he had started to leave out. He worked out the problems piecemeal, using many of the places and events that he knew well. It was not until he had reached the end of Book Two, MS-311, that he would confidently say that *he now knew how the story came out.*[4] At that point Frederic has just boarded the train returning to the front and the Caporetto disaster. Catherine Barkley is left pregnant in Milan. What had begun as Frederic's relationship with a priest, a doctor, and a nurse had changed drastically in six weeks' time. Catherine Barkley had been raised to a major character. Rinaldi and the priest would never again figure prominently in the novel, although Hemingway would periodically try to revive them. The story could no longer end at the Tagliamento, for Catherine's pregnancy had become a major consideration. Hemingway now knew that he had to carry the story through to Catherine's death in Switzerland.

Through the first nine chapters of *A Farewell to Arms*, Catherine Barkley sounds and acts suspiciously like Brett Ashley from *The Sun Also Rises*. Like Brett, Catherine is British; like Brett, she has lost a fiancé in the war. Both women are slightly neurotic V.A.D.'s. But in Book Two, Catherine's character begins to grow in other directions. Partly, Hemingway was able to use the physical beauty of Agnes Von Kurowsky, who was his nurse in Milan, but there were also qualities drawn from his first wife, Hadley Richardson. While he was creating Frederic's summer in Milan, Pauline, his second wife, was in the last two months

[4] Hemingway to Waldo Peirce, June 17, 1928.

of pregnancy with her first child. On June 28, just eleven days after Hemingway had written Waldo Peirce that he knew the end of the novel, Pauline suffered through eighteen hours of labor that ended with a Caesarian section. Mother and son survived. Although Hemingway had already used an emergency Caesarian in "Indian Camp" (1924), Pauline's operation provided the naturalistic basis for his conclusion. Thus during the summer of 1928, the character of Catherine Barkley expanded in depth and importance, and this change had considerable effect on the character of Frederic Henry. No matter how difficult his experiences had been, Frederic would be left alive to bear the burden of their disaster.

Between June 17 and July 25, Hemingway wrote 167 pages of manuscript, which covered the retreat from Caporetto and Frederic's desertion—the finest sustained narrative in the novel. But the heat, his new child, and the pressures of family life made him pessimistic about the novel. It did not seem any closer to completion than ever, he wrote Waldo Pierce.[5] On July 28, Hemingway left Pauline and the baby with her family in Piggott, Arkansas, and drove to Sheridan, Wyoming, where he could fish and write in solitude. Between July 30 and August 8, he pushed the novel from 478 to 548 pages—70 pages of new manuscript. After rowing up Lake Maggiore, Frederic and Catherine were safe in the high country of Switzerland.

Between August 9 and August 17 he averaged over 8 manuscript pages a day. When Pauline and his new son joined him in Sheridan on August 18, he was on MS-616. Catherine Barkley was in difficult labor in the Lausanne Hospital. For the next two days, while settling his family, he wrote nothing. Then, between August 20-22, he wrote the final 34 pages of manuscript. On August 22 he was able to tell Perkins that the novel was finished. A month later he was eager to begin the revisions, but he knew that it was too soon. As he had told Perkins in April, it was important for

[5] Hemingway to Peirce, July 23, 1928.

the book to cool off before he began reworking it.[6] With the manuscript completed, he was sure that the rewrite would go quickly, for each day he had written over the previous day's work.[7] This method of daily revision is important to keep in mind when discussing the manuscript, for otherwise one is misled by the apparent smoothness of large portions of it.

The holograph manuscript that was on deposit at the Houghton Library at Harvard has been placed by Mary Hemingway in the manuscript collection at the J. F. Kennedy Library. This manuscript is a pencil draft of 650 numbered pages with 4 unnumbered pages. It is written primarily on standard 8½ x 11 unlined paper. The sequence is as follows:

1-9	129a-129b	206-209 missing	425 bis
9 (double)	130-167	210-268	426-469
10-21	168 bis	268 (double)	470 insert
21 bis	169-172	269-283	470-477
22-103	174	[284]	478-479 missing
104a-104b	173	285-337	480-652
105-122	175-201	338-396	650 bis-652
123 insert	201b	397-398 missing	201-202 deleted pages
123-128	202-205	399-425	202-209 deleted pages

Of the 4 unnumbered pages, 2 contain working titles and possible epigraphs. Two pages are false starts on new chapters.

In spite of traveling to Chicago, New York City, Piggott, Key West, back to New York, Oak Park to bury his father, and finally returning to Key West, Hemingway had the first 400 pages of manuscript ready for typing on December 16. His wife, Pauline, and his sister, Sunny, worked steadily on the typed draft. On January 8, he wrote Perkins that he was

6 Hemingway to Perkins, April 21, 1928.
7 Hemingway to Perkins, Sept. 20, 1928.

working six to ten hours a day on the revisions. By January 10, 1929, the first twenty-nine chapters were in typed copy. On January 25, the novel was finished with exception of the last paragraphs, which were to be revised many times over the next few months.

With few exceptions, the serialized version of AFTA that appeared in *Scribner's Magazine* is identical with the hard-cover publication. If we compare both novel and magazine to the holograph manuscript, we find the difference is not more than a dozen words or phrases, except for the final paragraphs. This would seem to indicate that the Kennedy Library manuscript is the final revised draft that Hemingway's typists used in Key West. A detailed examination of the manuscript reveals something of the development of the novel as well as Hemingway's working habits.

The remarkable part about the manuscript is its incredible smoothness. Although there are heavily rewritten passages, forty-five percent of the first draft appears unrevised. Another thirty percent of the manuscript has only minor revisions, sometimes as little as a single word on a page. Seventy-five percent of the holograph manuscript went straight to publication with insignificant changes. From a writer who reputedly worked slowly, revising heavily, this apparent smoothness of the working draft is puzzling.

This puzzle is simplified by a reconstruction of Hemingway's working habits, which account for the apparent smoothness. The first draft was written and numbered sequentially. As he was writing, he would sometimes make minor additions or deletions that are in the same pencil as the draft. The following morning, as he told Perkins, he would rework the previous day's production. Sometimes this could be done on the same page, using the margins or interlinear space. However, on those incredibly smooth pages, there is the possibility that the second-day changes became so heavy that he recopied the manuscript on a fresh page. The numbering on these recopied pages would still be in sequence, for he had not yet begun the second day's writing. Of course, some pages were exactly right on the first draft, but not 300 out of 650. The first draft of the recopied page was probably destroyed. Thus, forty-five percent of the working draft will not support any conclusions about stylistic changes or narrative problems. Fortunately, the remaining portion of the manuscript tells us a good deal.

In August, when he was in the final hundred pages of the manuscript, Hemingway began rereading the novel from the beginning. On August 12, he made a note on the top of MS-109: "Seems fine so far." He was, perhaps, most concerned about the early portion, for it had been written before he knew exactly where the novel was going. Quite possibly as he read his way through the manuscript in August, he made some revisions, for the early chapters of the manuscript are the most heavily revised.

With the draft finished in August, Hemingway put it aside until sometime in late November, when the final revisions were begun. In the August draft, the pages were numbered sequentially; several major revisions during the rewrite period disrupted the first draft pagination. The first such revision occurs at MS-103. At that point Frederic is taking leave of Catherine for the front, where he will be wounded. Catherine gives Frederic a St. Anthony's medal, the patron saint of Italy. On the first draft, Hemingway had not made much of the medal. In the revision, he wrote an insert page of over twenty lines describing the medal and Frederic's conversation about it with his driver. First this page was marked "insert 102." Then it was changed to "103." The original MS-103 was changed to "104a" and MS-104, to "104b." The newly inserted page runs over on to the back side, something rare in the manuscript, but he did not want to have to insert yet another page. The last three lines of MS-103 are in three different pencils:

*I felt him in his metal box against my chest while we
drove.* Then I forgot about him. After I was wounded
I never found him. Some one probably got it at one of
the dressing stations.

Later on MS-162 when the priest is visiting the wounded
Frederic (p. 68), there is a passage about the St. Anthony
which Hemingway cut:

"~~See my Saint Anthony.~~"

where it lay   "You see my Saint Anthony."
I pulled the metal capsule out from/on my chest./He looked

at the thin gold chain.

"Perhaps he saved your life."

"Passini saved my life," I said. "He was between me and the burst."

"Poor Passini. You might remember him in your prayers."

"All right."

"I don't want to make you sad."

MS-162

Since the inserted MS-103 appears to have been done at
the revision stage, the last three lines of the page show
Hemingway coming back to the passage twice, each time
adding a slightly more ironic touch to the minor incident.
It is this attention to the possibilities of detail that kept him
working long hours during the revision stages.

A similar hiatus in the pagination occurs following
MS-128, where Frederic has just been blown up at Plava.
MS-129a appears to be the first draft of the explosion, for
it is written on the same Grisom Mill paper as MS-128.
MS-129b is on WAT/ALLS paper, indicating that it was
written during the revision stage. By the time Hemingway
had revised the passage in December, it looked like this:

(MS-128)
I ate the end of my piece of cheese and took a swallow of wine.

Through the noise I heard a cough, then came the chuh-chuh-chuh-

chuh—then there was a ~~roar and a white hot~~ flash, as ~~when~~ a blast-furnace

door is swung open, and a roar that started white ~~hot~~ and went red and on

                              (MS-129A)   my breath would not come
and on in a rushing ~~like~~ wind. I tried to breathe but ~~my chest would not~~

                    rush
open and I felt myself ~~go~~ out of myself and out and out and out

                    passing
and all the time the wind ~~roaring~~. I went out and on and on and I knew

                    Then I floated, hesitated and instead of going on
I was dead and that it had all been a mistake to think you just died./I

                    there was a long thin wire through the center of
felt myself slide back as though/my soul ~~was sliding down a long~~
The me that was gone out slid   twice it caught and stood still and once it
down that wire   nothing   turned completely over on the wire
~~tight wire~~/through ~~space~~ and the wind/and then
        jerked
it ~~slid suddenly~~ and stopped and
~~I breathed and~~ I was back.   ~~I took a breath~~.   The ground was

~~churned~~
torn up and in front of my head was a splintered beam of wood. ~~I heard~~
In the jolt of my head I heard   I thought somebody was screaming
somebody
~~somebody~~ crying. "~~Mamma mia! Mamma mia!" Somebody screamed,~~

~~then stopped, then screamed again.~~

Through revisions on MS-129b and in galleries, Hemingway trimmed his excesses to read:

I felt myself rush bodily out of myself and out and out
and out and all the time bodily in the wind. I went out
swiftly, all of myself, and I knew I was dead and that it
had all been a mistake to think you just died. Then I

floated, and instead of going on I felt myself slide back.
I breathed and I was back. The ground was torn up
and in front of my head there was a splintered beam
of wood. In the jolt of my head I heard somebody
crying. I thought somebody was screaming. (p. 54)

A year earlier, 1927, he had written of a similar experience in the short story, "Now I Lay Me":

... I had been living for a long time with the
knowledge that if I ever shut my eyes in the dark and
let myself go, my soul would go out of my body. I had
been that way for a long time, ever since I had been
blown up at night and felt it go out of me and go off
and then come back.[8]

Obviously, the experience is based on Hemingway's own
wounding on the Piave river in 1918. What is interesting in
the revisions is the writer's objective control. In the first revision, Hemingway had written a more detailed description
of this seminal experience than he ever published. If the
wounding was as traumatic as some believe,[9] it must have
been a difficult passage to write honestly, but even more
difficult to cut.

Another clear example of Hemingway's revisions can be
seen at MS-168 bis. The first draft of these three pages was
separated from the manuscript but saved by the author
(see Appendix B). In the deleted section Frederic and the
priest discuss love, but the emphasis falls more on Frederic's values than the priest's. Returning to this passage
when the novel was complete, Hemingway was able to
focus their conversation more precisely on the nature of
love and the importance of the high country—a crucial
touchstone for the novel.

[8] *Short Stories*, p. 363.
[9] See Philip Young, *Hemingway: A Reconsideration*.

In the revision, it is the priest's definition of love that
comes through so clearly:

*When you love you wish to do things for. You wish to
sacrifice for. You wish to serve.*

MS-169

Ultimately it is Catherine, not Frederic, who fulfills these
criteria. When Hemingway rewrote the conversation, he
knew that Frederic was not the hero of the novel. Here he
gives greater impact to Catherine's role, reinforcing her
sacrifice in the name of love, and at the same time he under-
lines the basic failure of Frederic Henry.

When the priest leaves, Hemingway adds the idyllic description of the Abruzzi, where there was fine hunting and
a less complicated way of life. Basing his description on a
feature story he had done five years earlier,[10] Hemingway
establishes the values that Frederic associates with the high
country. The total impact of this passage on the focus and
themes of the novel make it one of the most important revisions in the manuscipt.

The next irregularity in the manuscript occurs in Chapter
12, when Frederic is in the field hospital before being evacuated to Milan. There is a long deleted passage on
MSS-174-175 that reads:

I do not like to remember the trip back to Milan. ~~The train got into~~

~~the station early in the morning.~~ if you have never travelled in a

hospital train there is no use making a picture of it. This is not a

picture of war, nor really about war. It is only a story. That is why,

sometimes, it may seem there are not enough people in it, nor enough

[10] Hemingway, "More Game to Shoot in Crowded Europe than in
Ontario," *Toronto Star Weekly*, November 3, 1923, p. 20; rpt. in *The
Wild Years*, pp. 259-268.

unless it was quiet
noises, nor enough smells. There were always people and noises/and

always
always smells but in trying to tell the story I cannot get them all in/but

keeping
have a hard time ~~just sticking~~ to the story alone and sometimes it seems

But it wasn't quiet
as though it were all quiet ~~and nothing going on but what happened~~ If you

try and put in everything you would never get a single day done and ~~then~~

~~*the one who made it might not feel it so I will try to tell it*~~ (MS-175)

straight along and hope that the things themselves will give the feeling

Also when   a little out of your head
of the rest. ~~Besides when~~ you are wounded or ~~a little crazy~~ or in love

with someone the surroundings are sometimes removed and they only

come in at certain times. But I will try to keep the places in and

tell what happened. It does not seem to have gotten anywhere and it is

not much of a love story so far but it has to go on in the way it was

although I skip everything I can.

This entire passage was cut for obvious reasons. It is out of character; it sounds more like Hemingway talking to himself than anything we might expect Frederic to say. Although the novel is a first-person narrative, the reader seldom sees Frederic-as-author. This cut was probably made the day after it was written, when Hemingway reread and revised the previous day's work. In making the cut, he left one paragraph at the top of MS-174 and one paragraph at the bottom of MS-175. Because of the extensive cut, it would appear that the typists at Key West jumbled the pages. The published novel separates the paragraph on MS-174 from the paragraph on MS-175 with the entire

MS-173. As a result, there is a minor break in continuity between pp. 74-75 in the novel.

The next disruption of the manuscript is the result of eight pages Hemingway cut and revised at Key West. MSS-202 to 209 describe the first time Catherine goes to bed with Frederic in the Milan hospital. At Key West Hemingway realized his first draft was overwritten. His first revision attempt left the passage ambiguous. Finally he wrote the five page insert (MSS-201b-205), picking the first draft back up at MS-210. The revision makes the sexual relationship implicit in the dialogue without graphic description. (Compare pp. 91-93 of the novel with earlier version in Appendix B.) The revised pages are completely clean, with only one additional line added at the galley-proof stage.

Again this is a crucial scene in the novel, which had to convince the reader of the spontaneous love of Frederic and Catherine. Critics of Catherine have frequently said that the scene is unbelievable, that it is a fantasy for Catherine to leap into bed with Frederic the first time he asks. Although psychological motivation has been provided earlier for Catherine's behavior, the first draft does not make the sexual relations clear. Hemingway's final choice was to convey the sexuality of the scene by eliminating everything but the lovers' dialogue.

The next major revision made at Key West occurs when Frederic has returned to the front in October, 1917. On the evening of Frederic's first night back with his ambulance unit, Chapter 25 closes (MS-337) with Frederic saying good-night to the major in charge. In the manuscript there followed a lengthy (MSS-337, 337 bis, 338) description of how the Italian major looked and felt the next morning when waking. Although it is an effective character sketch of the sort that Hemingway did so well, it added nothing to the novel unless the major were to reappear later, which he did not. Moreover, the sketch created a point-of-view problem: the description is outside Frederic's knowledge.

Hemingway wisely cut out a piece of effective writing that did not contribute to the total effect of the book. The cut must have been made at Key West. Had it been made the day after it was written, he would not have kept the pages in the manuscript.

Two other breaks in the manuscript are the result, not of revisions, but apparently of Hemingway's misnumbering. It appears that he went from MS-396 to MS-399 from misreading his own numbering. Frederic and his enlisted men are in the middle of the Caporetto retreat. The last line of MS-396 reads:

"We would do best to start," the first one said.

The first line of MS-399 reads:

"We are starting," I said.

This same sort of page mistake occurs between MS-477 and MS-480. The last line on MS-477 is:

I found a man in the station and asked him if he knew what hotels were open. The Grand-Hotel & des Isles Borromees

The sentence is completed on MS-480:

was open and several small hotels that stayed open all the year.

The next break occurs after MS-425. Hemingway added MS-425 bis, which is a smooth copy of the previous page, perhaps done for the benefit of the typist. Another irregularity occurs when Hemingway deleted several lines of dialogue (see Appendix B) from MS-470. He added a page marked "insert 470." The change involves Frederic's problems upon reaching Milan after his desertion. In the deleted passage, he arranges for false leave papers, but at Stresa it is important that Frederic not have proper papers, not even phony ones. Hemingway probably made this change during the first draft, when he realized it would be easier to motivate Frederic's flight up the lake if he were more vulnerable to arrest.

The only other irregularity in the pagination occurs on the final pages of the manuscript. MSS-650 bis to 652 is an alternate ending to the novel that does not appear in the published novel.

Of the major disruptions in the mauscript pagination, most are the result of material added during the Key West rewrite. The disruption at MS-173 resulted from a lengthy deletion that confused his typists. There are four other significant deletions that did not alter the pagination and that were also made at Key West. The first major deletion begins on MS-231, describing Frederic's operation:

When I was awake after the operation I had not been away. You do not go away. They only choak you. *It is not like death's other kingdom,*[11] *nor is it like death* and afterward you might as well have been drunk except that when you throw up nothing comes but bile instead of alcohol and you do not feel better afterward. I saw sandbags at the end of the bed. They were on pipes that came out of the cast. *My legs hurt so that I tried to get back into the choaked place I had come from but I could not get back in there but threw up again and again and nothing came. They gave me water to rinse out my mouth and then I lay still and waited for the pain to reach the top and go down but there was no limit to the pain and it had long passed the point where pain had always stopped. I thought how our Lord would never send us more [than] we could bear and I*

11 A further indication that Hemingway while writing the novel was consciously aware of T. S. Eliot's crippled survivors: "Those who have crossed / With direct eyes, to death's other Kingdom / Remember us—if at all—not as lost / Violent souls, but only / As the hollow men / The Stuffed men." "The Hollow Men," 1925.

had always believed that [MS-232] *meant me,*
became unconscious when it became too bad, hence the
success of martyrs, but now it was not so but the pain
went way beyond what I could bear in the bone and
everywhere there was and then inside my chest it
started to jerk and jerk and then I cried and cried
without any noise, only the diaphragm jerking and
jerking and then it was better and I knew I could bear
it but gave no credit to our Lord. ~~When I was through~~
I did not think about our Lord but only that the pain
was less. ~~Crying and only my diaphragm still jerking a~~
~~little~~ *When I was through crying and lying still and*
trying to keep my diaphragm from jerking—it had
gone on crying after I was through—I saw Miss Gage
and said to her

Only the portion emphasized went into the novel. This
deletion, like so many of the major revisions and deletions
in the manuscript, is directly related to Frederic's feelings.
By deleting this and other passages Hemingway effaces
Frederic to the point that he is one of the least visible people in the novel. Only at crucial points is the reader told the
narrator's feelings or emotional responses. His conclusions
are minimal. This particular section is overwritten and out
of character. By deleting it, Hemingway does not let the
reader see Frederic's pain, which is consistent with his
theory of leaving out as much as possible while letting incident and dialogue carry the story.

The second major deletion is a similarly overwritten passage which follows the previous one. It begins on MS-233:

Nothing that you learn by sensation remains if you lose
the sensation. Sometimes pain goes and you cannot
remember it from the moment before but only have a
dread of it again. When love is gone you cannot
remember it but only remember things that happen
and places. There is no memory of love if there is no

love. All these things, however, return in the dark. In the dark love returns when it is gone, pain comes again and danger that has passed returns. Death comes in the dark. Countries that regret executions kill men in daylight when it is easier for them to go and often if the daylight is bright and there is a little delay in the execution so the sun is higher and the morning cool, [MS-234] the condemned man having been given rum, which often makes things right which are not right, there is not much horror. I have seen men shot, slumping quickly, and hanged, twirling slowly, and kneeling, arms behind the back, chest on a table, that tipped quickly forward the knife falling into a slot and thudding on wood while boy soldiers presented arms and looked sideways at the basket that had been empty and now had a head in it. If there was daylight it was not bad. But countries that believe in executions, where the men who execute and sentence to be executed think that they themselves will never be executed, and so have no pity, pity being the faculty of seeing yourself in the person of the pitied-one, in such countries they execute men at night. Such things will not be easily forgiven, nor will they, in the end, prevent the deaths of the executioners. They will all die, of course, and many of them, not knowing about death will be greatly surprised, and those who die at night will have lived to wish they had killed in daylight. [MS-235] I do not know just when night began to be bad for me but I suppose it must have been around this time. When I had first gone to war it had all been like a picture or a story or a dream in which you know you can wake up if it gets too bad. Also I had a feeling that other people died but that I did not die. I had the belief in physical immortality which is given fortunate young men in order that they may think about other things and that is withdrawn without notice when they need it most. After its withdrawal I was not greatly worried because

*the spells of fear were always physical, always caused
by an imminent danger, and always transitory. I was in
the second healthy stage, that of not being afraid when
I was not in danger. I suppose the third stage, of being
afraid at night, started about this point. I did not
notice it start because I was rarely alone at night. Fear
grows [MS-236] through recognition. It is not good for
a fear to talk about it and we talked about everything.
But it was not much of a fear at this time and I may
have used it and built it up as an argument for not
being alone although on the nights when I was alone I
was so tired that I slept heavily.*

This passage is curious for a number of reasons. The di-
gression on executions, only peripherally relevant to Frederic's later desertion, distorts Frederic's character and was
wisely cut. In it Hemingway obliquely refers to two inter-
chapters from *in our time*: Chapter Five, the execution of
the Greek ministers, and Chapter Fifteen, the hanging of
Sam Cardinella. Written in 1923, neither of the two executions were based on firsthand experience.[12] Nor had Hemingway seen a guillotine execution, although he was well
read on the French Revolution. He is attributing to Frederic firsthand knowledge that he had only imagined. The
diatribe on those who execute at night without pity has no
immediate relevance to the novel. Hemingway wrote this
passage in May, 1928, at Key West, where John Dos Passos,
among others, fished and drank with him when he was
through with his morning writing. Dos Passos, whose socialist conscience was finely tuned to what had been happening
to America in the Twenties, may well have discussed the
Sacco-Vanzetti executions, which had taken place the previous August.[13] The two Italian immigrants died in the electric chair shortly after midnight, August 23, 1927. Even
without Dos Passos, Hemingway must have been aware of

12 Baker, *Life Story*, p. 113.
13 See Dos Passos, "Camera Eye 50," *U.S.A.*

the massive protest by American writers, particularly against Judge Thayer, who sentenced the two men to death. Regardless of the reference, Hemingway was correct in cutting Frederic's philosophy of execution. Alternately maudlin and preachy, the entire passage has no place in the novel. By eliminating it, Hemingway left only residual indications of Frederic's nighttime fears, which were clues enough to his psychological state of mind.

There are no more major deletions in the manuscript until after Frederic and Catherine are secure in Switzerland. On August 14, 1928, he finished Chapter Thirty-nine, with two pages of dialogue in which Frederic and Catherine discuss the unborn baby. On August 15, he wrote three pages of manuscript, all of which he later cut at Key West:

We had a fine life; the things we did were of no importance and the things we said were foolish and seem even more idiotic to write down but we were happy and I suppose wisdom and happiness do not go together. Although there is a wisdom in being a fool that we do not know much about and if happiness is an end sought by the wise it is no less an end if it comes without wisdom. It is as well to seize it as to seek it because you are liable to wear out the capacity for it in the seeking. To seek it through the kingdom of heaven is a fine thing but you must give up this life first and if this life is all you have you might have remorse after giving it up and the kingdom of heaven might be a cold place in which to live with remorse. They say the only way you can keep a thing is to lose it and this may be true but do not admire it. The only thing I know is that if you love anything enough they take it away from you. This may all be done in infinite wisdom but whoever does it is not my friend. I am afraid of god at night but I would have [MS-587] admired him more if he would have stopped the war or never have let it

*start. Maybe he did stop it but whoever stopped it did
not do it prettily. And if it is the Lord that giveth and
the Lord that taketh away I do not admire him for
taking Catherine away. He may have given me Catherine but who gave Rinaldi the syphyllis at about the
same time? The one thing I know is that I do not know
anything about it. I see the wisdom of the priest at our
mess who has always loved god and so is happy and I
am sure that nothing will ever take God away from
him. But how much is wisdom and how much is luck to
be born that way? And what if you are not built that
way? What if the things you love are perishable. All
you know then is that they will perish. You will perish
too and perhaps that is the answer; that those who love
things that are immortal and believe in them are
immortal themselves and live on with them while those
that love things that die and believe in them die and
are as dead [MS-588] as the things they love. If that
were true it would be a fine gift and would even things
up. But it probably is not true. All that we can be sure
of is that we are born and that we will die and that
everything we love that has life will die too. The more
things with life that we love the more things there are
to die. So if we want to buy winning tickets we can go
over on the side of immortality; and finally they most
of them do. But if you were born loving nothing and
the warm milk of your mother's breast was never
heaven and the first thing you loved was the side of a
hill and the last thing was a woman and they took her
away and you did not want another but only to have
her; and she was gone, then you are not so well placed
and it would have been better to have loved God from
the start. But you did not love God and it doesn't do
any good to talk about it either, nor to think about it.*

In cutting this entire passage, Hemingway saved only the
opening sentence: "We had a fine life."

Although this is one of the more massive deletions from the manuscript, it is not unlike several minor false starts that characteristically occur immediately after a piece of finished action. Structurally it is as if Hemingway had written five tightly interrelated short stories. In the sequence prior to the above deletion, the action began at Stresa and ended at Montreux, following the classic short-story formula: conflict (the threat of arrest), rising action (the flight up the lake), climax (safe arrival in Switzerland), falling action (problems with customs), denouement (settling for the winter at Montreux). This pattern repeats itself five times with five separate climaxes: Frederic's wounding, Catherine's pregnancy, Frederic's threat of execution, the lovers eluding the lake patrol, and the onset of Catherine's labor pains. The first four climaxes either lead to a denouement that relieves the physical threat or, as with Catherine's pregnancy, postpones the threat. The final climax leads to the catastrophe that in one form or another has threatened one or both of the lovers from the beginning. Each time Hemingway builds the tension a little higher only to relieve it; but after each relief the tension remains higher than its previous level. Thus a graph of the action would be a jagged rising slope with five peaks. This structure is further confirmation that Hemingway plotted the book episodically, not knowing precisely where the next episode was going. Many of the letters he wrote during this period are dated at the end of such episodes, as if he took a break from the fiction for his correspondence. The manuscript shows that following each denouement Hemingway had difficulty beginning the next chapter, which frequently is characterized by a false start.

In the rejected philosophical passage above, he is once more attempting, through a modified stream-of-consciousness technique, to tie together loose ends and prepare the reader for Catherine's death. The central idea—those who choose the happiness of this world—finds its way back into the chapter later. Hemingway must have realized that there was no need to telegraph Catherine's death with such a heavy hand. Moreover, Frederic's wandering thoughts lack the impact that they have later when Catherine is actually dying. Here Frederic is full of self-pity with which the reader cannot identify. When Catherine is suffering in the hospital, Frederic's thoughts on the way of this world hit the reader much harder and ring truer.

It is interesting to see Hemingway once more trying to get Catherine, Rinaldi, and the priest into a kind of triad. He had attempted this once before at the beginning of Chapter Ten on a false start that he cut. Later in one of the false endings, he comes back to the same problem. Critics have long realized that these are the three "code" characters from whom Frederic learns about behavior under pressure. Because Hemingway had not plotted the novel through to its conclusion when he developed the characters of Rinaldi and the priest in Book One, he had no way to bring them back into the conclusion except in Frederic's thoughts. Each time he tried to do this, it proved awkward. Finally he must have realized that Rinaldi and the priest were implicitly present at the conclusion, for Catherine embodies both flesh and spirit. Frederic's internal argument about the spirit and the flesh in the closing chapters is directly related to what he had learned from those two in Book One.

The Biblical style and allusions of this passage may be an indication that Hemingway was beginning his usual search through the Bible for a title. He had found *The Sun Also Rises* in the Old Testament. It is not unlikely that he began reading through the New Testament for this novel's title. The several references to "the kingdom of heaven" support this argument. It is primarily in the Gospel of Matthew that this phrase appears. In the other three Gospels, the phrase is characteristically "the kingdom of God." When Frederic says: "They say the only way you can keep a thing is to lose it," he is paraphrasing Matthew x: 39: "He that findeth his life shall lose it: and he that loseth his life for my sake shall find it."[14] Throughout Matthew the central choice is between the things of this world and the Kingdom of Heaven. If a man chooses the Kingdom of Heaven, he must put aside the pleasures and objects of this life. This is the choice that Frederic is arguing in his head. Neither Frederic nor Hemingway found much solace in the Gospel of Matthew.

At crucial points throughout the novel, the possibility of prayer has been discussed. In Switzerland, Count Greffi, too old to pray, has asked Frederic to pray for him if he ever becomes devout. It is only when Catherine is dying that Frederic resorts to prayer, but the form runs contrary to the advice found in Matthew. Frederic prays:

> Don't let her die. Oh, God, please don't let her die. I'll do anything for you if you won't let her die. Please, please, please, dear God, don't let her die. Dear God, don't let her die. Please, please, please don't let her die. God please make her not die. I'll do anything you say if you don't let her die. You took the baby but don't let her die. That was all right but don't let her die. Please, please, dear God, don't let her die.[15]

In Matthew's version of the Sermon on the Mount, Christ tells the multitude that this is the improper form of prayer: "But when ye pray, use not vain repetitions, as the heathen do: for they think that they shall be heard for their much speaking. Be not ye therefore like unto them: for your Father knoweth what things ye have need of, before ye ask him." (Matthew VI: 7-8.) Frederic prays for the wrong

[14] Hemingway took two titles from Matthew later in the Thirties: "The Light of the World," and To Have and Have Not: "Ye are the light of the world. A city that is set on a hill cannot be hid." (Matthew V: 14.) "For unto everyone that hath shall be given, and he shall have abundance: but from him that hath not shall be taken away even that which he hath." (Matthew XXV: 29.)

[15] Hemingway, A Farewell to Arms (New York: Scribner's, 1929), Scribner Library Edition, p. 330. All further references to the novel will be from this edition and will appear parenthetically in the text.

thing in the wrong way. As he tells himself in this deleted passage, "those who love things that die and believe in them die and are as dead as the things they love."

The manuscript pages of the novel's final chapter are carefully dated and almost entirely clean of revision, indicating that Hemingway probably recopied each day's production after the following morning's revisions. With the exception of the final paragraphs, the only portion that bears heavy Key West revisions involves the birth of the baby. The paragraph describing Catherine's sutures got much of its detail in the revision. The emphasized portions were Key West additions:

> *I thought Catherine was dead. She looked dead. Her face was gray,* the part of it I could see. *Down below, under the light, the doctor was sewing up the great long,* forcep-spread, *thick-edged, wound.* Another doctor in a mask gave the anaesthetic. Two nurses in masks handed things. It looked like a drawing of the Inquisition. *I knew as I watched I could have watched it all, but I was glad I hadn't.* I do not think I could have watched them cut, but *I watched the wound closed into a high welted ridge* with quick skilful-looking stitches like a cobbler's, and was glad. When the wound was closed *I went into the hall* and walked up and down again. *After a while the doctor came out.*
>
> MS-636 / p. 325

The most curious deletion involves the baby himself. On MS-638, a nurse tells Frederic that the baby was born dead, choked on the umbilical cord. On MS-642, written the same day, the same nurse tells Frederic:

> *"The baby is alive you know."*
> *"What do you mean?"*
> *"It's alive that's all."*
> *"You want to be careful what you tell people."*

"I'm glad," the nurse said. "Did you see the doctor?"
"Yes," I said.
"I'm glad."

The baby apparently remained alive until Key West. There Hemingway cut this piece of dialogue and changed Frederic's prayer from: *"Take the baby* [my emphasis] but don't let her die" to: *"You took the baby* but don't let her die." A live baby would have been another loose end that Hemingway did not want. More importantly, a live baby would have been a sign of hope—life would go on. *A Farewell to Arms* is a massive defeat; there could be no sentimental hope left at the end.

The final paragraphs of the novel gave Hemingway more difficulty than any other single passage. The manuscript contains two endings that are similar but bear repeating:

There are a great many more details starting with my first meeting with an undertaker and all the business of burial in a foreign country and continuing on with the rest of my life—which has gone on and seems likely to go on for a long time. I could tell how Rinaldi was cured of the syphylis and lived to find that the technique acquired in wartime surgery is not much practical use in peace. I could tell how the priest in our mess lived to be a priest in Italy under Fascism. I could tell how Ettore became a Fascist and the part he took in that organization. I could tell what kind of singer whatisname became. I could tell how Piani got to be a taxi driver in New York. ~~I could tell you how I made a fool of myself going back to Italy~~. But they are all parts of something that was finished. ~~I suppose it was finished at the Tagliamento~~. I do not know exactly where but certainly finished. Piani was the least finished but he went to another country. Italy is a country every man should love once. I loved it once and lived through it. You ought to love it once. There

*is less loss of dignity in loving it young. I suppose
loving it or at least living in it is something like the
need for the classics.*

*I could tell you what I have done since March
nineteen hundred and eighteen and when I walked
that night in the rain alone, and always from then on
alone, through the streets of Lausanne back to the hotel
where Catherine and I had lived and went upstairs to
our room and undressed and got into bed and slept,
finally, because I was so tired—to wake in the morning
with the sun shining; then suddenly to realize what it
was that had happened. I could tell what has happened
since then but that is the end of the story.*

END

*Many things have happened. Things happen all the
time. Everything blunts and the world keeps on. You
get most of your life back like goods recovered from a
fire. It all keeps on as long as your life keeps on and
then it keeps on. It never stops. It only stops for you.
Some of it stops while you are still alive. You can stop
a story anytime. ~~Where you stop it is the end of that
story~~. The rest goes on and you go on with it. On the
other hand you have to stop a story. You have to stop
it at the end of whatever it was you were writing about.*

MSS-650-652

(FIRST REVISED ENDING)

*There are a great many more details, starting with my
first meeting with an undertaker and all the business of
burial in a foreign country and going on with the rest
of my life—which has gone on and seems likely to go
on for a long time.*

*I could tell how Rinaldi was cured of the syphylis
and lived to find that the technique learned in wartime
surgery is not of much practical use in peace. I could*

tell how the priest in our mess lived to be a priest in
Italy under Fascism. I could tell how Ettore [MS-
651 bis] *became a fascist and the part he took in that*
organization. I could tell how Piani got to be a taxi
driver in New York and what sort of a singer Simmons
became. Many things have happened. Everything
blunts and the world keeps on. You get most of your
life back like goods recovered from a fire. It all keeps
on as long as your life keeps on and then it keeps on
but you do not know about it. It never stops. It only
stops for you. Some of it stops while you are still alive.
The rest goes on and you go on with it. [MS-652 bis]
I could tell you what I have done since March
nineteen hundred and eighteen when I walked that
night in the rain back to the hotel where Catherine and
I had lived and went upstairs to our room and
undressed and got into bed and slept, finally, because
I was so tired—to wake in the morning with the sun
shining in the window; then suddenly to realize what
it was that had happened. I could tell what has
happened since then but that is the end of the story.

The first of these two drafts is heavily revised on the
page, with sentences added on the margin and interlinearly.
The second draft has nothing crossed out or revised—a
smooth copy that improves some changes from the first
draft. Both were written sometime after the manuscript had
been completed. With the exception of walking back to the
hotel in the rain, neither contributed significantly to the
ending that Hemingway finally wrote the following June.
Both have the wrong tone. They lack immediacy, and once
more they show Frederic-as-author, an exposure that Hemingway had attempted earlier and judiciously cut. Once
again he is attempting to bring back Rinaldi and the priest.
They were loose ends of the novel that he had developed
almost too well in Book One, when he did not know precisely where the story was going. In the first ending he is

tempted to draw on his 1922 and 1927 trips to Italy, when nothing had been the same, but he scratched that as a bad idea. He also gives a further clue to his original intentions when Frederic says, "I suppose it was finished at the Tagliamento." "It" obviously wasn't finished at the Tagliamento, but that may well have been where Hemingway had earlier intended to end the novel.

Both false endings attempt to reduce the tension built by Catherine's death. After this emotional peak, Hemingway wanted to let the reader back down softly—to allow the catharsis to work, as he was able to do later at the end of *The Old Man and the Sea*. In *A Farewell to Arms* he could not find this release, although he continued to search for several months.

At the Kennedy Library, Mary Hemingway has collected the numerous false endings of *A Farewell to Arms*. Although they are not arranged in chronological order and several are merely fragments, there appear to be thirty-two variant endings, plus two more in the holograph manuscript and one more in the *Scribner's Magazine* corrected galleys. Most of the variants are based on the first ending of the manuscript. However, one variant has the baby alive (see Appendix B). In the first draft of the manuscript, Hemingway had left the baby alive; by the time he wrote the first ending, he had rejected this idea. Sometime in May, 1929, he wrote an insert for MS-641, once more reviving the baby. Ultimately, of course, the baby appeared still-born.

One curious variant is the result of Scott Fitzgerald's suggestion when he critiqued the typescript: "Why not end the book with that wonderful paragraph on p. 241. It is the most eloquent in the book and could end it rather gently and well."[16] Fitzgerald was referring to the philosophical passage in which Frederic describes how the world eventually kills everyone impartially—the good, the gentle, and the brave. "If you are none of these you can be sure

[16] Fitzgerald critique, handwritten, undated, 1929.

it will kill you too but there will be no special hurry"
(p. 249). Hemingway liked the idea well enough to type it
up, giving the pages the proper numbers to fit them into the
typescript he had sent Scribner's. The suggestion was not a
bad one, but it, too, ended up in the pile of rejected
endings. Either Hemingway did not want to end the book
on a moralizing note, or he did not want Fitzgerald to be
given the credit. Fitzgerald had shaped the opening chapter
of *The Sun Also Rises* by urging Hemingway to cut the first
three galleys.[17] Hemingway's pride must have bridled at the
thought of his fellow writer being responsible for the ending of his second novel.

While he was still working on the ending, he received the
galleys for the novel's last installment in *Scribner's Magazine*. The galleys, dated June 4, 1929, have the second
variant ending printed above. On Galley 19, Hemingway
revised heavily in pencil but was unable to substantially
change his initial concept. It was not until June 24, 1929, ten
months after completing the first draft, that Hemingway got
the ending that went into print. One can sense the surge of
power on the manuscript page. The handwriting expands;
the pencil width broadens as if he were trying to push it
through the paper. There is a rush to get the words down;
one can almost feel the relief and pleasure there on the
page.

Falling back on his best technique, Hemingway wrote the
terse dialogue between Frederic and the surgeon with only
one final tight narrative paragraph:

But after I had got them out and shut the door and
turned off the light it wasn't any good. It was like
saying good-by to a statue. After a while I went out
and left the hospital and walked back to the hotel in
the rain. (p. 332)

17 See Philip Young and Charles W. Mann, "Fitzgerald's *Sun Also
Rises*: Notes and Comment," *Fitzgerald | Hemingway Annual* (Wash-
ington: NCR, 1970), pp. 1-9.

Frederic Henry, like so many twentieth-century fictional heroes, finds no catharsis. His failures have been inconsequential to everyone but himself; his personal loss has been massive, and he is left with no place to go.[18]

[18] Sheldon N. Grebstein's examination of the *A Farewell to Arms* MS in an appendix to his book, *Hemingway's Craft* (Carbondale: Southern Illinois University Press, 1973), appeared in print after my study had been completed. Certain conclusions of mine have been anticipated by Professor Grebstein; on other points we disagree. Where our observations overlap, footnotes will invite comparison.

Further Revisions

I always rewrite each day up to the point where I stopped. When it is all finished, naturally you go over it. You get another chance to correct and rewrite when someone else types it, and you see it clean in type. The last chance is in the proofs. You're grateful for these different chances.—Hemingway (*Paris Review* interview)

The textual problems of *A Farewell to Arms* are, at present, too complex to examine authoritatively. When it is possible to collate the holograph manuscript, the typescript, the galley proofs for the serialization, and the later galleys for the novel, it will be necessary to publish a new edition. The usual minor discrepancies can be explained and corrected. Several sentences and phrases that were apparently dropped by the two typists should be put back into the text. The one out-of-sequence paragraph can be reordered, and, hopefully, the full language of the novel will be restored. Based primarily on the holograph manuscript, this study is more interested in the kinds of revisions than in an authoritative text. The manuscript also raises the significant problems of epigrams and titles that appear in rough draft but not in final copy.

There is one indication in the manuscript that Hemingway's revisions did not proceed chronologically through the manuscript. On MS-452, he notes: "Start typist on page 222." MS-222 (p. 101) is the beginning of Chapter Sixteen, the night before Frederic's operation. What follows is the

cleanest copy in the manuscript, indicating that Hemingway had probably already revised and recopied much of
next hundred pages during the first draft. If the typing did
begin with Chapter Sixteen, it would have been because he
wanted to be certain of those opening chapters, pages of
which show two and three revisions.

Before he could start the typists, Hemingway had to reread the manuscript for two crucial points: chapter divisions and names. Throughout the first draft, he had difficulty recognizing the ends of chapters. Frequently he
would write through the ending and into the next chapter
before he realized that he had passed the natural breaking
point. He then went back, inserting the chapter number.
Some chapters are renumbered as many as three times, indicating that he had second and third thoughts about the
divisions.

More significant is the absence in the revised manuscript
of "Book" divisions. The published version is divided into
five Books, but in the manuscript there is only one indication (MS-467) that Hemingway might have intended to
break the novel into larger sections. This one notation appears to have been inserted during the final revision. When
the manuscript was typed, the typist included Book Four
at the beginning of Chapter Thirty-three. Hemingway
edited the notation out before sending the typescript to
Scribner's. The galleys for *Scribner's Magazine* publication
did not have book divisions, nor were they added when
Hemingway proofed them. (The novel was serialized in six
installments.) Book divisions appear for the first time as
handwritten additions in the galleys for the novel. These
galleys are dated May 6, 1929. The penciled additions are
not in Hemingway's handwriting. They were most likely
made by Max Perkins, but Hemingway must have agreed
to them, for he did not accept all of Perkins' suggestions.
Whatever he intended when he wrote the novel, he did not
think of it in terms of a five-act structure. Coming late as

they did, the book divisions were not a controlling factor in the structure of the novel.[1]

There was also the problem of names and spellings which Hemingway had to standardize before the typists began. Through the early part of the manuscript many of the characters had gone through name changes, and the spelling of *Catherine* alternated between *K* and *C*. In revisions, he made the following changes:

FIRST DRAFT	REVISED
Frances	Catherine, (Katherine)
Miss Reynolds	Miss Ferguson
Miss Watson, Lovell	Mrs. Walker
Piani	Moretti
J. Jepson, Kirby	Saunders
Manera	Passini
Rocky	Aymo
Menotti	Gavuzzi
Greppi	Greffi

The manuscript revisions are too numerous to be studied here completely, but there are types of revision that are significant to the artistry and intent of the author. The first type is the stylistic revision. For example, the opening paragraph of the novel, so carefully scrutinized by critics, looked somewhat different on its first draft:

In the late summer of that year we lived in a house in a village that looked across the river and the plain to the mountains. The river ran in channels in the bed of white pebbles and white boulders and there were always troops going by the house and down the rode road and the dust they raised powdered the leaves of the trees. The trunks of the trees too were dusty and the leaves fell early that year and I have seen the troops marching along the road and the dust rising and

[1] For an alternative analysis, see Grebstein, *Hemingway's Craft,* p. 206.

leaves falling and the soldiers marching and afterwards
the road bare and white except for the leaves.

The basic elements were present from the first: *house, river,*
troops, dust, trees, leaves. The revisions do not alter the relationship of these elements, but they do change the rhythm
of the paragraph. Much revised, the manuscript paragraph
looks like this:

In the late summer of that year we lived in a house in a village

~~in the night we heard the troops~~   The water in the river
that looked across the river and the plain to the mountains. ~~The~~
*   the river bed was white pebbles and dry white boulders and*
*   clear   the water was clear and swiftly moving and blue in the deep*
~~river ran~~ in/channels in the bed of white pebbles and white boulders   channels

*   T   went by*
~~and there were always~~ troops ~~going by~~ the house and down the ~~rode~~ road

and the dust they raised powdered the leaves of the trees. The trunks

*   and we saw*
of the trees too were dusty and the leaves fell early that year ~~and I have~~

*   stirred by the breeze*
~~seen~~ the troops marching along the road and the dust rising and leaves/

falling and the soldiers marching and afterwards the road bare and white

except for the leaves.

Still dissatisfied with the description of the river, Hemingway reworked the sentence until it finally read:

In the bed of the river there were pebbles and
boulders, dry and white in the sun, and the water was
clear and swiftly moving and blue in the channels.

The only substantial additions to the first draft—*sun* and
blue—do not change the meaning of the paragraph. It is the
poetics, not the content, that have been altered. The images
were present from the first, but it is not just the images that

establish the tone. The rhythm of the words, which gives emphasis to the imagery, is at least as important as the words themselves:

> In the late summer of that year
> we lived in a house in a village
> that looked across the river and the plain
> to the mountains.
> In the bed of the river
> there were pebbles and boulders,
> dry and white in the sun,
> and the water was clear
> and swiftly moving
> and blue in the channels.
> Troops
> went by the house and down the road
> and the dust they raised
> powdered the leaves of the trees.
> The trunks of the trees
> too were dusty
> and the leaves fell early that year
> and we saw the troops
> marching along the road
> and the dust rising
> and leaves,
> stirred by the breeze,
> falling
> and the soldiers marching
> and afterward
> the road
> bare and white
> except for the leaves.

Hemingway's published poetry is often neglected by critics as juvenilia. While it may not be significant as poetry, it does indicate his interest in poetics. Considering his relationship with Ezra Pound and Gertrude Stein, as well as his reading of T. S. Eliot, this interest is not surprising. Among

his unpublished literary remains there is a large body of
poetry that will probably never establish any firm credentials for Hemingway-as-poet, but that indicates the importance of poetry to him as a writer. Pound insisted that
poetry should be as well written as prose. Many of Hemingway's revisions insist that prose can be as rhythmical as
poetry.[2]

This is not to suggest that all of his revisions of *A Farewell to Arms* manuscript were made for the sake of poetics,
but many of the changes are similar to those of the opening
paragraph: they add rhythm rather than introducing new
detail. For example, there are Frederic's observations as he
is being evacuated back to the field hospital. The first draft
read:

> *I saw arched stone bridges over the river where
> tracks / turned off the road and we passed stone farm
> houses with chestnut trees growing around them.*

MSS-105-106

The revision looks like this:

> I saw the arched stone bridges over the river where the tracks
>
> turned off the road and we passed stone farm houses with ~~chestnut~~
> ~~spread~~ candelabraed   south
> pear trees ~~against~~ their (*unreadable*) walls ~~on the South side~~
> ~~trees growing around them.~~
>   *and ~~hedges~~ low stone walls in the fields.*

The final description reads:

> we passed stone farm houses with pear trees can-
> delabraed against their south walls and low stone walls
> in the fields.

Repeating the word *stone* and changing to the more sensu-
ous *pear* trees, Hemingway does not radically change the

[2] Grebstein reaches a similar conclusion, pp. 142-145, 168-169.

content of the original draft, but he improves its poetics.

This same type of change is apparent in the description of the cathedral square in Milan on the night Frederic returns to the front. The first draft reads:

> *There, instead of walking along in front of the shop windows, we crossed the tram tracks and walked along beside the cathedral. It was misty in the square and the cathedral stone looked damp.*

MS-292

In revision he junked almost all of the two sentences:

> *There were street car tracks and beyond them was the cathedral. It was white and wet in the mist.*

> ~~There, instead of walking along in front of the shop windows,~~ *we*

>   *on our left were the shops, their windows lighted, and*
> crossed the tram tracks ~~and walked along beside the cathedral.~~

> *the entrance to the galleria. There was a fog in the square and when we*
> ~~It was misty in the square and the cathedral stone looked damp.~~
> *came close to the front of the cathedral it was very big and the stone was wet.*

The only new observation is "the entrance to the galleria"; the first draft contains the essentials: *shop windows, tram tracks, cathedral, square, mist, wet stone.* The revisions change the rhythm of these observations by expanding the *it-was, there-were* constructions. Such revisions are matters of style, and the manuscript shows time and again Hemingway's careful attention to such matters.

A different type of revision, found throughout the manuscript, is one that reduces overwritten passages to the leanness associated with Hemingway. Usually these revisions move toward understatement, and they are found frequently in passages that had been done to death by the war novel genre. For example, the description of the bombardment at Plava:

There was a whistling that changed to an inrushing
scream of air and then a flash and crash outside in the
brick yard. Then a bump and a sustained incoming
shreak of air that exploded with a roar, the crash of
high explosive tearing steel apart on contact and
vomiting earth and brick.

MS-123

After several revisions, Hemingway backed off and wrote
an insert:

A big shell came in and burst outside in the brickyard.
Another burst and in the noise you could hear the
smaller noise of brick and dirt raining down. (p. 52)

With the theatrics eliminated, all that remains are the understated explosions.

There was always this temptation to slip into the overwritten prose of the popular war novel. Consciously aware
of the pitfall, Hemingway wrote a note to himself beside the
first draft above and then circled it for emphasis: *"Watch
out for this."* Many of the overwritten passages dealt with
the reactions of Frederic Henry. By eliminating these reactions to the point of understatement, Hemingway effaces
Frederic through the first three books of the novel. When
Frederic's thoughts and feelings are detailed, particularly
in Book Five, when Catherine is dying, they have greater
impact because the reader has come to expect Frederic's
stoicism.

Actually the problems raised by his narrator were more
perplexing for Hemingway than the published novel shows.
If, as evidence indicates, he did not have the novel plotted
to its present conclusion until well into Book Three, and if
he originally saw the novel ending with Frederic's death,
perhaps at the Tagliamento, then the stature of Frederic
would be expected to grow as the novel progressed. Once

Hemingway realized that it was Catherine who would die, he must have seen the problem posed by Frederic. One of the unnumbered manuscript pages contains a typed sentence focusing directly on the sore spot:

The position of the survivor of a great calamity is seldom admirable.

This is exactly Frederic's dilemma. He has survived, and in telling his story retrospectively, he simply cannot portray himself as a traditional hero. Left at the end in an emotional slough, his defeat is more thorough than that of Jake Barnes in *The Sun Also Rises*. Unlike Jake, Frederic has taken an active role in his disaster. Rail as he does against the anonymous forces of the universe and society, Frederic is left embarrassingly alive, and Catherine is dead because of Frederic's baby. He has done little that was heroic, nothing admirable or particularly virtuous, and it is he who is left alive to tell the story. Hemingway could not allow him to flounder in self-pity nor could he inflate Frederic's suffering. His role as ambulance driver is de-emphasized; he is allowed none of the ambulance-corps heroics found in so many autobiographic accounts from the western front. Even in his almost-heroic row up the lake, it is not Catherine whom Frederic is saving, but himself. Surviving is the only virtue permitted him, and many of the deleted manuscript passages would have enlarged Frederic's anguish.

On the same unnumbered manuscript page there is another typed quotation:

Henry James in conversation
with Preston Lockwood

New York Times
March 21, 1915
One finds it in the midst of all this as hard to apply one's words as to endure one's thoughts. The war has

used up words; they have weakened, they have deterioriated like motor car tires; . . . and we are now confronted with a depreciation of all our terms, or otherwise speaking, with a loss of expression through increase of limpness, that may well make us wonder what ghosts will be left to walk.

Despite the Jamesian circumlocution, the question of language is relevant to *A Farewell to Arms*. The polite and decorous language of the earlier period was no longer a useful tool to the post-war writer. The subtle problems of the Jamesian novel, with its impeccable drawing rooms, were no longer relevant. Fastidious manners and proper breeding were devalued by the war; niceness of distinction and language was of little use when faced with execution in another country. The novel of the American in Europe, James's forte, had to change after the war; *A Farewell to Arms* is that change.

Hemingway's novel is an answer to James's question about what language will remain. In one of the most heavily revised passages of the manuscript, Frederic restates the linguistic dilemma posed by James:

I was always embarrased by the words sacred, glorious, and sacrifice and the expression in vain. . . . There were many words that you could not stand to hear and finally only the names of places had dignity. . . . Abstract words such as glory, honor, courage, or hallow were obscene beside the concrete names of villages, the numbers of roads, the names of rivers, the numbers of regiments and the dates. (pp. 184-185)[3]

Neither of the typed quotations appear in *A Farewell to Arms*, although Hemingway might have been intending to use them for epigraphs. His previous novel, *The Sun Also Rises*, had started with three epigraphs that were cut to two

[3] Grebstein reaches a similar conclusion, pp. 206-207.

for publication. Hemingway felt afterward that these epigraphs had misled readers, who read the novel as a chronicle of the "Lost Generation" while not understanding the statement in Ecclesiastes about the earth abiding forever.[4] For whatever reasons, Hemingway did not use epigraphs in *A Farewell to Arms*, but these two potential epigraphs reveal something of the author's attitude toward his material. Neither are concerned with the love story or with the war story—the apparent dichotomy of the novel that has bothered critics. Both quotations focus on the aftermath of the war: what will be left after the catastrophe. Writing from the perspective of 1928, Hemingway knew very well what had been left. He had seen the disaster in Europe and America's retreat into isolation. The pre-war values, both European and American, had died in the trenches. By 1928, the heroic rhetoric of Teddy Roosevelt and Woodrow Wilson had become a joke.

A less subtle problem in the manuscript was language— not the sort that Henry James was worried about but those profane and obscene words which are the natural speech of men at war. Hemingway had battled this problem head-on with Scribner's before the publication of *The Sun Also Rises*. Perkins, a master of tact, had written Hemingway: "The majority of the people are more affected by *words* than things. I'd even say that those most obtuse toward *things* are most sensitive to a sort of a *word*. I think some words should be avoided so that we shall not divert people from the qualities of this book. . . . You probably don't appreciate this disgusting possibility because you've been too long abroad, and out of that atmosphere. And papers now attack a book, not only on grounds of eroticism which could not hold here, but upon that of 'decency,' which means *words*. In view of this, I suggest that a particular adjunct of the bulls . . . be not spelled out, but covered by a blank."[5] The bull's "balls" had been changed to "horns" and other

4 Hemingway to Perkins, Nov. 19, 1926.
5 Perkins to Hemingway, June 29, 1926.

words had gone to blanks. Now, two years later, Hemingway wrestled with the same problem of language but with words even more offensive. As he had told Perkins, he never used certain *words* unless they were irreplaceable. Certain *words* were not ornaments and were used by him only when absolutely necessary.[6] That necessity was clearly present in *A Farewell to Arms* if it were to remain true to experience. The conversation of Frederic's ambulance drivers during the retreat was ultimately reduced to blanks, but in the manuscript Hemingway wrote the only way he knew:

"Tomorrow we'll sleep in the king's bed," Bonello said.
"Tomorrow maybe we'll sleep in shit," Piani said.
"I'll sleep with the queen," Bonello said.
"You'll sleep with shit," Piani *said sleepily.*

MSS-377-378

"The first thing we will see will be the ~~fucking~~
cavalry," Piani said.
"I don't think they've got any cavalry."
"I hope to Christ not," Bonello said. *"I don't want to*
be stuck on a lance by any fucking *cavalry."*

MS-410

"Never mind. That's one thing I can always
remember. I killed that son of a bitch *of a sergeant."*

MS-411

"Take him back there with the others," the first
officer said. *"You see. He speaks Italian with an*
accent."
"So do you, you cocksucker," I said.

MSS-445-446

All of the words emphasized eventually were blanked, but Hemingway fought for their use.

[6] Hemingway to Perkins, July 24, 1926.

Another problem not easily solved was the choice of a title. *A Farewell to Arms* is in neither the first draft nor any of the revisions. There is no clear indication that he found his title before December, 1928, by which time he was well into the process of revision. The title, taken from a Geroge Peele poem, is appropriate, but Hemingway continued to have misgivings about it. Perkins assured him in late February, 1929: "As for the title, I think it is very good indeed, though it is one of those titles that is better after you have read the book than before. But even at first sight it is a fine title. Everyone here thinks so too."[7]

Characteristically, Hemingway turned to the *Bible* and *The Oxford Book of English Verse* when searching for titles. *A Farewell to Arms* he found in the verse collection, but it was not the only title that Hemingway had considered. In the holograph manuscript there are four typed titles which were apparently found during the revision period at Key West. The other titles, apparently under consideration, were: *The World's Room, Nights and Forever, A Separate Peace, The Hill of Heaven*. "A Separate Peace" would have been a fine title, and one can only speculate why Hemingway did not use it when it had close associations with *in our time*:

> Nick turned his head and looked down at Rinaldi. "Senta Rinaldo; Senta. You and me we've made a separate peace." Rinaldi lay still in the sun, breathing with difficulty. "We're not patriots." Nick turned his head away, smiling sweatily. Rinaldi was a disappointing audience.   (*in our time*, p. 81.)

Perhaps Hemingway did not use the title because of its ambiguity. If "A Farewell to Arms" implies the arms of war and the arms of love to many readers, "A Separate Peace" would surely suggest the alternate spelling, "Piece," which would have been a sardonic statement about the love affair.

[7] Perkins to Hemingway, Feb. 27, 1929.

The other three titles found in the holograph manuscript
—"The World's Room," "Nights and Forever," and "The
Hill of Heaven"—were taken from *The Oxford Book of
Ballads*.[8] "The World's Room" comes from the ballad "Edward, Edward"; "Nights and Forever" appears to be taken
from a refrain line in "A Lyke-Wake Dirge"; "The Hill of
Heaven" is from "The Deamon Lover." "Edward" concerns
the death of the young lord who leaves his wife and child to
beg through the world. "The Deamon Lover" destroys the
woman who had been unfaithful. "The Lyke-Wake Dirge"
concerns the condition of a man's soul.

Neither the rejected titles nor the final title had any in-
fluence on the writing of the novel. The rejected titles were
typed on unnumbered pages, indicating that they were
probably done at Key West in December. Two of them—
"The World's Room" and "Nights and Forever"—do appear
in the holograph manuscript written on the front cover
from a tablet of writing paper, Old Irish Linen. This is the
same paper that Hemingway used for the last few pages of
the manuscript. A separate page in Hemingway's hand lists
thirty more possible titles (see Appendix B) that seem to
have been compiled during the revision stage of the manuscript. For the most part they were found in *The Oxford
Book of English Verse*. Buried between *Sorrow for Pleasure* and *Late Wisdom* is *A Farewell to Arms*. This evidence merely supports what the author said about his practice of titling:

Interviewer: Do the titles come to you while you're in
the process of doing the story?
Hemingway: No. I make a list of titles *after* I've
finished the story or the book—some-

---

[8] *The Oxford Book of Ballads*, ed. Arthur Quiller-Couch (Oxford,
1910), pp. 125, 138, 290-291; Hemingway could have been using any
of the reprints of 1919, 1924, or 1927; "Edward" and "The Lyke-
Wake Dirge" also appear in the 1910 edition of *The Oxford Book of
English Verse*. "The Deamon Lover" appears only in the ballad collection.

                times as many as 100. Then I start elimi-
                nating them, sometimes all of them.

Interviewer: And you do this even with a story whose
                title is supplied from the text—"Hills
                Like White Elephants," for example.

Hemingway: Yes. The title comes afterwards.[9]

[9] George Plimpton, "An Interview with Ernest Hemingway," *Paris Review*, 18 (Spring, 1958), p. 83.

Publication: Words and other Words

After a while I went out and left the hospital and walked back to the hotel in the rain.

When Max Perkins picked up the typed manuscript at Key West in January, 1929, the first period of Hemingway's career was over. For ten years he had struggled with his style and his pocketbook. His first novel, *The Sun Also Rises*, continued to make money, but the royalties all went in a divorce settlement to his first wife, Hadley. Most of his expenses in 1928 had been paid for by Pauline and her family, and although he continued to let Uncle Gus Pfeiffer pick up the bill on his African safari in the Thirties, Hemingway would never again be financially dependent on anyone.

On February 13 Perkins wired Hemingway: "WISH TO SERIALIZE STOP FIRST INSTALLMENT BEING SET WITH SOME BLANKS STOP MAY ASK PERMISSION ON TWO OR THREE BRIEF PASSAGES IN LATER ONES BUT ONLY WITH YOUR APPROVAL STOP PRICE PROPOSED $16,000."

A Perkins letter followed on the same day:

Dear Ernest,
I am writing at the first possible moment to say we are keen to serialize. There are certain words, some of which we spoke of, which must be concealed by a white space, and there are several passages later which we will have to raise the question of omitting, chiefly

because they contain certain words which could not be
deleted without spoiling the sense of the passages.
There are never more than two, three, or four lines
anyhow, and I am positive they are nothing that any
magazine would not have to deal with in the same way
as we propose.

14 FEBRUARY 1929
AWFULLY PLEASED PRICE OK ERNEST
HEMINGWAY

Hemingway wrote Perkins on February 16, thanking him
for some books the Scribner bookstore had sent him and
repeating his pleasure at the serialization price. He sensed,
however, another fight beginning on the use of "certain
words." In *The Sun Also Rises* he had been badgered into
making changes in language to protect the ears and eyes of
his American readers, and he saw the same battle in front
of him. He told Perkins that each omission would have to
be discussed specifically, but that he would not be unreasonable. For unavoidable omissions, blanks would have to
be inserted, but he resisted the idea of dropping an entire
passage. Every part of the book depended upon every other
part. If a passage had to be dropped, then a blank should
indicate the deletion. He was thinking in terms of the *Scribner's Magazine* serialization at this point, for he speculated
that blank passages might make readers more eager to buy
the novel to see what had been left out. He reminded Perkins that emasculation was a simple operation in men, ani-
mals, and books, but that the effects were very great. It was
not an operation to be performed unintentionally, particularly on books. For the magazine he would accept blanks;
both of them, he was sure, had the same interests at heart.

On February 19, 1929, Robert Bridges, editor of *Scribner's Magazine*, mailed Hemingway the galley proofs for
the first installment of the novel with a cover letter explaining the deletions: "You will note that in accordance with

Perkins, we have in several places put in dashes instead of
the realistic phrases which the soldiers of course used. This
was not done from any particular squeamishness, but we
have long been accepted in many schools as what is known,
I believe, as 'collateral reading,' and have quite a clientage
among those who teach mixed classes. Things which are
perfectly natural and realistic in a book are not viewed
with the same mind in a serial reading." Bridges suggested
that one paragraph be omitted altogether in deference to
the magazine's readers: "On galley 12, I would suggest that
you omit the paragraph circled with lead pencil, inserting
several dashes to fill out the line after 'Please,' resuming
with: 'That is how it ought to be, etc.' "

The passage that Bridges deleted was part of Frederic's
daydream in Chapter Seven when he is visualizing a week-
end in bed with Catherine:

> Because we would not wear any clothes because it was
> so hot and the window open and the swallows flying
> over the roofs of the houses and when it was dark
> afterward and you went to the window very small bats
> hunting over the houses and close down over the trees
> and we would drink the capri and the door locked and
> it hot and only a sheet and the whole night and we
> would both love each other all night in the hot night in
> Milan. (p. 38)

The passage was an important one for the novel, for this
daydream would be acted out later in Milan under less than
ideal conditions. The reality of the hotel room would not
match the illusion, and the passage was necessary for
comparison.

On February 23, Hemingway returned the galleys to
Bridges with permission to omit the offending paragraph,
replacing it with dashes. At the same time he asked Perkins
once more if the title was right, for this would be his last
opportunity to change it. Perkins replied that the title was

fine. As for the deleted passage, Perkins said: "[It] will do very well for the book and it is necessary really. But anyhow, I would never ask you to take out anything, not even a word, unless it seemed to me that it simply had to be done; and I should not be just playing safe. I should play the other way, in fact."

On February 27 Perkins wrote Hemingway concerning the cuts that Bridges had suggested, trying to anticipate Hemingway's reaction. Perkins assured Hemingway he understood the difficulties of his art: "There was a great deal of hostility to 'The Sun.' It was routed and driven off the field by the book's qualities, and the adherence which they won. The hostility was very largely that which any new thing in art must meet, simply because it is disturbing. It shows life in a different aspect, and people are more comfortable when they have got it all conventionalized and smoothed down, and everything unpleasant hidden. . . . It was the same failure to be understood that a wholly new painter meets. People simply do not understand because they can only understand what they are accustomed to." Perkins enclosed an advance check of $6,000 on the serialization. In all of 1928, Hemingway had made only $8,942 in royalties from Scribner's and most of that had gone to Hadley from *The Sun Also Rises*.

But even the advance check could not placate Hemingway when he saw the galleys for the second installment of *A Farewell to Arms*. He found that Bridges had made two cuts—one of six lines and the other of ten. The result was that the dialogue did not make sense—two consecutive lines of dialogue were spoken by the same person. Hemingway was enraged that he had not been consulted. The manuscript lines had not even been set up in the galley. He demanded that the galley proofs be set as he had written the manuscript; then deletions could be discussed. He would rather return the money than have arbitrary changes made in his published work.

These two passages in the second installment that

Bridges had altered were not corrected for magazine publication. The first passage takes place in the field hospital when Rinaldi is giving Frederic advice on women. The italicized parts were deleted:

"Truly? I tell you something about your good
women. Your goddesses. *There is only one difference
between taking a girl who has always been good and a
woman. With a girl it is painful. That's all I know.*" *He
slapped the bed with his glove. "And you never
know if the girl will really like it.*"
"Don't get angry."
"I'm not angry. *I just tell you, baby, for your own
good. To save you trouble.*"
"*That's the only difference?*"
"*Yes. But millions of fools like you don't know it.*"
"You were sweet to tell me."
"We won't quarrel, baby. I love you too much. But
don't be a fool."   (pp. 66-67)

The second deletion was made in the first meeting of Frederic and Catherine in the Milan hospital. In what may be the shortest seduction scene in literature, Bridges made the passage even shorter leaving the reader wondering what, if anything, had taken place:

"Feel our hearts beating." [Catherine]
"I don't care about our hearts. I want you. I'm just mad
    about you."
"*You really love me?*"
"*Don't keep on saying that. Come on. Please. Please,
    Catherine.*"
"*All right but only for a minute.*"
"*All right,*" I said. "*Shut the door.*"
"*You can't. You shouldn't.*"
"*Come on. Don't talk. Please come on.*"
Catherine sat in a chair by the bed.   (p. 92)

On April 16, Perkins wrote Hemingway, assuring him that the galleys for the novel followed the original copy exactly. Perkins was hopeful that the Literary Guild or Book-of-the-Month Club might be interested in the book, but the turmoil caused by the magazine serialization must have killed any hope for book-club interest. In spite of Bridges' delicate excisions, in spite of blanks, and in spite of words left out, the June issue of *Scribner's Magazine* was banned from the Boston book stands by the superintendent of police, Michael H. Crowley. Certain passages in *A Farewell to Arms* were deemed salacious. Ironically, the June installment contained the passages that Bridges had most heavily edited.

Hemingway's problems with language were not over with the magazine publication. Words came in two categories: those which could not be used in the magazine and those which could not be used in hard cover. Bridges would not allow: *balls, cocksucker, fuck, Jesus Christ, shit, son of a bitch, whore,* or *whorehound* to appear in the magazine. For the most part Hemingway understood Bridges' dilemma and did not make an issue of the point. Bridges did print *damn, God, goddamn, bastard,* and *good Christ.* When the galleys were set for the publication of the novel, some of the words were put back in. Perkins, working under Scribner policy, put back *Jesus Christ, son of a bitch, whore,* and *whorehound.* The other words were still too strong for the public in 1929. This decision was a disappointment to Hemingway.

On May 2, 1929, Perkins told Hemingway that the galleys were being set from the manuscript, "disregarding magazine corrections." He was concerned that Hemingway might have made corrections in the magazine galleys that he wanted to include in the novel. When Hemingway returned the galleys on June 7, he was upset about several deletions.

Perkins apparently suggested omitting the reference to the earthier side of hospital life:

"Would you like to use the bedpan?"
"I might try."

(p. 86)

Hemingway said that he had cut out at least two thousand words about hospital life that had dominated the chapter. This was the only incident he had left in. The bedpan should stay. It was the same with the other words Perkins wanted to delete. Hemingway insisted that he had used discretion throughout the novel. All of the words were in print elsewhere—in Shakespeare, for example. He was particularly concerned about the publication in Germany of Remarque's *All Quiet on the Western Front*. It had sold in the thousands in Germany and was doing very well in England. Hemingway emphasized to Perkins that *A Farewell to Arms* would be competing with Remarque that fall in the U.S., and Remarque had used most of the words that Hemingway wanted to use. The commercial and artistic value of his own work might be killed by such emasculation. Hemingway insisted that he did not want his novel suppressed, but, short of that, he wanted everything he could get. There had always been good writing, he told Perkins, and then there had been American genteel writing.

Hemingway was adamant about the conversation between Frederic and his drivers during the retreat from Caporetto. If that were changed, it would be ruinous he felt. Any changes in this dialogue would be made without his consent. The changes were made.

Then there was the problem about the *balls*. In the manuscript Frederic's confrontation with Miss Van Campen reads as follows:

"Have you ever had jaundice, Miss Van Campen?"
"No, but I've seen a great deal of it."

"You noticed how the patients enjoyed it?"
"I suppose it is better than the front."
"Miss Van Campen," I said, "did you ever know a man who tried to disable himself by kicking himself in the balls?"

(p. 144)

In *Scribner's Magazine*, the word *balls* appears as a blank. Hemingway again felt that the word was crucial to the scene. Here was a woman who had always been protected from such language by virtue of her sex and her position.

Hemingway reminded Perkins that it was the same word that had caused so much trouble in *The Sun Also Rises*. In that novel, during the fiesta a drunken conversation went like this:

"Tell him the bulls have no balls!" Mike shouted, very drunk from the other end of the table.
"What does he say?"
"He's drunk."
"Jake," Mike called. "Tell him bulls have no balls!"

Under pressure Hemingway changed *balls* to *horns* for the 1926 publication. (Sometime later Scribner's reinserted the original wording.) But in 1929 the same word was causing trouble. Hemingway's point was that the strictures needed to be tested; he wanted a return to the full use of the language. If they had tried the word in 1926 with *The Sun*, they would know if it could be printed in the United States. One must keep in mind that Scribner's was not attempting to protect its readers so much as it was trying to publish books that would not be banned or censored. They did not want a court fight or adverse publicity. The compromise in *A Farewell to Arms* substituted *scrotum* for *balls*.

An even more impossible word in 1929 was *cocksucker*. Hemingway argued that he was eliminating most of the lan-

guage used by men, but to eliminate the language entirely
was to emasculate the novel. When Scott Fitzgerald saw the
galleys for the novel, he told Hemingway that he simply
could not use the word. The novel would be suppressed
immediately.[1] In his June 7 letter to Perkins, Hemingway
suggested that if the word would lead to suppression, then
c---s----r would serve. Even that was apparently too strong
for the 1929 readers, for only a blank appeared in the novel
when it was published.[2]

In addition to the problem of language, there was the further irritation to Hemingway of others telling him how to
rewrite his book. This advice came not from malice but
from good intentions—which only made it worse. First
there was Owen Wister, who had become an admirer in 1927
although his reaction to *in our time* had been initially
negative. In a letter to Barklie Henry in 1927, Wister wrote:
"Do you remember sending me a collection of Ernest Hemingway's selections to read and my not setting any value on
them. Now I must eat humble pie. His recent tale in the *Atlantic* and the book *The Sun Also Rises* are both perfectly
extraordinary. I don't know any young writer whose style
and gift seem to me to approach him. Were I 30, that's the
way I should wish to write. I hope he has a long career of
development ahead of him. And that he will become interested in more varieties of human nature. So far he reveals
a somewhat limited field of action."

On February 18, 1929, Wister wrote Perkins enthusiasti-
cally about the serialization of Hemingway's new novel.
This was barely four days after Hemingway himself had
accepted the offer. Wister went on to tell Perkins: "Kipling,
who was hostile to E. H. on account of *The Sun Also Rises*
until I reasoned with him, sent a message: 'Tell him that
since you vouch for him, I'll believe in him.' Intend some
day to deliver but not until I have seen the new book." Perkins relayed this interest, but one wonders how delighted

[1] Fitzgerald to Hemingway, undated, 1929.
[2] See Grebstein, pp. 208-209.

Hemingway might have been with Kipling's left-handed acceptance.

Early in 1929, Wister got a set of galley proofs of *A Farewell to Arms* from Perkins. Perhaps Perkins wanted to use the Wister endorsement in publicity for the novel, or perhaps he was merely being nice to the older writer. Whatever the motive, Hemingway does not appear to have been consulted on the matter. On April 30, Wister wrote Perkins a glowing appreciation of the new novel, although he felt some of the medical details were too outspoken. But this was a minor reservation: "When you wish to call on me, if you shall so wish, I will do my best to frame my enthusiasm into something you can use to help him and his book and his publisher."

On May 6 Wister wrote again to Perkins, this time having finished the novel, which he apparently had not done in his first burst of enthusiasm. He was still very much impressed and had written Hemingway telling him so. But there were parts of the last chapter that bothered him. There were, he felt, certain details that should be omitted, certain portions that should be changed. He had made suggestions for such changes to Hemingway. Wister was also concerned about the two themes—love and war—that did not seem to come back together at the end.

One can only imagine how Hemingway took such paternal enthusiasm from Wister, but we know that he was, at that very time, agonizing over the last chapter. The portions that Wister wanted softened were the very portions he was most sure of. But Perkins, too, was having some critical problems with the book. He wrote Wister on May 17: "The serious flaw in the book is that the two great elements you named—one of which would make it a picture of war, and the other of which would make it a duo of love and passion—do not fully combine. It begins as one thing wholly, and ends up wholly as the other thing. This was a point I had meant to make when I sent him the galley proofs for the book. . . . my idea was that the war should be somehow carried over into the last part of the book."

As he told Wister, Perkins tactfully brought up the proposed addition to Hemingway in a letter of May 24: "The book is so remarkable that if you want to work further on any parts of it, you ought to do it. . . . The first point relates to the combination of the two elements of the book—Love and War. They combine, to my mind, perfectly up to the point where Catherine and Lieutenant Henry get to Switzerland; thereafter, the war is almost forgotten by them and by the reader, though not quite. And psychologically it should be all but forgotten; it would be by people so profoundly in love, and so I do not think what I at first thought that you might bring more news of it or remembrance of it into this part. Still, I can't shake off the feeling that war, which has deeply conditioned this love story—and does so still passively—should still do so actively and decisively. It would if Catherine's death might probably not have occurred except for it, and I should think it likely that the life she had led as a nurse, and all the exposure, etc. might have been largely responsible. If it were, and if the doctor said so during that awful night, in just a casual sentence, the whole story would turn back upon the war and realization of Henry and the reader.

"I say this with the realization that a man in this work may make a principle into an obsession, as professors do. Unity? Nothing is so detestable as the *neat* ending. . . . I know, by the way, that Wister wrote you about these two elements of War and Love, and that he saw the question differently, as if the story were really only of love with war as the impressive and conditioning background, or almost only that. But I could not quite see it that way."

Perkins went on to suggest that Catherine's pain in the last chapter might be made a little less visible. He did not want the shock of the physical suffering to overpower the reader at the end.

If such friendly advice from Owen Wister and Max Perkins were not enough, Hemingway got further instruction from Scott Fitzgerald, who had convinced him to cut the opening chapter from the manuscript of *The Sun Also*

Rises. This time Hemingway did not let Fitzgerald see his novel until Scribner's had the typescript. Perhaps he was becoming a little piqued by the implications that he had learned much about writing from Fitzgerald. There is some kidding to this effect in several letters to Fitzgerald in the Twenties.

Fitzgerald responded in his own fashion. There was much in the book that he found over-written and self-indulgent. Some of the minor characters in Milan needed to be eliminated. The day at the race track was unnecessary: "This is definitely dull . . . It's dull because the war goes further and further out of sight every minute. 'That's the way it was.' It's no answer. This triumphant truth that races were fixed!"

Frederic's conversation with the British major at the Anglo-American Club also needed revision: "This is a comedy scene that really becomes offensive for you have trained everyone to read every word—now you make them read the word *cooked* (and fucked would have been as bad) *one dozen times.* It has ceased to become amusing by the fifth . . . yet the scene has possibilities, reduced to five or six cookeds it might have rhythm like the word wops in one of your earlier sketches. You're a little hypnotized by yourself here."

Fitzgerald found much of Catherine's dialogue simple and unbelievable. Moreover, the book was not 160,000 words long as Hemingway had thought; rather, Fitzgerald told him, it was more like 80,000 to 100,000. The ending was not right for the novel. There was a place earlier where the novel should have stopped. And finally Fitzgerald could say, "A beautiful book it is!" Hemingway's only recorded comment is written on the bottom of Fitzgerald's last page. He wrote: "Kiss my ass."

With Wister, Perkins, and Fitzgerald all giving paternal advice, it is a wonder that Hemingway was able to control his temper as well as he did. The advice had no effect; the changes that Hemingway made were his own, except for those words he was forced to omit. On June 24, 1929, he wrote Perkins that the final draft of the conclusion was written. Once he had finished rewriting the ending, he realized that the advice had been well-intentioned. He asked Perkins to destroy the letter in which he had blown up about Wister's suggestions. That letter is not in the Scribner file. Already Hemingway was discovering that his first violent reactions were impulsive and frequently wrong. He would learn this lesson time and again in his life and still be able to forget it. Unfortunately, it is those impulsive answers which have become literary history while the second-thought apologies are forgotten.

With the book finished and in galleys, Hemingway began to worry about things other than style. After the *In Our Time* stories, in which there were recognizable characters, and after *The Sun Also Rises*, with its thinly veiled personalities, he had learned that he was taking a chance with libel suits any time he wrote a story. Before there had been little to risk, for there had been no big money involved. This time was different. There was already the $16,000 payment for the serial; the book should sell for him. On September 9, 1929, Hemingway wrote Perkins asking his opinion about a disclaimer at the front of the novel. This suggestion was too late to be included in the first edition which was published on September 27, 1929. The first printing was 31,050 copies.

September 28, 1929
Perkins to Hemingway
FIRST REVIEW SPLENDID STOP PROSPECTS
   BRIGHT

October 3, 1929
ALREADY GETTING REORDERS STOP VERY
   FINE PRESS

The second printing in September of 10,000 copies included the following note: "None of the characters in this book is a living person, nor are the units or military orga-

nizations mentioned actual units or organizations. E. H."
This note disappeared from subsequent printings and editions of the novel.

When Hemingway got a copy with the dust jacket, his
reaction was similar to his reaction when he first saw the
dust jacket of *The Sun Also Rises*. The bull on the cover of
that earlier book, Hemingway had felt, looked emasculated.
He had even sent pictures of bulls to the artist to improve
the bull's virility. The dust jacket of *A Farewell to Arms*
was equally displeasing to him. He felt the title and author
had been sacrificed to the artist's picture. Moreover, the
woman looked unattractive and decadent, with large mis-
placed breasts. Hemingway said that the cover alone would
be a challenge to anyone who wanted to suppress the book.
Her legs, he thought, were awful and her belly muscles
gigantic, but then, as he admitted, he was probably over-
reacting.

On October 4, Hemingway took up the point of the "alibi
note" again with Perkins. He said that his real worry was
the Italian government, which had suppressed all references to Caporetto in the official histories of the war. He
did not want to be sued by Italy. The possibility of that was
very slim, he said, but still his contract held him responsible
for libel suits. The note would be a kind of insurance. He
left the matter up to Perkins' judgment for further printings. Hemingway assured Perkins there were no names of
anyone he had ever seen or known in the book. There had
been an American Red Cross hospital in Milan, he said, but
it had not been founded until June of 1918, and all the action of the novel took place prior to 1918.

October 15, 1929
Perkins to Hemingway
SALE AT END OF LAST WEEK 28 THOUSAND
COPIES STOP HAVE PRINTED IN ALL FIFTY
THOUSAND STOP PROSPECTS EXCELLENT

By October 22, the sales reached 33,000. November 12, sales were 45,000 with 70,000 printed. November 21, sales passed 50,000.

By the end of November there were rumors in Europe that Hemingway was leaving Scribner's for another publisher. During the following weeks Hemingway wrote Perkins several times, assuring him that he had no such intentions and that the rumors were malicious. Perkins replied that Scribner's was not worried.

On November 30, Hemingway once again wrote Perkins, asking him to reinsert the disclaimer and, in fact, make it stronger. He did not even claim to have been in Italy. He was only using it as a setting for his fiction, a tradition that had been followed by writers for hundreds of years. It was not intended to be a picture or judgment of Italy.

December 7, 1929
SALES 57 THOUSAND

December 9
SALES 59 THOUSAND

December 11
SALES 62 THOUSAND

On December 15, Hemingway wrote Perkins that his own fears about libel were probably exaggerated. Still it would not hurt anything to put some disclaimer at the beginning.

December 19
SALES 65 THOUSAND

By January 8, 1930, the sales of the novel had passed 70,000 copies. Hemingway had become a best seller in his own country. By 1961 the novel would have sold 1,383,000 copies in various editions and reprints.

The first reviews of the novel were overwhelmingly favorable. Malcolm Cowley, Clifton Fadiman, and Henry

Canby were impressed and positive about the novel.[3] It is amusing to read through the early reviews, not for their appreciation of the novel, but for the misconceptions of Hemingway-as-writer that were already current. He was anti-intellectual; he had learned too much from Gertrude Stein; he was an autobiographic writer; he wrote well naturally, but did not understand the process; he was unread; the image was full blown by 1930, and, if it was not true, it did not hurt his sales.

The one really negative review was done by the second-generation American realist Robert Herrick in *Bookman* under the title—"What Is Dirt?"[4] Herrick began by saying that he was adamantly opposed to censorship, but there were times when it was necessary. *A Farewell to Arms* was one of those times. He found much of the physical detail in the novel to be "unpleasant garbage." Comparing the novel with Remarque's *All Quiet on the Western Front*, parts of which had been deleted for American publication, Herrick found the German author had produced a work of art, whereas Hemingway had produced "mere dirt." It would have been "no great loss" if *A Farewell to Arms* had been suppressed. With the assurance by now familiar in guardians of morality, Herrick said that he had not read past Book Two of the novel, for he had had enough by then.

To a certain degree Herrick reflected the conservative reaction of "middle America" that has characterized public outrage to *avant garde* literature in the twentieth century. Scribner's received numerous letters from readers outraged by either the magazine publication or the hard cover version. From Elizabeth, New Jersey a lady wrote: "I am discontinuing my subscription to a magazine which

[3] Henry S. Canby, "Chronicle and Comment," *Bookman*, 70 (Feb., 1930), p. 644; Malcolm Cowley, "Not Yet Demobilized," *NYHTBR* (Oct. 6, 1929), pp. 1, 16. Clifton Fadiman, "A Fine American Novel," *Nation*, 129 (Oct. 30, 1929), pp. 497-498.

[4] Robert Herrick, "What Is Dirt?" *Bookman*, 70 (November, 1929), pp. 258-262.

I have read since its first number. . . . your choice of fiction is most distasteful. You will reply that you cater to popular demand, that you 'hold the mirror up to nature.' I admit it. Generally literary taste is degenerate, and nature has its moments of indecency, which may better be unrecognized. Specifically I object to this serial 'A Farewell to Arms,' . . . I cannot allow a magazine containing such vileness to be seen in my house. I have burned the offending number. There is no excuse for printing indecency."

From Mobile, Alabama, the General Secretary of the Young Men's Christian Association wrote to cancel their subscription: "It is with keen regret that I am now obliged to withhold Scribner's from the magazine tables . . . I refer particularly to Ernest Hemingway's 'A Farewell to Arms' which, in my judgment, is absolutely lacking in literary merit and vulgar beyond expression. Everyone who thinks realizes that such conditions exist, but why a magazine like yours should exploit such disgusting situations, is hard to understand."

A Maine reader compared Hemingway's writing to the act of picking through sour milk, moldy bread, and rotting vegetables to be found in some kitchens. "I know there are kitchens where things look like that, and if I get a chance to help clean them up I shall."

It is well to remember letters such as these, for without them the concern of Bridges and Perkins about *words* would now seem very puritanical. In 1929 the battles were all still to be fought in America, and Scribner's was risking considerable loss in publishing *A Farewell to Arms*. There was no guarantee that the sales would be as large as, in fact, they were. Hemingway was vaguely amused by the magazine cancellations, and jokingly offered to make up the subscription loss from his own pocket.

In February, 1930, Hemingway was the most talked about young author in America. He had written a good novel that had outstripped Fitzgerald's *Gatsby* in sales. He was financially secure for the first time since he had begun writing. Although the great depression was sweeping America and Europe, he was making good royalties, and the dollar was becoming more valuable every day. The first period of his career was over; in six years he had published two collections of short stories, one satire, and two novels—everything that he had set out to do. Africa, the *Esquire* letters, the Spanish Civil War, two more divorces, and all of the literary feuds were hidden in his future. The Twenties were over. One era had passed away and another was being born.

SECTION TWO

1918-1928: The Making of the Novel

The Italian Front: 1915-1916

In the late summer of that year we lived in a house in a
village that looked across the river and the plain to the
mountains.

I

In this often-quoted first sentence of *A Farewell to Arms* a
number of questions are raised that readers have not yet
attempted to answer in any systematic way. In the late summer of what year? in which village? looking across what
river to which mountains? So much emphasis has been
placed on the symbolic value of Hemingway's mountains
and plains that the historical denotation of the words has
never been established. Yet such a definition is necessary to
appreciate Hemingway's technique in writing the novel.

It is valuable, for example, to realize that the novel begins
in the late summer of 1915 and that Catherine dies in the
spring of 1918. Since Italy did not enter the war until the
summer of 1915, Frederic Henry served at the front from
the very beginning. Those critics who would have him undergo total disillusionment at the Tagliamento river when
faced with his execution have ignored the two years he
spent driving dead and dying men back from the front
lines. One does not live two years at the front and maintain
one's illusions about war. Catherine Barkley has been "at
the war" even longer than Frederic, and her illusions about
war were dissolved when her fiancé was blown to bits on
the western front in 1914. When Frederic first meets her,
Catherine's trauma is obvious; she seems a little "crazy" to

Frederic. It is difficult to argue that the novel moves from illusion to disillusion when its specific dates are brought into focus.

From the reader's point of view it is important to visualize the geography and chronology of events as Hemingway has written about them; for the critic it is interesting to discover just how accurate this geography and chronology were for a period of the war and a part of the country Hemingway had never seen. Although Hemingway's experience in 1918 at Schio and Fossalta contributed to the first chapter of *A Farewell to Arms*, nothing that he had seen firsthand could have resulted in the geographic and military accuracy of the novel. When superimposed upon a map of the Italian front of 1915, Hemingway's description matches the existing terrain conditions with remarkable verity (Map 2). The First Battle of the Isonzo (June 23 to July 7, 1915), which resulted in heavy Italian losses, established the front lines of the Austro-Italian conflict. The immediate Italian goal had been Gorizia, but the Austrian defense had stopped the Italians short of the Isonzo river. The Second Battle of the Isonzo (August 3, 1915) cost the Italians 60,000 casualties and produced negligible results.

"In the late summer of that year" there were two villages that looked across the Isonzo river toward the mountains: Lucinico and Gradisca (Map 3). Both towns were just inside the Italian front, and from both towns troops moved into Gorizia when it fell in 1916. However, Lucinico was in an exposed position and as a result was leveled by Austrian artillery fire in 1915. Gradisca, on the other hand, was an artillery base and command post for the Italians because it was less vulnerable to Austrian fire. The view from Gradisca across the river in 1915 was recorded in the diary of Gino Speranza, an Italian-born American journalist: "In front lay the Isonzo, with fields running down to its banks, across it, a low livid red mountain, the Carso, and farther away to the left (north), under the protection of the Aus-

Map 2
Battles of the Isonzo

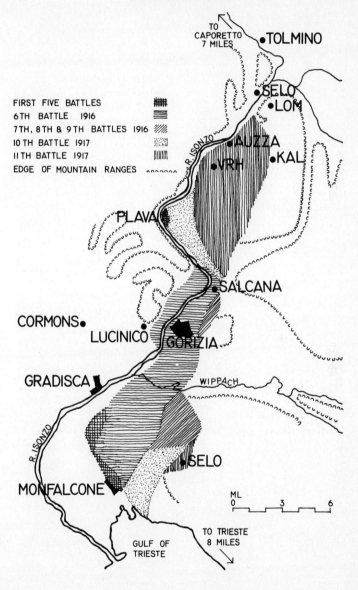

Map 3

Frederic Henry's war zone from 1915 to October, 1917. The Italian Second Army's area of responsibility was north of Gorizia on to the Bainsizza Plateau. The Third Army eventually occupied the Carso Plateau to the south.

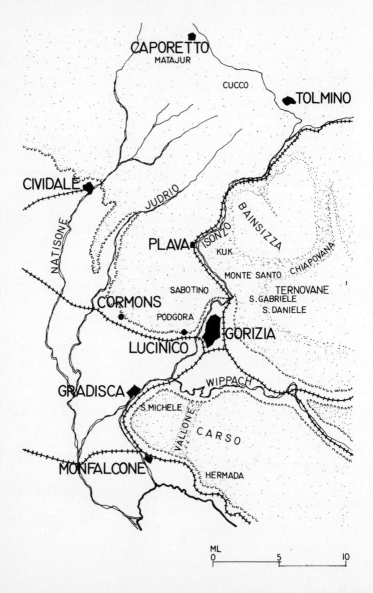

trian mountains, Gorizia!"¹ This view is not unlike the view from Frederic Henry's nameless village at the same time and the same place.

Speranza also recorded the view of the Friulian plain which Frederic described as being rich with crops and fruit orchards. Speranza's view across the plain in 1916 is remarkably similar: "Before me spread the lowlands of the Friulian plain, . . . Beyond rose the mountains, tall, imponderable . . . all I could see was a picture of peace, of normal life, of beauty . . . I saw nothing but fields and orchards and villages and streams."²

As we return to the terrain of Chapter One (Map 3), we see that there is a valley north of both Gradisca and Lucinico that flows down from the mountains on the Italian side of the Isonzo river. These mountains are dominated by Monte Sabotino, which was heavily fortified by the Austrians and which they held against the Italian attack well into 1916. From June through October of 1915, there was fierce fighting on the slopes of Sabotino. This coincides perfectly with the view that Frederic had from his village in 1915: "To the north we could look across a valley and see a forest of chestnut trees and behind it another mountain *on this side of the river.* There was fighting for that mountain too, but it was not successful" (p. 4; my emphasis). The view from Gradisca across the river toward Gorizia and north to Monte Sabotino is very like Frederic's view in the opening chapter.

In addition to geographic accuracy, Chapter One is accurate on several historical points. Just as Frederic relates, King Victor Emmanuel did live in Udine during 1915 so that he could be close to the front. Acting as commander-in-chief, he made daily visits to the front lines to encourage the troops. He frequently stopped at the British Red Cross hospital outside of Cormons, along with the Duchess of

¹ Gino Speranza, *The Diary of Gino Speranza,* ed. F. C. Speranza (New York: Columbia U. Press, 1941), I, p. 233.
² *Ibid.,* pp. 224-225.

Aosta whose husband, the Duke of Aosta, commanded the Italian Third Army on the Carso. Hemingway describes such a visit by the King in Chapter One:

> If one of the officers in the back was very small and
> sitting between two generals, he himself so small that
> you could not see his face but only the top of his cap
> and his narrow back, and if the car went especially
> fast it was probably the King. He lived in Udine and
> came out in this way nearly every day to see how
> things were going, and things went very badly. (p. 4)

While Hemingway's description of the king is not flattering, it is similar in attitude to a passage from Speranza's diary:

> The King, accompanied by a general and a colonel, was
> passing on foot. With all respect I feel for His Majesty,
> I cannot think him a kingly figure. Small, almost badly
> shaped, dressed in a general's field uniform, he was
> walking along the dusty road, carrying a camera that
> seemed too big for him.[3]

Just as Hemingway stated, the king found that things were going very badly at the front in 1915. Between June and December, 1915, the Italian losses were 66,000 killed, 190,000 wounded, and 22,500 missing in action. None of the Italian objectives had been taken, and the front line had remained almost static (Map 2). Attacking barbed wire with garden clippers and without mortars and with little heavy artillery, the Italians suffered enormous losses.

The heavy battlefield losses were complicated by the outbreak of cholera in the winter of 1915. The Italian medical corps was initially unprepared to handle the epidemic; entire units had to be taken out of the front lines to be placed in quarantine. The British Red Cross unit at Villa Trento

[3] Speranza, I, p. 321.

outside Cormons was strained by the unexpected cholera victims, for the epidemic came at a time when the Red Cross drivers were moving a thousand battle casualties a week. Unit Six of the British Red Cross cared for hundreds of cholera victims in a week during the peak month of November. One ambulance hauled 80 cholera victims back from the lines in a single night. Although Hemingway did not experience the epidemic, he used it to close his first chapter with ironic understatement:

> At the start of the winter came the permanent rain and with the rain came the cholera. But it was checked and in the end only seven thousand died of it in the army.
> (p. 4)

In the first two pages of the novel Hemingway has displayed a precise geographic and historic sense of place that is all the more remarkable for his never having experienced the time and never having seen the place. Without giving place names and dates, he has woven accurate details into the fabric of his chapter. His analysis of the military situation is in harmony with the historian's view. This accurate sense of being in northern Italy in the fall of 1915 with the unvictorious Italian army could not have been accomplished without precise and detailed knowledge. Such detail sets the pattern for the remainder of the novel, but at no times does Hemingway allow history to distract his reader. The historical facts are in the novel, but they are kept beneath the surface of the story.

II

Chapter Two of *A Farewell to Arms* begins: *"The next year there were many victories"* (p. 5). The "next year" was 1916, and the Italian army did achieve several important victories. The mountain fighting north of Gradisca and Lucinico forced the entrenched Austrians back almost to the

Isonzo (Map 2) before the Italians finally pushed across the river in August, 1916. Hemingway writes: "The mountain that was beyond the valley [Monte Sabotino] and the hillside where the chestnut forest grew were captured" (p. 5). Johnson's *Battlefields of the World War* describes the action: "Northwest of Gorizia the brilliant assault was equally successful. The hills of Podgora and the supposedly impregnable stronghold of Monte Sabotino were carried by storm. The last of the natural outworks of the Bainsizza bastion were in Italian hands."[4] The victories that Frederic mentions "beyond the plain on the plateau to the south" (p. 5) were also important for the Italians in 1916. After the August offensive, the Italians were in possession of San Michele and Boschini heights north of it. By August 10, a large section of the Austrian defense on the Carso plateau collapsed, giving the Italians a sizable strategic gain. But the most important conquest for the Italians in 1916 was the town of Gorizia.

Gorizia fell during the Sixth Battle of the Isonzo, which began on the morning of August 6, 1916. For the first time in the war General Cadorna had the heavy artillery and the trench mortars necessary to blast open the Austrian defenses. When Gorizia fell two days later, Cadorna had finally taken what had been his initial objective since the beginning of the war. With great simplicity and accuracy Hemingway writes: "we crossed the river in August and lived in a house in Gorizia" (p. 5).

Gorizia is located just as Hemingway portrays it. The Isonzo river runs behind it, and the fighting was in "the next mountains." But Hemingway's accuracy goes beyond simple location. Frederic narrates: "I was very glad the Austrians seemed to want to come back to the town sometime, if the war should end, because they did not bombard it to destroy it but only a little in a military way" (p. 5). This description

---

[4] D. W. Johnson, *Battlefields of the World War*, American Geographical Society Research Series No. 3 (New York: Oxford U. Press, 1921), p. 566.

of Gorizia's condition, which Hemingway had never seen, is verified by a British artillery officer's description of the town in August, 1916: "The suburbs of the town were badly knocked about, but the centre was not at this time much damaged. Gorizia lies in a salient of the hills, with the Austrians looking down upon it from the tops of most of them. But, still hoping to win it back, they do not shell it heavily or often. There are special reasons . . . Gorizia is a sort of Austrian Cheltenham, whither Austrian officers retire in large numbers to pass their last years in villas which they take over from one another's widows. So the Austrian officer class has a sort of vested interest in the preservation of the place."[5]

It is worth remembering that Frederic calls on Catherine at the British hospital, which "was a big villa built by Germans before the war" (p. 18). Later Frederic speculates on the marble busts that line the walls: "This had been the villa of a very wealthy German and the busts must have cost him plenty" (p. 28).

Hemingway's accuracy on the point of the German villas in Gorizia conceals the fiction of a British hospital in Gorizia. The British Red Cross had a unit in Gorizia in 1916, but most of the unit were ambulance drivers who lived in an old boarding house on the Via Ponte Isonzo. As far as can be determined, there were no British nurses or V.A.D.s stationed in Gorizia in 1916-1917, nor was there a British hospital there. The British Red Cross hospital, which was staffed with a number of V.A.D.s, remained at the Villa Trento outside of Cormons and only Ambulance Unit One from this hospital was moved into Gorizia. As will become obvious later, Hemingway probably knew of this arrangement, but he took liberty with the facts in order to move Catherine into close proximity with Frederic in Gorizia.

Of Gorizia's condition, Frederic notes that the civilians had remained in town and that there were cafés open. Dal-

[5] Hugh Dalton, *With British Guns in Italy* (London: Methuen, 1919), pp. 55-56.

ton's description of the town in his book, *With British Guns in Italy*, also noted: "There was still a fairly large civilian population in the town, and one restaurant still keeps open."[6] Frederic also describes the "shell-marked iron of the railway bridge, the smashed tunnel by the river where the fighting had been, the trees around the square and the long avenue of trees that led to the square" (pp. 5-6). Almost every military description of Gorizia makes note of the blown bridges across the Isonzo. Dalton's book has a picture of the twisted steel of the railway bridge. The British Red Cross report says: "The roadway of the iron bridge which spanned the Isonzo had been shot through again and again and was almost impassable for any save foot passengers."[7] Dalton's description of the bridge notes that not only was the railway bridge "broken down by shell fire" but the other two bridges across the river also had spans destroyed by fire.[8] A Library of Congress photograph from WWI shows the Italian cavalry riding into the town square shortly after the capture of Gorizia in 1916. The street and square are tree-lined exactly as Hemingway says they were.

Frederic laconically reports that "the whole thing going well on the Carso made the fall very different from the last fall when we had been in the country. The war was changed too" (p. 6). Frederic's understated evaluation once more coincides with the evaluation of military historians. Villari says that the victories on the Carso and the taking of Gorizia did more than improve the strategic position of the Italian army; these victories made significant improvements in the morale of the army and the nation. For the first time in the war, the Italian army had taken a sizable piece of territory from the enemy and had occupied one of his principal towns.

[6] *Ibid.*, p. 56.
[7] *Reports by the Joint War Commission of the British Red Cross* (London: n.p., 1921), p. 435.
[8] Dalton, p. 55.

These autumn victories were consolidated just as the snow began to fall at the higher altitudes in October, 1916. Because of snow and winter weather, "all large scale operations were held up, and only small isolated actions took place from time to time amid the deep snows."[9] Frederic accurately portrays the situation as the snow begins to fall at Gorizia. "We knew it was all over for that year," he says. He notes that "Up the river the mountains had not been taken" (p. 6). On the map (Map 2) one can see that the Austrians still held some mountainous territory on the Italian side of the Isonzo up river from Gorizia, and that none of the mountains on the Austrian side up river had fallen to the Italians at the end of 1916.

When Frederic Henry returned from his extended winter leave in the spring of 1917 (Chapter Three), his unit was still in Gorizia; the spring offensive had not yet begun. Frederic saw "the town with the hill and the old castle above it in a cup in the hills with the mountains beyond" (p. 10). The "old castle" was the walled *castello* of the Counts of Gorizia, a landmark prominent in all tourist guides and every visitor's report of the town. When Speranza visited Gorizia in August, 1917, he took particular note of the castle, the relatively rebuilt town, and the twenty-two hundred inhabitants.[10]

Frederic returned to the front just in time to participate in the spring offensive that General Cadorna was supposed to coordinate with Allied offensive on the western front, but that he had delayed for a full month. The attack at Plava did not begin until May 12, 1917. The Italian plan called for massive artillery bombardment to precede the Tenth Battle of the Isonzo. The Gorizia command, which was largely the Second Army, was responsible for attacking the Bainsizza heights between Plava and Gorizia, including Monte Kuk, Monte Vodice, Monte Santo, and Monte San Gabriele. On

9 Luigi Villari, *The War on the Italian Front* (London: Cobden, 1932), p. 98.
10 Speranza, *Diary*, II, pp. 82-83.

the Carso plateau, the Italian Third Army held responsibility. Frederic is briefed on the attack plan as soon as he returns to Gorizia: "The division for which we worked were to attack at a place up the river [Plava] and the major told me that I would see about the posts for during the attack. The attack would cross the river up above the narrow gorge and spread up the hillside [Monte Kuk]" (p. 17).

When Frederic reconnoiters the terrain at Plava in Chapter Five he gives an accurate appraisal of the tactical situation:

> I had been up the river to *the bridgehead at Plava*. It was there that the offensive was to begin. It had been impossible to advance on the far side the year before because *there was only one road leading down from the pass to the pontoon bridge* and it was under machine-gun and shell fire for nearly a mile. It was not wide enough either to carry all the transport for an offensive and the Austrians could make a shambles out of it. *But the Italians had crossed and spread out a little way on the far side to hold about a mile and a half on the Austrian side of the river.* It was a nasty place and the Austrians should not have let them hold it. I suppose it was mutual tolerance because *the Austrians still kept a bridgehead further down the river.* The Austrian trenches were above on the hillside only a few yards from the Italian lines. *There had been a little town but it was all rubble. There was what was left of a railway station and a smashed permanent bridge* that could not be repaired and used because it was in plain sight. (My emphasis; p. 23.)

The accuracy of Hemingway's detail can be verified on the map (Map 2), but he had never seen Plava either before or after the war. On a small-scale map, the two bridgeheads are conspicuous points of the military posture. The single bridge at Plava is distinctive. The small town reduced to rubble was Zagora on the slopes of Monte Kuk. Speranza saw the same town in July, 1917, about two months after the offensive in which Frederic was wounded. Speranza describes the scene: "The Isonzo at this point is a very narrow gorge, green, serpentine stream flowing down a defile between Monte Sabotino on the west and Monte Kuk, the Vodice, and Monte Santo, on the east. . . . Zagora, a village on the slopes of Monte Kuk, held partly by the Austrians and partly by the Italians before the advance of the latter, is almost razed to the ground."[11]

Although Frederic makes light of the "show" at Plava when he takes leave of Catherine, the attack was a major one that the Italians had been planning all winter. The strategic importance of the objectives can be appreciated on a battle map. The Carso plateau was the key to the liberation of Trieste, which had been the watchword and goal of the Italian army from the beginning of the war. The key, in turn, to the Carso was the Bainsizza plateau. Before either plateau could be brought under attack, the Italians first had to root the Austrians out of the mountain bastions that protected the plateaus: Kuk, Vodice, Santo and San Gabriele.

Wounded unheroically before the battle really began, Frederic Henry is later told that the effort was "enormously" successful and that nearly a thousand prisoners had been taken (p. 63). Contemporary accounts also called the attack successful; Monte Kuk was taken along with 6,000 prisoners in a five-day period. A contemporary historian has seen the Tenth Battle of Isonzo as a fiasco in which the Italians lost 157,000 men to the Austrian losses of 75,000. This was, however, an assessment of the attack all along the projected front. At Plava itself the attack was successful inasmuch as the objective of Monte Kuk was taken.

When Frederic was wounded, he turned his ambulances over to a British officer whose unit also had ambulances at Plava. Although the point is a small one, it is significant be-

11 *Ibid.*, pp. 58-59.

cause it shows how detailed Hemingway's knowledge of the Plava attack was. The annals of the British Red Cross document the point: "The Italian attacks upon the high positions occupied by the Austrians were delivered from the bases of Gorizia and Plava, centres from which the ambulances of Unit 1, . . . worked as far forward as it was possible for any cars to go. The number of cases carried from May 12 to May 28, inclusive dates of the offensive, was 5,486 in the Gorizia area and 3,933 in the Plava area."[12]

This type of accuracy in the novel reflects the journalist's bias for facts, and, once the reader is aware of it, he may account for other points in the novel on an historical basis rather than a literary one. For example, one reason Catherine Barkley is a British V.A.D. is that in 1917 there were no American Red Cross nurses at the front in Italy. There were, however, a number of British V.A.D.s in Italy in 1917. It would have been historically inaccurate for Catherine to have been anything other than British or Italian. For the same kind of reason, Frederic Henry had to be in the Italian army. He could not have been an American Red Cross driver, as Hemingway himself had been, for there were no American Red Cross drivers in Italy during 1915-1917.

This does not mean that Hemingway was a slave to historical fact. When the structure of the novel demanded, he could bend and stretch historical facts to suit his needs. For example, there is the matter of the hospital in Milan. When Frederic is transferred from the field hospital to the "American hospital," America had just entered the war. The Plava bombardment began on May 12, and America did not

---

12 *Reports by the Joint War Commission*, p. 435. Rather than clutter this chapter excessively with footnotes, the author has eliminated the supporting authority for much of the data. In addition to texts cited, the following sources were used throughout this chapter: Cyril Falls, *The Battle of Caporetto* (Philadelphia: Lippincott, 1966); Ronald Seth, *Caporetto* (London: Macdonald, 1965); *Fortnightly Review*, "History of the War," 108 (1917), p. 154; Charles Bakewell, *The American Red Cross in Italy* (New York: Macmillan, 1920), pp. 25-31.

enter the war until April 1, 1917. When Frederic departs
for Milan, he is told that he "would go to an American hospital in Milan that had just been installed. Some American
ambulance units were to be sent down and this hospital
would look after them and any other Americans on service
in Italy" (p. 75). In point of fact, however, the American
Red Cross hospital did not open in Milan until July of 1918,
a full year later than Hemingway fictionalizes it. Hemingway himself, who was wounded on July 8, 1918, was the
first patient at the new hospital that had been established
in the response to the disaster at Caporetto. There being no
assurance that the Piave river line would hold in December, 1917, the American Red Cross established four units
of ambulance drivers and the Milan hospital in anticipation
of future casualties. But there was no American hospital in
Milan in 1917, and Hemingway knew it. He has foreshortened an historical fact for the sake of his plot, but he has
not done it out of ignorance.

This detailed historical accuracy continues through the
Milan confinement to the end of the novel. Although Hemingway knew Milan firsthand from his own war experience,
he still had no firsthand knowledge of the Italian campaign
during 1917. Frederic's knowledge of the fighting at the
front continues to be accurate while he is in the hospital, for
he keeps informed through the newspapers.

Throughout Book Two of *A Farewell to Arms* there is a
motif of newspaper reading. The morning that Frederic is
examined by the three conservative doctors, he has first sent
the porter out for "all the papers he could get" (p. 95).
During his summer recuperation, he reads of "many victories in the papers" and remarks that it is his daily habit
to read newspapers. At one point Frederic is seen reading
the Boston papers filled with stale news of American training camps and old war news (p. 136). Much later, when
Frederic and Catherine are at Stresa, he reads of continued
Italian disasters in the paper: "The army had not stood at

the Tagliamento. They were falling back to the Piave"
(p. 253). Even when he is safe in the Swiss alps, Frederic
cannot ignore the news accounts of the Italian front:

> I read the *Corriere della Sera* and the English and
> American papers from Paris. All the advertisements
> were blacked out, supposedly to prevent communica-
> tion in that way with the enemy. The papers were bad
> reading. Everything was going very badly everywhere.
> I sat back in the corner with a heavy mug of dark
> beer . . . and read about disaster. (p. 292)

When Frederic took Catherine from Montreux to Lausanne, he bought newspapers: "I . . . read the papers I had
bought at the station. It was March, 1918, and the German
offensive had started in France" (p. 308). When Catherine
begins to hemorrhage in the hospital, Frederic is in a café
reading the paper of the man opposite him: "It was about
the break through on the British front" (p. 329).

Frederic's predilection for newspapers can be explained
in several ways, but the most obvious service performed by
the newspapers is a structural one. Through the papers
Frederic and the reader are never allowed to forget the
war; no matter how far removed Frederic becomes from
the war physically, the fighting at the front continues to impinge upon his consciousness. The details that Frederic
reads are no less accurate than the details found in Book
One. At every point Hemingway has gone to some lengths
to insure historical accuracy, and his accuracy always
points up the war.

When Frederic and Catherine are trysting in his hospital
bed, he cannot avoid the news from the front:

> At the front they were advancing on the Carso, they
> had taken Kuk across from Plava and were taking the
> Bainsizza plateau. . . . The Italians were using up an
> awful amount of men. I did not see how it could go on.

Even if they took all the Bainsizza and Monte San
Gabriele there were plenty of mountains beyond for the
Austrians. (p. 118)

This is an accurate picture of the front's progress during the
summer of 1917. (Map 2) Between June and September,
General Cadorna pursued the bloody Eleventh Battle of the
Isonzo. The Italian Second Army made substantial gains on
the Bainsizza, but both the Second and Third Army absorbed staggering losses during the summer.

In August, General Capello at the head of the Second
Army succeeded in pushing the Austrians to the eastern
edge of the Bainsizza. By the end of August the Italians
controlled the western slope of Monte San Gabriele, while
the Austrians retained possession of the northern and eastern slopes. This is exactly what Frederic reads in the September newspapers in Milan:

> The fighting at the front went very badly and they
> could not take San Gabriele. The fighting on the
> Bainsizza plateau was over and by the middle of the
> month [September] the fighting for San Gabriele was
> about over too. They could not take it. . . . A British
> major at the club told me the Italians had lost one
> hundred and fifty thousand men on the Bainsizza
> plateau and on San Gabriele. He said they had lost
> forty thousand on the Carso besides. (p. 133)

The facts could be no more accurate if they were in a military history, which is where Hemingway very likely found
many of them.

From this general survey of the historical accuracy of the
novel, it becomes obvious that Hemingway researched his
material, but this initial observation leads to questions with
less certain answers. Why did he choose to write about an
experience that he had to research? If he wanted to write
about the war in Italy, he could have relied on his own ex-

periences there. If he had set the novel in 1918, he could
have written with very little research, and he would have
been on certain ground. Catherine could have been a Red
Cross nurse like her prototype Agnes von Kurowsky, instead of a V.A.D. The front could have been the Piave river
line, which Hemingway knew from experience. The engagements were no less bloody and the rain no less wet in October 1918 than they were in 1915-1917. Frederic could have
been wounded at Asiago or Grappa or Fossalta. He could
have participated in the victory of Vittorio Veneto, in which
the Italians won back almost all the territory they had given
up to the Austrians in the Caporetto disaster. Instead of defeat, Hemingway could have used the Armistice celebration.

In view of the novel's fabric, there can be only one structural reason for Hemingway's choice: he wanted to use the
retreat from Caporetto as the crisis of his story. He must
have deliberately chosen not to use the victory at Vittorio
Veneto because he wanted to place Frederic in the midst
of a beaten and partially paralyzed army, not a victorious
one. In order to place Frederic in the middle of the
Caporetto retreat, Hemingway had to do a considerable
amount of reading on the first three years of the war. He
also had to research in minute detail the five-day retreat
from the Bainsizza to the Tagliamento. Before attempting
to analyze the structural significance of this choice, however, we will find it valuable first to compare the historical
fact of the Caporetto retreat with Hemingway's fictional
version.

The Retreat from Caporetto

"I'm trying to do it so it will make it without you knowing it, and so the more you read it, the more there will be."—*A Moveable Feast*

I

Book Three of *A Farewell to Arms* is more than an impressionistic over-view of what retreats are like. Those readers who maintain that Hemingway's version of the Caporetto retreat is based on his Greek war experience ignore the many references to specific places, times, conditions, and attitudes that permeate Book Three. The sum of these references represents a total knowledge of the military situation in northern Italy that is more detailed than any one observer could have had at the time of the retreat. Frederic and the reader are better informed on many points than were contemporary military leaders. For example, Chapter Three recognized all of the probable causes that led to the disaster at Caporetto, but these are causes which have come out in retrospect and that were by no means so clear before the Austrian attack as they appear in the novel.

The most obvious defect in the Italian strategy is made clear to Frederic as soon as he takes his ambulance crew onto the Bainsizza plateau on October 23, 1917. It is one day before the Austro-German attack, and Gino, Frederic's driver, analyzes the strategic disadvantages of the Italian defenses:

Our troops were still in the attacking position. There was no wire to speak of and no place to fall back to if

there should be an Austrian attack. There were fine
positions for defense along the low mountains that
came up out of the plateau but nothing had been done
about organizing them for defense. (pp. 182-183)

Gino's analysis is confirmed by the Italian General Caviglia,
who took part in the battle and who described it after the
war. He too states that the Italian positions were suited for
the offensive, but were totally unreasonable for a defensive
position:

> The first line was inevitably bad at many points because
> it represented the extreme advance of the last Italian
> victory, yet it was held by the majority of the troops,
> whereas the second line, generally well-sited and
> strong, depended for its defenses on divisions scattered
> all over the place.[1]

During the retreat, Frederic made discoveries of tactical
mistakes for himself when he found bridges unblown and
crossing points unprotected by a rear guard:

> "Why isn't there somebody here to stop them?" I said.
> "Why haven't they blown the bridge up? Why aren't
> there machine guns along this embankment? . . . Down
> below they blow up a little bridge. Here they leave a
> bridge on the main road. Where is everybody? Don't
> they try and stop them at all?" (p. 211)

Frederic's charge is a serious one, but it is not unsup-
ported. A German captain by the name of Erwin Rommel
was equally amazed at the shortsightedness of the Italian
defenses. In his account of the battle, Rommel states that if

---

[1] Caviglia is summarized in Cyril Falls, *The Battle of Caporetto*
(Philadelphia: Lippincott, 1966), pp. 30-31; also see James E. Edmonds, *Military Operations in Italy 1915-1919* (London: H.M. Stationery Office, 1949), pp. 46-47.

the Italians had dug in machine-gun positions behind the first line, they could have stopped the German advance in the mountains.[2] Historians later established that the Italian rear guard, who fought valiantly and desperately at some points, had at other strategic crossings deserted their posts. Particularly within the province of the Italian Second Army to which Frederic was attached, several bridges were left unblown. Other bridges were so poorly destroyed that they did little to impede the Austro-German advance.

These military mistakes were the outward effects of more deepseated causes to which the Fascist government after the war became very sensitive. One of the reasons *A Farewell to Arms* was banned in Italy for so many years was its accurate assessment of the causes for the breakdown in morale that allowed Caporetto to take place. Hemingway embodies in his narrative the same points that the British historian G. M. Trevelyan, who witnessed the retreat, later isolated as direct causes of the disaster. Trevelyan listed the causes as socialist activity on the home front, a food shortage at the front lines, enemy propaganda, and ineffectual leadership.

The socialist rancor against the war is a covert presence throughout *A Farewell to Arms*. Two of Frederic's Italian ambulance drivers—Piani and Bonello—are socialists from Imola who are proud of their beliefs: "We're all socialists. Everybody is a socialist. We've always been socialists" (p. 208). In Piani's words, the socialists "don't believe in the war anyway" (p. 217). Hemingway's fictional portrayal of socialist unrest is an accurate reflection of the conditions in Italy in the fall of 1917. In August, socialists in Turin had led food strikes that had resulted in violence. Thousands of munition workers who had participated in the Turin strike were transferred to the front lines at Caporetto as punishment. Caporetto was thought to be the quietest part of the front, and there they could cause the least trouble. The Ital-

[2] Erwin Rommel, *Infantry Attacks*; quoted in Falls, *Battle of Caporetto*, pp. 39-40.

ian government chose to minimize the slogan of the strikers at Turin: "There shall be no third winter in the trenches." But the impressed strikers in the trenches at Caporetto made no secret of their dissatisfaction; their officers knew that these men had no intention of fighting a war. Hemingway notes the dissatisfaction in Milan and Turin when Frederic details how badly things were going in September: "There were riots twice in the town against the war and bad rioting in Turin" (p. 133).

This socialist dissension on the home front was instrumental in lowering troop morale all along the fighting front. Hemingway indicates this loss of morale in the conversation between Frederic and the priest when Frederic returns to the front in Book Three. The priest says that he does not see how the fighting can go on much longer and hopes that it will stop on both sides. Frederic replies that he does not think it will end that way. The priest responds: "I suppose not. It is too much to expect. But when I see the changes in men I do not think it can go on" (p. 178). The changes to which the priest refers include the general lowering of morale which the socialist turmoil encouraged.

Another factor in the breakdown of troop morale was the food shortage at the front during 1917. In 1916 each Italian soldier was rationed 700 grams of bread and 350 grams of meat a day. In 1917 the rate was reduced to 400 grams of bread per day and 200 grams of meat twice a week. On other days his diet was made up of salt fish, sardines, or vegetables. Once more Hemingway demonstrates his careful research when Frederic and Gino discuss the food shortage the night before the attack at Caporetto began:

[Frederic] "Has the food really been short?"
[Gino] "I myself have never had enough to eat but I
am a big eater and I have not starved. The mess is
average. The regiments in the lines get pretty good
food but those in support don't get so much. Something

THE RETREAT FROM CAPORETTO   109

is wrong somewhere. There should be plenty of food."
"The dogfish are selling it somewhere else."
"Yes, they give the battalions in the front line as much
as they can but the ones in back are very short. They
have eaten all the Austrians' potatoes and chestnuts
from the woods. They ought to feed them better. We
are big eaters. I am sure there is plenty of food. It is
very bad for the soldiers to be short of food. Have you
ever noticed the difference it makes in the way you
think?"
"Yes," I said. "It can't win a war but it can lose one."
"We won't talk about losing. There is enough talk about
losing." (p. 184)

Gino's complaint is modest, but Gino, Frederic reminds us,
is a patriot who was born a patriot. If a patriot can talk this
way about the food, how must the less patriotic have
spoken?

The socialist unrest and the food shortage were capital-
ized upon by the Austro-German propaganda, which General Cadorna, the commander-in-chief of the Italian Army,
knew was eating at the morale of his troops. In his post-war
account of his command, he listed the propaganda as one
of the main reasons he did not pursue his summer victory
on the Bainsizza plateau. Cadorna also attributed part of
the Caporetto disaster to the effectiveness of the enemy
propaganda. Cadorna was blamed for failing to counter
the enemy propaganda, which "fostered sedition and
treachery within the ranks of his command."[3]

Propaganda leaflets, which were delivered by shellburst
and dropped from airplanes, were apparently most effective among the troops at Caporetto. One such leaflet read:
"At the request of the Italian government, English and
French soldiers have been firing, at Milan and Turin, for
two days with machine guns upon old Italian soldiers who,

[3] Johnson, *Battlefields of the War*, p. 570.

when called up, refused to go to the front, as well as upon
people who took their part. Countless killed and wounded."[4]

Even more insidious was the propaganda plea for peace,
which argued that it took two armies to make a war. If only
both sides would lay down their arms, there would be no
war. This false hope for peace is used by Hemingway in the
conversation between Frederic and the priest the night before he goes up on the Bainsizza (p. 178), but it is more
explicitly stated in the earlier conversation between Frederic and his ambulance team moments before he was
wounded in the spring of 1917. Passini and Manera remind
Frederic that there have already been troops who refused
to fight. Frederic says: "I believe we should get the war
over with. It would not finish it if one side stopped fighting.
It would only be worse if we stopped fighting" (p. 49). Passini cannot agree with Frederic. With defeat everyone
would go home, he reasons. Defeat is not so bad, and the
government could not hang everyone. Passini argues:

> "War is not won by victory. . . . Did you see all the far
> mountains today? Do you think we could take them all
> too? Only if the Austrians stop fighting. One side must
> stop fighting. Why don't we stop fighting? If they
> come down into Italy they will get tired and go away.
> They have their own country. But no, instead there
> is a war." (pp. 50-51)

Passini's sentiments are an accurate reflection of both the
socialists' complaints and the enemy propaganda.

The general unrest in the army was compounded by the
poor quality of Second Army leadership both during the attack at Caporetto and during the subsequent retreat. There
appear to have been whole sections of the front line at
Caporetto "who, in accordance with a previously formed
intention, abandoned their duty, and surrendered on pur-

[4] "Enemy Wiles on the Italian Front," London Times (Nov. 5,
1917), p. 2; dateline Oct. 21, 1917.

pose. This was 'Caporetto' in the narrower and more strict-
ly accurate sense. For it was only in the geographical zone
that such betrayal occurred, but unfortunately Caporetto
was the key to the whole strategic position."[5] The failure of
the leadership to control the dissidents in the trenches
contributed to the success of enemy breakthrough; although
the line may have given way with the most determined
Italian troops, for the German gas attack lasted well beyond
the hour and half time-limit of the Italian gas-masks.

Proper leadership could have salvaged the situation and
prevented the total breakthrough that occurred. During the
retreat the disaffection of the Second Army troops was mul-
tiplied by the disintegration of the leadership structure.
The responsibility for the chaos of the retreat has been
placed on the "failure of the senior staff officers to issue ade-
quate orders . . . and to the lack of road control. . . . In some
sectors the Italian leadership had broken down completely
and whole divisions disappeared with artillery. . . . Many
artillery batteries had ridden away with their officers at
their head, deserting the infantry."[6]   This evaluation
matches the experience of Frederic Henry on his way back
to the Tagliamento river. In Frederic's own words: "There
was no need to confuse our retreat. The size of the army
and the fewness of the roads did that. *Nobody gave any
orders"* (my emphasis; p. 216).

And to a certain extent Frederic Henry's own leadership
during the retreat reflects microcosmically the general
breakdown in the Second Army command. When he leaves
Gorizia, Frederic is charged with the delivery of three ambulances and his three enlisted men—Aymo, Bonello, and
Piani—to the far side of the Tagliamento. Enroute his three
ambulances become hopelessly mired in the mud of side
roads chosen by Frederic. Of the two sergeants picked up

[5] G. M. Trevelyan, "Italy's Breakdown at Caporetto," *The Great
Events of The Great War*, eds. C. F. Horne and W. F. Austin (New
York: National Alumni, 1920), p. 313.
[6] Falls, *Caporetto*, pp. 60-61.

by Frederic enroute, one is shot deserting and the other deserts successfully. Aymo is killed by his own Italian rear guard. Bonello deserts to the advancing enemy. Frederic reaches the Tagliamento with only Piani. As a record of leadership under pressure, Frederic's performance is the epitome of the general performance of the Italian Second Army during the retreat. It is important to note that such a breakdown occurred for the most part only within the Second Army. Had Frederic been assigned to either the First or the Third Army, he would have experienced a more orderly retreat.

These several points where the novel and historical circumstances coincide are preliminary to an examination of the retreat itself, but they show that Hemingway had a total grasp of the military, social, and political situation that resulted in the debacle at Caporetto. In fact, Frederic's understanding of his own situation is probably more comprehensive than one could reasonably expect of a man caught up in a retreat. All of the causes of the disaster are present in the novel, but they were by no means so clear before the historians had analyzed the event. Frederic possesses knowledge that one gains after the fact. But no matter how accurate Hemingway is in the matter of socialist revolt, food shortage, propaganda, and poor leadership, it is in the concrete details—"the people, the places, and how the weather was"—that Hemingway's historical accuracy must be tested.

II

In Book Three of *A Farewell to Arms*, Frederic Henry joins his ambulance detachment on the Bainsizza plateau on October 23, 1917, the day before the Austro-German offensive began at Caporetto. Frederic's exact position on the Bainsizza is difficult to pinpoint. We are told he is working somewhere above Ravne where the British ambulances are stationed.

As the attack begins on the morning of October 24, Frederic narrates the conditions:

> The *wind* rose in the *night* and at *three o'clock in the*
> *morning* with the *rain* coming in sheets there was a
> *bombardment* and the *Croatians* came over across the
> mountain meadows and through the patches of woods
> and into the front line. They fought in the dark in the
> rain and a counterattack of scared men from the
> second line drove them back. There was much shelling
> and many rockets in the rain . . . between the gusts of
> wind and rain we could hear *the sound of a great*
> *bombardment far to the north.* (my emphasis; p. 186)

Although most authorities agree that the attack began at two a.m., rather than three a.m., Hemingway's accuracy is still rather remarkable for either fiction or history. His description of the weather conditions is absolutely correct. A contemporary account describes the weather for the same time period: "Light rainfall had begun early, but then turned to a heavy downfall with snow storms on the heights and mist in the valleys. Visibility even when day dawned was very poor."[7] Hemingway was equally aware of the changes; he describes the rain shifting to snow: "I felt the rain on my face turn to snow. The flakes were coming heavy and fast in the rain" (p. 186).

Although the infantry assault on the pressure point at Caporetto did not begin until eight a.m., the Second Isonzo Army of the Austro-Germans on the Bainsizza moved forward in advance of the main assault. Hemingway is historically accurate, therefore, in placing the infantry attack on the Bainsizza in the pre-dawn hours. The second attack he describes was repulsed before daylight, and there was not another attack that day, Frederic tells us. Hemingway states, then, that on October 24, when the break occurred in the Italian line at Caporetto, the front line held on the

[7] James E. Edmonds, *Military Operations in Italy*, p. 52.

Bainsizza. German battle maps show that the front line on the Bainsizza did not change on the 24th, just as Hemingway indicates. The enemy advance on the Bainsizza did not start until the Italian Second Army was forced to pull back by the breach at Caporetto.

The bombardment that Frederic could hear to the north was the furious pounding that preceded the attack at Caporetto. A two-hour gas attack was followed by a concentrated artillery attack that left the Italian front lines a shambles. On the night of October 24, Frederic learned that the "Austrians had broken through the twenty-seventh army corps up toward Caporetto" (p. 187). Italian battle maps locate the twenty-seventh corps' area of responsibility as just north of the Bainsizza. On the morning of October 24, "a 15-mile gap had been nipped out of the Italian front and, in the absence of anything of the nature of battle police to stop the fugitives, the four divisions of the Italian IV Corps which held this sector disappeared, involving *the left division of the XXVII Corps in their flight*" (my emphasis).[8] Hemingway does not belabor his factual details; they are woven into the fabric of the narrative in an unobtrusive manner.

After the Austro-Germans had cut the gap in the Italian line at Caporetto, there followed a period of confusion during which it is difficult to make generalizations about the Italian front. While wholesale desertion was taking place at Caporetto, on the Bainsizza plateau, where Frederic was stationed, the line held firm. The Italian general staff under the leadership of General Cadorna passed through three stages of recognition that are again fairly well reflected in the novel.

First, General Cadorna recognized that the line had been breached at Caporetto and that some measures must be taken to reform the line. Cadorna's immediate reaction was to provide for a defensive line to which the front could fall back without giving up any more territory than was neces-

THE RETREAT FROM CAPORETTO

sary. At six p.m. on October 24, General Cadorna ordered the Carnia zone to make ready the defense of Monte Maggiore. This is exactly the rumor that Frederic hears from the medical officer: a strategic withdrawal is being planned and the troops will fall back to "hold a line across the mountains from Monte Maggiore" (p. 187). The medical officer's information is said to have come from Division Headquarters.

Although General Cadorna's initial withdrawal was planned to hold a line in the mountains, he saw that he might be forced further back. At the second stage of his planning, he set up three lines of defense, each of which was still in the mountains. However, Cadorna took the further precaution to ready the defenses on the west side of the Tagliamento river in case the withdrawal should be forced back that far. Cadorna watched the progress of the action through October 25, ordering troops back as was tactically necessary. At some point on the 25th, Cadorna realized the gravity of the situation and prepared the order to retreat beyond the Tagliamento river. As the order was about to be put into effect on the night of October 25, Cadorna was advised by the commander of the Second Army that the mountain line of defense could be held somewhat longer. In consequence Cadorna held up the general order.

However, Cadorna did order certain elements of the front lines to begin to pull back toward the river on the night of the 25th. On the Carso, the Third Army began to withdraw its heavy artillery from the forward positions. Thus Hemingway maintains his accuracy when he has Frederic Henry pull off the Bainsizza on the night of the 25th.

It is worth noting that the weather on October 25 was warm and almost sunny. And, although the atmosphere of Hemingway's retreat is saturated with rain, he makes no mention of the weather on the 25th. The entire day is foreshortened rather noticeably to achieve intensity, for Hem-

ingway throughout the retreat selects carefully those portions which best suit his artistic purpose. It did not suit his
purpose to have October 25 warm and sunny. However, the
critics have made more of the October rains than they perhaps will bear. Carlos Baker has firmly established Hemingway's symbolic use of the rain in *A Farewell to Arms*,[9] and
Philip Young calls Hemingway's use of the rain "the old
'pathetic fallacy' put to new use. . . . Good and bad weather
go along with good and bad moods and events. It is not just
that, like everyone, the characters respond emotionally to
conditions of atmosphere, light, and so on, but there is a
correspondence between these things and their fate. They
win when it's sunny, and lose in the rain."[10] The critics' attitude seems to be that Hemingway has arranged the rain
to suit his artistic purpose, that he turns it off and on like
some stage-prop spigot. What most critics overlook are
those portions of the retreat when it is not raining, for it
suits their critical purpose to see the entire retreat as under
a steady downpour. A close examination of the rain during
the retreat shows, however, that Hemingway was following
a rather exact timetable provided by the battle accounts.
Not once during Book Three of *A Farewell to Arms* does
fictional rain fall when actual rain did not.

In Book Three rain and snow began to fall in the early
morning hours of October 24 (p. 186). On the 25th, Hemingway does not mention the weather during the day, but
that night the rain resumes and continues until the morning
hours of October 27 (pp. 188-191). On the morning of the
27th the rain slackens: "The rain was falling not so heavily
now and I thought it might clear" (p. 199). By noon of the
27th the rain had stopped: "The rain had stopped during
the forenoon and three times we had heard planes coming"
(p. 203). Twice during the afternoon of October 27, Frederic mentions the sun's attempts to come through the cloud
cover (pp. 205, 207). By the night of the 27th the rain has

9 Baker, *Hemingway: The Writer as Artist*, pp. 105-106.
10 Young, *Hemingway: A Reconsideration*, p. 92.

resumed and it continues to fall through the 28th (pp. 214, 218, 221). It is still raining when Frederic jumps into the Tagliamento. Thus, out of five days, it has rained three. One day has been cloudy but has had only partial rain; one day has not been mentioned.

The historical facts of the weather conditions during the retreat match Hemingway's fictional account in every respect. As we have already seen, the attack on the 24th took place in rain and snow. One account of weather controls over the fighting zone says: "Several days of stormy weather were followed by a fine spell, which favored a rapid advance on the part of the Teutonic troops, across the mountains and through the valleys. During the early part of their retreat, the Italians suffered greatly from the cold torrential rains."[11] More specifically, the rain cleared during the day of October 25; on the night of the 25th there were stars and a moon visible on the Carso.[12] A clear night on the 25th does not correlate with Frederic's fictional experience on the Bainsizza; however, the geographic difference between the two locales may account for this difference. By most accounts, the rain resumed on the 26th sometime during the early morning hours. The solid weather front degenerated into heavy rain squalls across the Friuli plain on the 26th.[13] However, on October 27, the rain stopped during the day; by most accounts the afternoon of the 27th was clear enough for enemy aircraft to bomb the retreat and to direct fire for the enemy artillery. On the evening of October 27, the rain resumed and continued through the 28th. The rain fell intermittently through the entire retreat with the exception of two times: the day of October 25 and the afternoon of October 27.[14]

Hemingway may have learned about rain during retreats

[11] Robert De C. Ward, "Weather Controls Over the Fighting in the Italian War Zone," *Scientific Monthly*, 6 (Feb., 1918), p. 104.

[12] Dalton, *With British Guns in Italy*, pp. 98-100.

[13] Perceval Gibbon, "Italy's Breakdown at Caporetto," *Great Events of the Great War*, v, p. 318.

[14] Falls, pp. 37-55. Dalton, pp. 101, 108-109; Edmonds, p. 63.

from reporting the rain-drenched retreat in Greece, but to have followed so accurate a timetable of the Italian conditions required more than analogous knowledge; it required something like an accurate history book.

If the fictional rain of *A Farewell to Arms* falls on an accurate historical timetable, Frederic's movements during the retreat are equally synchronized with the military history. From the morning of October 24 when the attack begins, Frederic and history are marching to the same drum. When Frederic takes his ambulances down off the Bainsizza plateau in the early morning of October 25 (p. 188), he is following the evacuation timetable set up by General Cadorna: "The Commando Supremo ordered the 2nd Army Command to withdraw the Bainsizza forces on to the line of main resistance, and if necessary to recross the Isonzo."[15]

It takes Frederic and his ambulance crew thirty-six hours to make the trip off the plateau to Plava and down the river gorge to Gorizia. The distance, at most, is about twenty-five kilometers. This slow rate of travel is in keeping with the actual disengagement from the Bainsizza, which was orderly but which moved at something less than a kilometer an hour in the rain. Frederic describes the first day of the retreat: "The retreat was orderly, wet and sullen. In the night, going slowly along the crowded roads we passed troops marching under the rain. . . . There was no more disorder than in an advance" (p. 188). Frederic's fictional experience is similar to the actual difficulties experienced by a British ambulance unit at Cormons trying to evacuate to the Tagliamento: "Owing to the congestion of the roads several hours elapsed before the last party to leave Villa Trento were able to make any progress."[16] Hugh Dalton experienced the same frustrations as he struggled to get his British artillery unit on the Carso plateau back across the

15 Villari, *War on the Italian Front*, p. 153.
16 *Reports by the Joint Commission*, p. 436; see also Villari, p. 155; T. N. Page, "The Disaster of Caporetto," *Italy and the Great War* (New York: Scribner's, 1920), p. 313.

Map 4

Frederic Henry's retreat route from the Bainsizza Plateau to the rail line at Latisana.

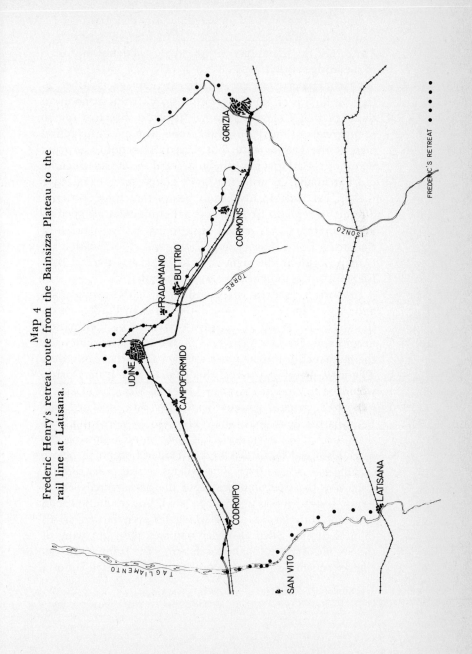

Latisana bridge on the Tagliamento. It took Dalton four and one-half days to move from the Carso to Latisana, a feat certainly comparable with Frederic's fictional four days to the bridge at Codroipo.

When Frederic entered Gorizia at noon on October 26 (p. 188) he was on schedule with history. It was at noon on the 26th that General Cadorna "issued a directive to the commanders of the Third and Second Armies . . . for retirement to the Tagliamento. The directive was not to be acted upon until Cadorna gave the final word to retreat which he did not finally do until the night of the 26th."[17] Selective withdrawal had already begun before that time. Material difficult to replace, like the hospital equipment assigned to Frederic Henry, was moved back somewhat in advance of the main body. For example, the actual evacuation of Gorizia began on the night of October 25, and the last British ambulances did not leave until the 27th.

In Gorizia, Frederic is responsible for withdrawing three ambulances loaded with hospital supplies to Pordenone on the west side of the Tagliamento river. This destination necessitates Frederic's crossing the river at Codroipo. On the map such a retreat route appears somewhat contrived. The most direct way across the Tagliamento from Gorizia would be to cross the river at Latisana. However, General Cadorna's general evacuation order had assigned the Latisana bridge to the Italian Third Army retreating from the Carso. Thus Hemingway is once more following the strict historical fact when he has Frederic go north before turning toward the river. The general retreat order did not even give the Codroipo bridge to the beleaguered Second Army; instead it was assigned to small bridges at Bonzicco, Pinzano, and Carnio, all of which lie even farther north than Codroipo. Such an order required the right wing of the Second Army to flank march across the front of the oncoming enemy forces. Once the retreat turned into a

17 Edmonds, pp. 56-57.

debacle, many of the Second Army troops took the Codroipo bridge anyway, just as Frederic and Piani do.

Frederic does not get his three ambulances on the road out of Gorizia until 9:30 p.m. on October 26 (p. 192). In the slow-moving and frequently stalled main line of the retreat, Frederic realizes how vulnerable he is: an air attack could effectively stall the entire retreat by disabling a few vehicles. Leaving the main road, Frederic chooses to use side roads to make quicker progress. Fifteen hours after leaving Gorizia, his ambulances are ten kilometers from Udine. The geography between Gorizia and Udine is the least distinct of any in the novel. It is impossible to correlate accurately the narrative of the novel with a small-scale map. For example, there was no main road between Gorizia and Udine, as Hemingway implies. Even the main body of the retreat must have been using secondary roads that followed the outlines of squared fields and the boundaries of canals. If Hemingway knew this, he chose to ignore it. The important point was to position Frederic on the outskirts of Udine on the afternoon of October 27 when the German advance guard was about to enter the city.

A few kilometers outside of Udine, history and fiction join once more in firm conjunction. Historically, it was on the afternoon of October 27 that General von Berrer, commander of the German Alpenkorps, received a false report that Udine had already fallen to the advance guard. On the basis of this information, von Berrer moved out ahead of his troops in an open staff car, driving the main road between Cividale and Udine. At the entry to Udine, General von Berrer was shot and killed by the Italian rear guard who still occupied the city although most of the town had been evacuated. Hemingway was aware of the circumstances surrounding the death of the German general, for in "A Natural History of the Dead," published three years after A Farewell to Arms, he singled out "von Behr" [sic] as a brave man "who commanded the Bavarian Alpenkorps at the battle of Caporetto and was killed in his staff car by the Italian rear guard as he drove into Udine at the head of his troops."[18]

General von Berrer (Behr) makes his fictional appearance in *A Farewell to Arms* right on historical schedule. It would not have been within Frederic's point of view to have known who he was, nor would it have been plausible to have Frederic close enough to Udine to witness his death. Still, Hemingway includes the historical fact at exactly the right time and right place. As Frederic and his drivers approach the road between Udine and Cividale, Frederic sees the staff car:

> Ahead across the wet countryside I could see Udine in the rain. Across the bridge I looked back. Just up the river was another bridge. As I watched, a yellow mud-colored motor car crossed it. The sides of the bridge were high and the body of the car, once on, was out of sight. But I saw the heads of the driver, the man on the seat with him, and the two men on the rear seat. They all wore German helmets.   (p. 210)

Frederic identifies the car for Aymo, one of his drivers, as a German staff car. It is Aymo who is about to be shot to death by the same Italian rear guard who killed von Berrer.

At this point Hemingway's use of historical fact is so oblique as to be almost unrecognizable. But in fact, his history is consistently understated throughout the novel. In the opening section the reader is not told what year or which war or what river. In Book Three the accuracy of the historical detail is always subordinate to action and theme. The accuracy is inherent in the story, but it never distracts the reader or gets in the way of the author.

[18] Ernest Hemingway, "A Natural History of the Dead," *The Short Stories of Ernest Hemingway*, Scribner Library Edition (New York: Scribner's, 1953), p. 446.

As Hemingway said in his *Paris Review* interview: "I always try to write on the principle of the iceberg. There is seven-eighths of it under water for every part that shows. *Anything you know you can eliminate and it only strengthens your iceberg. It is the part that doesn't show.* If a writer omits something because he does not know it then there is a hole in the story"[19] (my emphasis). In *A Farewell to Arms* Hemingway has left a good deal out and the "iceberg" is strengthened by his omissions. Beneath the surface of the novel, the geography and history unobtrusively support the exposed surface.

III

At noon on October 27, 1917, Frederic Henry abandoned his three ambulances ten kilometers outside of Udine. Just as during the actual retreat: "The rain had stopped during the forenoon and three times we had heard planes coming, seen them pass overhead, watched them go far to the left and heard them bombing on the main highroad" (p. 203). Hugh Dalton's firsthand account of the retreat recounts similar air attacks on the afternoon of the 27th: "Enemy bombing planes came over frequently. One came right over us and then turned down the Vallone, and there was a series of heavy explosions, and great clouds of brownish smoke leapt up beneath her track."[20]

From this point forward in the novel, Hemingway's use of geographic detail becomes so precise that Frederic's movements can be easily followed on a small-scale map. Ten kilometers out from Udine places Frederic's group in the vicinity of Buttrio just south of the Torre river. Frederic narrates:

[19] George Plimpton, interviewer, "The Art of Fiction xxi: Ernest Hemingway," *Paris Review*, 5 (Spring, 1958), p. 84.
[20] Dalton, p. 105.

Later we were on a road that led to a river. . . . The
river was high and the bridge had been blown up in
the centre; the stone arch was fallen into the river and
the brown water was going over it. . . . Up ahead I
knew there was a railway bridge. . . . We went up to the
bank and finally we saw the railway bridge. . . . It was
a long plain iron bridge across what was usually a dry
river bed.   (p. 209)

Although Hemingway had never seen the Torre river when
he wrote of it, he was an expert map reader, and most maps
show the Torre as a dry river bed where it passes outside
of Buttrio. During the week of the retreat, however, all
streams and rivers were at flood stage as a result of the
steady rains. There were two bridges at Buttrio across the
Torre just as Hemingway said there were.

Once across the bridge Frederic was approximately
seven kilometers from Udine. Although Hemingway had
never seen Udine when he wrote the description, what
Frederic sees from the plain is a perfectly accurate description of the town: "We walked along the railroad track. On
both sides of us stretched the wet plain. Ahead across the
plain was the hill of Udine. The roofs fell away from the
castle on the hill. We could see the campanile and the clock
tower" (p. 212). There is a castle on the top of Udine's hill,
and there is a prominent clock tower that can be seen for
some distance. The campanile is also there.

Frederic and his Italian drivers follow the railway that
runs from Gorizia through Cormons to Udine. At the Torre
river the railroad and the road to Udine are parallel and
run in close conjunction until they reach the town of Pradamano, where they separate. Frederic describes this topographical feature rather exactly: "The railway moved south
away from the highway now and we could not see what
passed along the road. A short bridge over a canal was
blown up but we climbed across on what was left of the

span" (p. 213). It is just past the canal that Frederic is able
to see "the line of the other railroad" ahead of him (p. 213).
This observation gives the map reader another accurate fix.
The "other railroad" must be the one that runs from Cividale to Udine. It could not be the one on Frederic's left, to
the east, which runs from Palmanova to Udine because that
is in no way "ahead" of Frederic's position.

Frederic continues to describe the countryside as he
moves in the direction of Udine:

> *To the north was the main road* where we had seen the
> cyclists; *to the south there was a small branch road*
> across the fields with thick trees on each side. I thought
> we had better cut to the south and work around the
> town that way and across country toward *Campoformio
> and the main road to the Tagliamento.* We could avoid
> the main line of the retreat by keeping to the secondary
> roads beyond Udine. I knew there were plenty of side-
> roads across the plain. (My emphasis; p. 213)

The geographic point described here can be found where
the road north from Pradamano rejoins the railway that
Frederic is following. As Frederic indicates, there is an
abundance of side roads around Udine on the south side of
the town, all of which would lead eventually to Campo-
formio and the Tagliamento.

Frederic's plan seems sound, but he has not taken the
Italian rear guard into consideration. Aymo is shot and
killed by his own troops, which forces Frederic to rethink
his plan. He and his two remaining drivers hide in an abandoned barn for the rest of the day. During the night of October 27, Frederic and Piani manage to make their way in
the dark around the *north* side of Udine. The geography is
foreshortened during this part, for it takes place in the
dark. The next firm geographic point is the road between
Udine and the Tagliamento river: "We got past the town

to the north without seeing any Italians, then after a while came on the main channels of the retreat and walked all night toward the Tagliamento. . . . We were going along the side of a road crowded with vehicles and troops" (p. 218). Frederic's descriptions of the road conditions throughout the retreat have been praised for their detail; however, Hemingway actually understates the confusion of the retreat and the mass of debris left behind by the re-treating army. German pictures taken at the time (Figs. *1* and *2*) give some indication of the crowded condition of the road for the advancing army and also show the aban-doned gear left by the fleeing Italian army.

The next precise point is at the Codroipo bridge across the Tagliamento. It was here that battle police set up check points to filter the mass of people moving west. As the Ger-man advance neared the bridge head, the Italians blew the bridge, stranding some men and stores on the east bank. It is here that Frederic chooses to desert rather than die. He plunges into the swollen river near the east bank. When he comes out of the water he still must cross the river; "I knew there was no bridge across the river until Latisana. I thought I might be opposite San Vito" (p. 227). The map shows that between Codroipo and Latisana there is no bridge. San Vito is on the west bank of the river and would therefore have been opposite Frederic when he came out of the river.

When Frederic reached the rail line at Latisana, Heming-way was forced into his first really awkward topographical situation. There was a railway bridge across the Taglia-mento at Latisana; between Frederic and the rail line was the main road that led to the vehicular bridge at the same point. Frederic had to get across this road to get to the rail line. On October 28, 1917, the main road was jammed with refugees and a large part of the Italian Third Army, which was making its way slowly across the bridge. Hemingway knew of these conditions but chose to ignore them. It would

1. Material abandoned by the retreating Italian Second Army between Udine and Codroipo, October, 1917. *Courtesy of Library of Congress.*

2. Typical road conditions during the retreat from Caporetto. Here the advancing Austro-German troops make their way between Udine and the Tagliamento River. Note abandoned Italian materiel in the ditch. *Courtesy of Library of Congress.*

have been pointless to have put such an obstacle between Frederic and his goal at that point.

Once Frederic is on the train, he takes refuge under a tarp that covers heavy artillery pieces. He thinks: "They must have been sent ahead from the third army" (p. 230). On October 25, Cadorna had ordered the Third Army to get its less mobile artillery to the other side of the Piave river. Although the Third Army did not begin to pull back in numbers until October 27, it had its big guns clear of the front and on their way back to the Tagliamento line by the 28th, which is when Frederic smashes his head against one of them on the train to Mestre.

IV

The particularity of Hemingway's topographical and meteorological details alone should put to rest any arguments that Hemingway used the Greek retreat as the basis of his fiction. However, his description of the retreat goes beyond the setting to portray the mood and physical circumstances of the Caporetto retreat with equal accuracy.

The crowded conditions that Frederic discovered on the roads were not peculiar to the route of the Second Army, but Frederic's area was less coordinated than any other area of the retreating front. Orders were lacking, for the most part, and those which were given were being continually countermanded. The transportation available for moving the army to the rear was totally inadequate to the task. The advancing German officers were amazed at the confusion of the Second Army, which allowed them to take large numbers of prisoners who simply had no place to go.

When Frederic first took his place in the retreat of the Second Army, it had not yet degenerated into confusion. Outside Gorizia, the retreat was simply stalled:

I could see the stalled column between the trees in the rain. . . . The column did not move, although, on the other side beyond the stalled vehicles I could see the troops moving. . . . This block might extend as far as Udine. . . . Several hours later I heard the truck ahead of us grinding into gear. . . . we started, moving a few yards, then stopping, then going on again. . . . The column stalled again in the night and did not start. (pp. 194-195)

The correspondent from the *London Times* on the scene saw much the same thing: "[The road] was black with men and horses and guns and wagons. It would have been humanly impossible to keep formation in such a press. Those on foot slipped forward as best they could, in and out among the tangle of carts. *When they were too tired they climbed up on any vehicle on which there was still room.*"[21] (My emphasis.)

Frederic's detachment of ambulances becomes the epitome of the general experience. His Italian drivers pick up stragglers—two virgins and two sergeants—representing the two components of the retreat: refugees and soldiers. Like his real counterparts, Frederic finds his way clogged by the refugees who jammed the roads. It has been estimated that 350,000 troops and 400,000 civilians flooded the roads, trying to get to the Codroipo bridge.

Like many of those in the actual retreat, Frederic leaves the main road to make his way cross country on side roads toward Udine. A day later, after losing his ambulances and two drivers to the vicissitudes of the retreat, Frederic discovers that the road between Udine and the river is, if anything, worse than that from Gorizia. In the actual retreat: "The two main roads from Palmanova and Udine converged on the bottle-neck of Codroipo, and a mass of artillery and transport of both the Third and Second Armies were moving down them and getting blocked in the town, so that as each unit came along it simply abandoned its transport, adding it to the tail of the block, and

21 "Packed Roads," *London Times* (Nov. 7, 1917), p. 2.

the men struggling through as best they could."[22] German photographs of the Udine-Codroipo road taken in the wake of the retreating Italians testify to the correspondence between the fictional and the actual experience of the retreat.

In addition to the clogged roads and the absence of road control, the actual retreat was under the intermittent threat of air attack. As the weather cleared, enemy planes were able to harass the barely mobile line. Frederic realizes that an air attack could permanently block the column's progress, and on the afternoon of the 27th he sees the planes bombing the main road. In the actual circumstances there were more planes than Frederic reports, although they did little damage. The retreating troops on the main line to Codroipo were bombed and machine-gunned, but the enemy planes attacked from so great an altitude that the damage was more psychological than real.

Another aspect of the retreat that Frederic accurately observes is the widespread looting that took place after the civilian population had abandoned their homes. This civilian exodus did not become epidemic until the 27th, and it is on the 27th that Frederic first observes the problem. As his group leaves an abandoned farmhouse, one of the sergeants steals a clock that Frederic forces him to put back. This is the only incident of wanton looting in the novel, although Frederic and his drivers take advantage of abandoned farms to secure the food they require. For the actual retreat, food also became a problem. In Hemingway's fictive version, Frederic and his men find two meals in abandoned farms. In the same house to which the clock is returned, Frederic appropriates a large cheese and a bottle of wine that he divides among the men. On the night of the 27th, Frederic, Piani, and Bonello spend the night in an abandoned farmhouse outside Udine: "There were ashes of a fire on the big open hearth. The pots hung over the

22 Edmonds, *Military Operations in Italy*, p. 67.

ashes, but they were empty. I looked around but I could not find anything to eat" (p. 215). Later Piani finds some wine and a sausage which he and Frederic eat for supper.

Hemingway needed to know little of retreats to have imagined that such looting as this took place, and his accuracy does not indicate that he researched this point. However, his use of looting is one more point in a pattern of accuracy that goes beyond superficial or hearsay knowledge and that shows a thorough historical understanding of the conditions prevalent during this particular retreat.

There is the point of the rear guard, for example. All the military historians note that the rear guard varied from one sector to the next in its effectiveness. In some cases they were able to impede the advancing Austro-German army for crucial periods through heroic sacrifices. In other cases the rear guard abandoned their posts before the enemy appeared, leaving key bridges and cross roads undefended. Hemingway is accurate in both the time and position of the rear guard that Frederic encounters outside Udine. It is ironic that Aymo should be killed by his own troops, just as it is ironic that the only killing that Frederic sees during the retreat is Italians killing other Italians. The enemy is a presence more felt than seen, and no contact is ever made with him.

The lack of road control, the air attacks, the looting, and food shortage, the rear guard—these are all characteristics which conceivably could have been found in the annals of any mass retreat. There was, however, one aspect of the Caporetto retreat to which the Italian government was particularly sensitive, and which Hemingway portrayed with accuracy: the breakdown in discipline that led to Frederic's desertion.

Although the breakdown at Caporetto took place within the Second Army, Hemingway quite accurately does not show the confusion becoming general until the army reaches the plain. During the actual retreat a German field officer, Erwin Rommel, was at one point surrounded by armed Italian soldiers outside of Cividale who wanted to surrender. An Italian officer who resisted the will of his troops was shot down by his own men. Poor leadership at the crisis had apparently destroyed the faith of many enlisted men in their officers; their will to fight had been seriously eroded.

This loss of will is graphically portrayed in the gradual dissolution of Frederic's group. With the breakdown in the Second Army's will to fight, such desertions were not uncommon. By the time the Austro-German force reached the Tagliamento river on October 30, it had taken 265,000 Italian prisoners. In a seven-day period, Italy had lost 75,000 more prisoners than did Great Britain during the entire war.

While the Italian Third Army was able to retreat in fairly orderly fashion toward the Latisana bridge, the Second Army developed serious morale problems once it became mired in the confusion of refugees on the Friulian plain. Falls, with British disdain, says that "a high proportion of the Italian Second Army set out for their homes to get into civilian clothes."[23] T. N. Page fixes the geographic area where the breakdown of morale became most serious: "It was mainly after leaving Cividale that the Second Army began to break up. After Udine was abandoned, though units fought gallantly, it broke up completely as an army and, possessed by the idea that all was lost, flung away their arms and accoutrements, and, self-disbanded, spread over the country, headed for the Tagliamento and home."[24]

To belabor what must now be obvious, Hemingway's narrator is witness to the disintegration of the Second Army at exactly the right time and place. Frederic has watched his men desert; he has seen the roads unguarded, the bridges unblown, the orders ungiven. Between Udine and the Ta-

23 Falls, p. 61.   24 T. N. Page, p. 313.

gliamento, he is caught up in the panic of the retreat and the mindlessness of war. He hears soldiers shouting:

> "*Andiamo a casa!*" a soldier shouted.
> "They throw away their rifles," Piani said. "They take them off and drop them down while they're marching. Then they shout."
> "They ought to keep their rifles."
> "They think if they throw away their rifles they can't make them fight."
> In the dark and the rain, making our way along the side of the road I could see that many of the troops still had their rifles. They stuck up above the capes.
> "What brigade are you?" an officer called out.
> "*Brigata di Pace!*" someone shouted. "Peace Brigade!"
> (pp. 219-220.)

These deserters, both real and fictional, were rounded up at the Codroipo bridge. The *London Times* headline read: ITALY RESTORES ARMY DISCIPLINE BY EXECUTIONS. The lead began: "Discipline has been restored to the Italian army by ruthless execution of deserters and the situation is improving. . . . The retreat is now methodical." The deserters were "reorganized" by the military police, and only those who refused to cooperate were shot. Included in the actual executions were suspected German infiltrators and officers who were not with their troops. Hemingway was aware of this aspect of the retreat, for Frederic had noted earlier the rumor of German infiltrators in Italian uniforms (p. 216). At the bridgehead Frederic's experience once more epitomizes the general condition. First, he is an officer who is not with his command, and such officers are being shot summarily. Moreover, Frederic is not an Italian; he speaks with an accent and he is in an Italian uniform, which qualifies him as a German infiltrator in the eyes of the battle police. Thus, Frederic's fictional experience be-

comes more and more a synthesis of the actual group experience in the retreat from Caporetto.

As Frederic approaches the river, he finds a wooden
bridge "nearly three-quarters of a mile across, and the
river, that usually ran in narrow channels in the wide
stony bed far below the bridge, was close under the wood-
en planking" (p. 221). Edmond's description of the river
during the actual retreat matches Hemingway's fictional
description: "The Tagliamento . . . is a torrent rather than
a river; its bed is of great width, as much as 3,000 yards and
more in the Friuli plain, stony and traversed by many
branches, fordable in ordinary weather, but after heavy
rain raging torrents carrying all before them."[25] Although
no contemporary description of the foot bridge at Codroipo
is available, a German photograph taken when they
reached the river shows just such a wooden bridge as Frederic describes. (Fig. 3)

But Hemingway had never seen that bridge when he described it. He had never crossed the Tagliamento, had
never been in Udine or Gorizia, had never seen the Bainsizza plateau. Here is accuracy so fine that it goes beyond
realism, but it is accuracy that lies mostly below the surface
of the novel, supporting the visible iceberg. The obvious
conclusion is that Hemingway used secondary source material in writing the novel, and this is not the popular portrait of the artist that we have always been given. The
question remains: what were the sources and how were
they used? Hemingway himself pointed out two of them in
print—*The Red Badge of Courage* and *The Charterhouse
of Parma*—but no one paid any attention. It must have
given him some amusement to know that no one in his
lifetime had seen what he had done in *A Farewell to Arms*.
As with all seemingly easy tricks, the only difficult part was
the execution.

[25] Edmonds, p. 63.

3. The wooden bridge at the Tagliamento after the river had receded. It was at this bridge that Frederic went into the water. Debris is aftermath of the retreat. *Courtesy of Library of Congress.*

4. View of the balcony of the Red Cross hospital, Milan, 1918. *Courtesy of Library of Congress.*

Sources for the Fiction*

I started out very quiet and I beat Mr. Turgenev. Then I trained hard and I beat Mr. de Maupassant. I've fought two draws with Mr. Stendhal, and I think I had an edge in the last one.—Hemingway (in Lillian Ross' *Portrait of Hemingway*)

It is no longer possible to say of Hemingway: "He simply went out and lived his experiences, thought about them, and then wrote them down like the good reporter he's been since his good training at seventeen."[1] *A Farewell to Arms* is, in part, a researched novel, and eventually one must ask what sources Hemingway used to write of places he had not seen and battles he had not fought. Partial answers to this question are possible on the basis of what is known and what is suggested by Hemingway's earlier fiction and non-fiction.

In 1920, Hemingway wrote a feature for the *Toronto Star Weekly* entitled "How to be Popular in Peace Though a Slacker in War," which indicates one direction of source study: *"Buy or borrow a good history of the war. Study it carefully and you will be able to talk intelligently on any part of the front. . . .* With a little conscientious study you should be able to prove to the man who was at first and second Ypres that he was not there at all. You of course are

---

* Most of the biographic data in this chapter is taken from Carlos Baker's *Hemingway: A Life Story*. This data is unfootnoted but can be found between pp. 38-64.

1 William F. Dawson, "Petoskey Interview," *Michigan Alumnus Quarterly Review*, 64 (Winter, 1958), p. 123.

aided in this by the similarity of one day to another in the army."[2] (My emphasis)

Five years after this newspaper story, Hemingway published "Soldier's Home" in which he came back to the same point of reading war histories:

> [Krebs] sat there on the porch reading a book on the war. It was a history and he was reading about all the engagements he had been in. It was the most interesting reading he had ever done. *He wished there were more maps. He looked forward with a good feeling to reading all the really good histories when they would come out with good detail maps. Now he was really learning about the war.*[3] (My emphasis)

There is evidence to indicate that Hemingway himself did just this type of reading during the twenties and that this reading became the background for *A Farewell to Arms*.

Besides histories of the war, Hemingway also had access to newspaper accounts, as well as his own feature stories written after the war. When the Caporetto retreat took place, Hemingway had just begun work as a cub reporter on the *Kansas City Star*. The *Star* carried the Italian story on the front page during the last week in October and into November, 1917. Considering Hemingway's interests and his own eagerness to get into the war, it seems likely that he would have read the *Star* accounts of the retreat. He may even have read them off the wire service copy. However, a survey of the *Kansas City Star* in 1917 shows that it did not carry the Caporetto story in enough detail to have been a major source of the novel. Still Hemingway had access not only to the *Kansas City Star* but also to the morgue files of the *Toronto Star* between 1920-1923, when he most likely

---

[2] Ernest Hemingway, "How to be Popular in Peace," *Toronto Star Weekly* (March 13, 1920), p. 11; the irony of this advice is that Hemingway gives the impression that he fought on the western front which he had not.

[3] Ernest Hemingway, "Soldier's Home," *Short Stories*, p. 148.

began his reading on the Italian war. One also recalls that Frederic Henry is continually reading newspapers to stay informed about the front. Beyond a general knowledge of the Italian war, it is impossible at this point to say that Hemingway used these two newspapers as sources for specific points in *A Farewell to Arms*. However, he did incorporate into the novel portions from his own newspaper feature stories that he wrote after the war for the *Toronto Star*.

Besides secondary written sources, Hemingway also had access to friends and acquaintances who knew about Caporetto. Ted Brumback, Hemingway's ambulance-driving friend who knew Hemingway had not taken part in Caporetto, explained Hemingway's description of the Italian disaster as coming from secondary sources: "He obtained his information from officers and men who had taken part in the fiasco."[4] Although such sources could not have provided the kind of accuracy found in the novel, Hemingway must have learned more from such sources than is commonly supposed. While he was in Italy, he certainly had the opportunity to talk with veterans who had taken part in Caporetto, although Hemingway's limited Italian would have been a handicap. The most obvious source, of course, is Hemingway's own experience in Italy during the war. This source has been overvalued in past criticism, but there remain certain aspects of Hemingway's war experience that have not been fully correlated with the novel.

History, newspaper stories, first- and second-hand experiences—these are the primary sources for *A Farewell to Arms*. With the exception of personal experience, these are the same sources that Stephen Crane had available to him when he wrote his researched war novel, *The Red Badge of Courage*. One recalls that Hemingway praised Crane's use of such source material: "Crane wrote [*The Red Badge of Courage*] before he had ever seen any war. But he had

[4] Ted Brumback, "With Hemingway Before *A Farewell to Arms*," *Kansas City Star* (Dec. 6, 1936), p. 20.

read the contemporary accounts, had heard the old soldiers
. . . talk, and above all he had seen Matthew Brady's wonderful pictures."[5]

Like Crane, Hemingway also had his picture books.
While he was in Italy he collected postcard photographs of
the battle zones. Sometime after he returned to Oak Park,
he pasted these into a scrap book that included other war
mementos, including his Italian medals. This scrap book
was with him in Paris when he began the novel and was
very likely with him when he finished it.[6] Hemingway discovered other picture books the winter of 1926 in the
Vorarlberg. In a letter to Fitzgerald, he described two illustrated German war books: one of them covered the mountain fighting on the Italian front, the second was the history
of the Wurttemberg artillery. Although his German was
minimal, Hemingway was enthusiastic about the mountain
pictures. He promised Fitzgerald that he would send him
copies, for the pictures outweighed the German text. Hemingway looked forward to the book due to appear on the
Sturmtruppen.[7] It was in the months immediately following
this letter to Fitzgerald that Hemingway began to change
his plan for his war novel. It was to the mountains he had
seen in the picture books that he moved the opening chapters. To discover all the sources that Hemingway used in his
novel is not feasible; yet, within the categories suggested
above, several specific sources are apparent.

I

History

In the biography, Carlos Baker notes that Hemingway
was proud, among other things, of "his medical and military
knowledge, his skill in map reading, navigation, and the siz-

---

[5] Hemingway ed., *Men at War*, p. xvii.
[6] The author was shown the scrap book by Carlos Baker, who had
it on loan from Mrs. Mary Hemingway.
[7] Hemingway to Fitzgerald, Feb. 1926.

ing up of terrain."[8] In his descriptions of Plava and Gorizia, we have already seen his ability to describe terrain on the basis of a contour map. Now it is important to understand his grasp of military history.

Soon after he returned wounded from Italy, Hemingway must have begun, like his fictional character Krebs, to read the war histories that proliferated during and immediately after the war. By 1922 in a *Toronto Daily Star* feature, "A Veteran Visits Old Front," Hemingway was already making specific references to action that took place on the Italian front during the 1915-1917 period. He had also begun to imply that he had witnessed that action, a habit he continued all his life. By 1923 he was giving Ezra Pound advice on military strategy. His authority in military matters grew steadily. As a reporter he sent stories back from the Greco-Turkish War, the Spanish Civil War, the Sino-Japanese War, and World War Two in Europe. His library at Finca Vigia in Cuba numbered about six thousand volumes, many of which were military histories.

When Alberto Moravia visited Finca Vigia after Hemingway's death, he described the library as typical for a writer of the 1930s: "There are no philosophy books, no works of science, none of the essays or literary criticism that one finds today. Narrative fiction predominates. All the classics of the English, French and Russian novel are there, in modern editions which look as if they had been read and reread by their owner. *One is not surprised to find as well a great number of travel books, diaries and narrative accounts of explorations. Hemingway as a journalist had developed a taste for facts and lived experiences*"[9] (my emphasis). He had developed more than a taste for accurate facts. By the time he wrote *A Farewell to Arms*, they had become a key ingredient in his fiction, and many of those facts had come from his reading.

[8] *A Life Story*, p. viii.
[9] Alberto Moravia, "The Ghost of Hemingway," *Atlas*, 11 (1966), pp. 337-338.

When Hemingway returned from Italy in 1919, he "read everything in the house—all the books, all the magazines, even the *A.M.A. Journals*" from his father's office. From the library he checked out great numbers of books, very much like Krebs.[10] From July through December of 1919, Hemingway was in and out of the family summer house near Petoskey, Michigan. At the lake house he found that the family had bound together collections of various journals for summer reading.

Thus, his first winter home from the war, Hemingway found that his most available reading was magazines from the war years. With his growing interest in military history, it seems likely that he would have paid particular interest to the accounts of battles he found there. In Petoskey, he very likely used the public library, as did his fictional character Yogi Johnson in *Torrents of Spring*. We know that he was familiar with the library, for he lectured on his war experiences there to the Ladies Aid Society in December, 1919.[11]

Whether or not the Petoskey library carried a subscription to the *Century Magazine*, Hemingway indicates some familiarity with the periodical in *Torrents of Spring*:

As she [Diana] looked out of the window, a copy of the *Century Magazine* dropped from her nerveless hand. The *Century* had a new editor. Glenn Frank had gone to head some great university somewhere. There were more Van Dorens on the magazine.[12]

Century ran a detailed description of the Caporetto disaster in an article by G. Ward Price, "The Italians at Bay."[13] Price, a British correspondent who took part in the Italian

10 M. H. Sanford, *At The Hemingways* (Boston: Little, Brown, 1962), p. 179.
11 Mrs. Constance Montgomery to MSR, April 22, 1970.
12 *Torrents of Spring*, p. 87.
13 G. Ward Price, "The Italians at Bay," *Century*, 73 (1917), pp. 635-652.

retreat, gave specific information on the initial attack at Caporetto, the retreat from the Bainsizza plateau, the road
conditions, the confusion, the weather, the looting, the
enemy aircraft, and the spirit of the retreat. In the article
were pictures of Caporetto and Gorizia, including the castle
there and the stone arch of the destroyed bridge. There is
nothing to indicate that Hemingway read this specific article, but in the course of his reading he must have read
articles similar to it, for the Italian retreat was a war story
of the first magnitude, and no news magazine ignored it.

But the magazine stories seldom provided the kind of detail found in *A Farewell to Arms*. At some point in the
Twenties, Hemingway must have read one or more of the
better military histories to find this information. Of the numerous historical sources available, he could have read
Douglas W. Johnson's *Battle Fields of the World War*
(1921), which was a reliable source on the military events
of the disaster and which contained maps and pictures of
the battle line along the Isonzo. In 1920 a five-volume collection appeared called *The Great Events of the Great War*,
which included essays by Perceval Gibbon and G. M. Trevelyan, two Englishmen who participated in the retreat and
wrote firsthand accounts of it. It would appear that Hemingway read at least the Trevelyan article, for there is one
passage that finds a strong echo in *A Farewell to Arms*. This
passage was Trevelyan's description of the breakdown in
the Second Army:

"The army of the Bainsizza, San Gabriele, and Gorizia,
who had no thought of giving way when the enemy offensive began in the last week of October, successfully resisted
the attacks made on their positions, until the order came
from Cadorna to retreat beyond the Tagliamento. They
carried out irreproachably the difficult retirement across
the Isonzo gorge and out of the hills; but as they proceeded
over the plain, hustled by the victorious enemy pouring
down on their flank from Cividale, they were gradually
infected by the sense that all was lost. Mainly between

Udine and the Tagliamento, they gave way at length to the war-weariness which had so long been at strife with their valor and patriotism, flung away their rifles wholesale, and passed round the word, *'Adiamo a casa'* ('We're going home')."[14]

This passage is perhaps the informing source that Hemingway used in describing the disintegration of the Second Army. The lines are worth comparing. Hemingway wrote:

"We're going home. The war is over."
"Everybody's going home."
"We're all going home."

. . . .

"Adiamo a casa!," a soldier shouted.
"They throw away their rifles," Piani said. "They take them off and drop them down while they're marching. Then they shout." (p. 219)

If Hemingway did not read Trevelyan, he must have read an account like that of Thomas N. Page, who, in a single page, caught most of the details that Hemingway used in his chapter:

"The greater part of [the Second Army] had now, all semblance of organization lost, *thrown away their guns and* were simply making their way westward. . . . A panic had spread through the countryside, and the stricken *population abandoned their homes* and, taking such movables as they could carry, headed westward . . . The *roads were packed with vehicles*; in places thousands of farm vehicles and driven stock mingled . . . with army cars, caissons, ambulances; pedestrians carrying all they had left in the world. . . . The pace of the slowest, which was hardly ever more than half a mile an hour, set that of the entire retreat. The autumn rains had begun and poured down steadily. *At times there was a complete block, and the melancholy procession came to a stand for hours, or numbers straggled off cross the sodden fields to seek some country lane that offered the illusory promise of a quicker way to safety. Many abandoned their vehicles to make better time on foot.* . . . It was mainly after leaving Cividale that the Second Army began to break up. *After Udine was abandoned, . . . it broke up completely as an army, and possessed by the idea that all was lost, flung away their arms and accoutrements, and, self-disbanded, spread over the country, headed for the Tagliamento and home*"[15] (my emphasis).

Another source, unlikely though it may seem, is *Baedeker's Guide to Italy*. In *Across the River and Into the Trees*, Hemingway satirized the Baedeker tourists, using the word as a pejorative. Yet at one point in *A Farewell to Arms* he found the Baedeker guide very useful, for a comparison of Hemingway's description of Udine (which he had not seen in 1928) and the Baedeker guide forces one to conclude that he either used this travel guide or one similar to it. When Frederic first sees Udine, he is seven kilometers out on the plain: "Ahead across the plain was the *hill of Udine.* The roofs fell away from *the castle on the hill.* We could see the *campanile and the clock tower*" (my emphasis, p. 212). Baedeker's description of Udine includes the same landmarks: "Udine . . . In 1915-1917 it was the G.H.Q. of the Italian army. Among the chief buildings are the Cathedral, *with a hexagonal campanile* . . . above the picturesque Piazza Vitorio Emanuele, *with a clock tower* resembling that at Venice, rises the *Castello*"[16] (my emphasis). Hemingway's description of this unfamiliar town is too exact not to have come from the travel guide.

A more extensive source book that Hemingway was unlikely to have missed is Charles Bakewell's *The Story of the American Red Cross in Italy*, published in 1920. In 1920 Hemingway was in Toronto and Chicago, still in touch with several of his ambulance-driving friends from the Italian front. One of them probably discovered the Bakewell book,

15 *Italy and the Great War*, p. 313.
16 Karl Baedeker, *Guide to Italy* (New York: Scribner's, 1928), p. 87.

which listed in its appendices all the Americans and British who took part in the Red Cross war effort in Italy. In Appendix Nine, Bakewell lists the members of the ambulance service and the rolling canteen. Under Ambulance Section Four appear the names of Hemingway, Ted Brumback, Howell Jenkins, and other names from the Hemingway biography. Beside the name of Ernest Hemingway there is an asterisk, indicating that he received the Italian Silver Medal. In Appendix Ten, which lists American and British personnel other than ambulance drivers, there appear the names of Catherine DeLong, Charlotte Heilman, Elsie MacDonald, Agnes Von Kurowsky, and all the other nurses who were known to Hemingway when he was confined to the Milan hospital.

Thus Bakewell must have reminded Hemingway of the people and places he had been involved with in Italy. Apart from nostalgic interest, Hemingway could have found in the Bakewell book many of the details that years later he would use for his description of the retreat from Caporetto. For example, Hemingway found Bakewell drawing a strong parallel between the Napoleonic wars in 1809 and the military situation in 1917: "Napoleon, long years before, had discovered the strategic importance of Caporetto. He wrote in 1809 to Prince Eugene . . . warning him of the danger of a break at that point, which would let the Austrians through the valley of the Natisone and force a retreat to the Piave . . . Shortly after this warning was sent Austria did break through at Caporetto and everything happened exactly as Napoleon had foreseen."[17] Hemingway picked up the Napoleonic parallel and used it in Frederic's meditation: "Napoleon would have whipped the Austrians on the plains. He never would have fought them in the mountains. He would have let them come down and whipped them around Verona" (p. 118).

Bakewell could also have provided Hemingway with a list of the causes that resulted in Caporetto. Hemingway

---

[17] Bakewell, *The American Red Cross in Italy*, p. 19.

could have found information on the food riots in Turin, and he could have gotten a detailed analysis of the food shortage at the front. Bakewell also gave him information on the Austrian propaganda campaign: "Leaflets were dropped over the trenches in which the Italians were told that the Austrians themselves were sick of the war and longing for peace, that they were friends, and that peace would come if they only came together and threw down their arms and refused to fight."[18] It is such an awareness of the Austrian propaganda that informs much of the pacifist discussion in *A Farewell to Arms*.

Bakewell describes the behavior of the Second Army during the retreat in a way that is remarkably similar to Hemingway's fictional version: "Some of the soldiers threw away their guns as they ran, and sang and shouted 'Peace! We are going home. The war is over. One man can't fight alone.' Others cursed . . . Here were others, wolves in sheeps clothing. Austrians and Germans disguised in Italian uniforms, giving contrary orders."[19] The idea of infiltrators reappears in the novel twice. First, Frederic comments: "we had heard that there had been many Germans in Italian uniforms mixing with the retreat in the north" (p. 216). The second time occurs at the bridge, when Frederic realizes that he has been mistaken for just such an infiltrator.

Bakewell is also the most available source for the executions that took place at the Tagliamento bridge, a little-publicized part of the retreat. Almost none of the contemporary histories mentions the executions, and only one English newspaper article has been discovered that said anything of them. Bakewell, who served the Red Cross as an historian and head of the Department of Public Information, may have had Italian sources not readily available after the war. In any case the executions that he reports as truth are very similar to those found in *A Farewell to Arms*: "Some of the soldiers had thrown away their guns in the

18 *Ibid.*, p. 21.
19 *Ibid.*, p. 22.

flight before the enemy, an unpardonable offense in a soldier. These were caught at the bridge crossings. And more than once, in the early dawn, regiments were drawn up on three sides of a hollow square as these unfortunates were led out before them to face the firing squad. There was nothing . . . heroic in their last moments. They did not go to their deaths with head erect and defiant, but cowering and sadly bewildered."[20]

Hemingway's account of these executions appears almost as an answer to Bakewell's rhetorical account. Hemingway shows both the brave man and the coward facing death. The lieutenant colonel does face death defiantly: "If you are going to shoot me, . . . please shoot me at once without further questioning. The questioning is stupid" (p. 224). Another officer breaks into tears when he is condemned to die. Frederic's reaction is neither brave nor cowardly, for he sees the firing squad not as a test of his courage but as a test of survival. The Bakewell version is rhetorical, with no true feeling for the individuals involved. Hemingway's artistry can be measured by the changes he works upon his source. His version is both personalized, yet objective; there is no touch of sentimentality. But, more importantly, Hemingway is always focused on the individuals.

In the Bakewell book Hemingway also could have read of the death of Lieutenant Edward McKey, one of the few Red Cross men killed on the Italian front. Because Hemingway served in the same sector with McKey in 1918, he probably knew the story of his death firsthand, but the Bakewell account would have refreshed his memory. In examining the biography of McKey, one is struck with the numerous parallels between his experiences and those of Frederic Henry.

Edward McKey had been an artist before the war, living in France and Italy; Frederic Henry had been studying architecture in Italy before the war. McKey was in Paris when the war began, and he volunteered immediately to drive ambulances for the Italian army. Both McKey and

[20] *Ibid.*, p. 23.

Frederic Henry were fluent in Italian. Both men are similar to those founders of the Norton-Harjes ambulance group in France who volunteered at the beginning of the war.

McKey was one of the drivers who had arrived in Italy with the ferry load of ambulances that had been sent from France in December, 1917. The following March, McKey volunteered to take a rolling canteen unit to the front lines to provide hot meals, chocolate, coffee, and cigarettes. When the major Austrian offensive opened on June 15, 1918, McKey's rolling canteen was on the crossroads between Fornaci and Fossalta, not far from the Piave. It was there, on June 16, that McKey was killed instantly when an Austrian artillery shell exploded at his side. He was the first Red Cross man to die in Italy, and he became something of a topical hero, whose last words were reported to have been: "How splendidly the Italians are fighting!"

It was about June 16 that Hemingway became bored with his duties at Schio and applied for the rolling canteen service. He was eventually assigned to the same area that McKey had been in charge of when he was killed. It is rather unlikely that Hemingway did not know of McKey's death, for it was carried in the Red Cross Bulletin and in Red Cross newspapers of the day. It may have been chance that took Hemingway to the same sector, but he also may have gone at his own request. When other ambulance drivers became bored with the canteen duty on the Piave and went back to Schio, Hemingway remained, determined to see his adventure through. On July 8, he got himself blown up just as had McKey; and even more spectacularly, Hemingway lived to receive his decoration.

At his death Hemingway had in his possession the *Report of the Department of Military Affairs* put out by the Commission of the American Red Cross, covering the period January-July, 1918. In it both Hemingway and McKey appear. There is also a curious unpublished poem that Hemingway apparently wrote in 1919-1920, titled "Killed. Piave —June 15, 1918." McKey was killed on June 16, 1918. Later

Hemingway changed the date of the poem to July 8, 1918, the date of his own wounding. Since it is unlikely that he had forgotten when he was blown up in the night, one speculates about the first date and whether it might not refer to McKey. Certainly something of McKey's circumstances were used in the background and circumstances of Frederic Henry.

Although he had no need for a source, Hemingway could also have found statements in the Bakewell book that would have reminded him of the speeches that Frederic found obscene in comparison with the reality of war. Bakewell, for example, quotes King Emmanuel's order to his troops as he took command at the beginning of the war: " 'The solemn hour of Italy's vindication has come. . . . Soldiers, yours will be the glory of raising the Italian tri-color on the sacred frontiers that nature itself has set as the boundary of our country. Yours will be the glory of completing the work your fathers with such great heroism began.' "[21] Bakewell, writing with the sure hand of a public relations man, kept up a steady patter of such rhetoric through his book, and it was this sort of rhetoric which Frederic found so nauseating. Hemingway needed no reminder on this point, but, if he did, the Bakewell book would have supplied it.

A second historical study that probably served as a source for *A Farewell to Arms* was Hugh Dalton's first person narrative, *With British Guns in Italy* (1919). If Hemingway did not discover the book for himself, his attention was probably drawn to it by his British friend "Chink" Dorman-Smith, who was a professional military man with artillery service in Italy. Dorman-Smith would have been aware of the book and would also have known of Hemingway's interest in the period. In the early Twenties the two men were in correspondence and vacationed together at least twice. What Hemingway found in the book was a description of Gorizia as it appeared in August, 1916, information he badly needed. He also found a detailed account of the

[21] *Ibid.*, p. 8.

Third Army's retreat from the Carso during which they suffered from the same conditions as the Second Army, with the exception of the desertions.

In the Dalton book, Hemingway also found the name Rinaldo Rinaldi, which he used for an infantryman in an *in our time* sketch and for the Italian doctor in *A Farewell to Arms*. In the novel Frederic calls Rinaldi by his first name, Rinaldo, on page 171; and the priest also used both names three pages later. More important to Hemingway's purpose, the Dalton book contained a detailed picture of Gorizia. This was information that Hemingway had to have, for he had never seen Gorizia, and he needed better information than tour guides supply. In Dalton he found what Gorizia was like in wartime: the people, the buildings, the streets, the bridges, the feeling that prevailed. He also learned about the Austrian villas that had not been destroyed or shelled by the retreating Austrians. All of this information appears in *A Farewell to Arms* and Dalton was the most available source.

The most important information Hemingway found in *With British Guns in Italy* was an unbiased, detailed account of the retreat from the Carso across the bridge at Latisana. Dalton supplied Hemingway with an exact timetable for the retreat; Hemingway learned the precise sequence of when the preparation orders were received and when the execution of those orders began. He learned the military priorities of the retreat. Dalton gave him an exact timetable of the rains, and details on how hard it rained and when it let up. There was exact information on the activities of enemy aircraft and their effectiveness. Dalton described the road conditions, the lack of road controls, the lack of food, and the general confusion of the retreat. It was this kind of information that Hemingway used to establish the authenticity of Frederic Henry's fictional retreat from the Bainsizza plateau.

A seemingly improbable source, but one that Hemingway may have used, is the *Report by the Joint War Commission of the British Red Cross* published in 1921. If he did not use this exact source, Hemingway must have used something very like it, for *A Farewell to Arms* contains accurate information on British Red Cross activities at the Italian front in 1917. For example, when Hemingway put his fictional British hospital in Gorizia, he located it in a large villa that resembled the Villa Trento, where the British Red Cross hospital was located at Cormons, not far from Gorizia. The *Report* described the Villa Trento in some detail just as it described the cholera epidemic of 1915. The British Red Cross unit moved into Gorizia when it fell in 1916, just as did Frederic Henry. The house where the unit lived was shaded by the same sort of chestnut trees that Frederic observed in Chapters One and Two.

During May, 1917, the British ambulances from the British unit in Gorizia moved up to Plava for the spring offensive. One recalls that when Frederic was wounded at Plava, he turned his ambulances over to a British officer in charge of some British ambulances there. In the fall of 1917, the *Report* states that "the motor ambulances of the Unit were divided between two localities, half being stationed at Gorizia, the remainder at Ravne."[22] When Frederic went up on the Bainsizza in October, 1917, we are told that "the British cars were working further down the Bainsizza at Ravne. He had great admiration for the British" (p. 181). Hemingway's accuracy in having the British ambulances at Plava and at Ravne calls for a source like the *Report*.

During the retreat following Caporetto, the British cars were among the last to leave Gorizia on October 27. Frederic's ambulance unit left Gorizia on the night of October 26. During the retreat the British units encountered the very difficulties that plagued Frederic:

"Dr. Brock received orders . . . to evacuate the hospital, and to hold himself in readiness to leave with the whole staff at the shortest notice. In the evening *these instructions*

22 *Report by the Joint War Commission of the British Red Cross,* p. 436.

*were countermanded but on the 27th new orders were re-
ceived* . . . to transfer the hospital to Conegliano on the far
side of the Tagliamento. . . . *Owing to the congestion of the
roads several hours elapsed before the last party to leave
Villa Trento were able to make any progress.* It was impossible to save the bulk of the material, the wounded had all
been evacuated, the nurses already sent off; and the column
of ambulances, *with such stores as they could carry,* en-
deavoured to make its way along the crowded roads to the
bridge across the Tagliamento. *To secure the safety of the
personnel some of the cars had to be abandoned* . . . *Such
material as had been carried away from Villa Trento was
lost en route.*"[23] (My emphasis)

This historical account finds its fictional counterpart in
the experience of Frederic Henry. Stalled lines of traffic,
countermanded orders, valuable hospital equipment, and
abandoned ambulances are all part of Frederic's retreat. If
his account struck no discordant note with readers who had
taken part in the retreat, it was because Hemingway had
relied on sources that provided him with the kinds of specific information seen above.

In addition to finding source material in historical non-
fiction, Hemingway used two other printed sources when
he wrote *A Farewell to Arms*: his own newspaper feature
stories from the Twenties and Stendhal's *The Charterhouse
of Parma*. Robert O. Stephens, in *Hemingway's Nonfiction*,
has already established Hemingway's use of his own journalism in the novel. Stephens shows that the feature stories
that Hemingway wrote about Germany, Switzerland, and
Italy during the early Twenties found their way into the
novel.[24]

Stephens does not suggest that Hemingway had copies
of the articles at hand when he wrote *A Farewell to Arms*,
but some of the parallels are so extended that such a sug-

23 *Ibid.,* p. 436.
24 Robert O. Stephens, *Hemingway's Nonfiction* (Chapel Hill: University of North Carolina Press, 1968), pp. 254-269.

gestion seems reasonable. After one reads the Young-Mann inventory of Hemingway's literary remains, the suggestion seems a certainty, for Hemingway was a "saver." Young says that the author "kept nearly everything from novel to note from the 1919 Chicago days . . . to the bitter end."[25] Item 122 of the inventory includes notes, background material, and typescript for several *Toronto Star* articles. Item 305 covers numerous folders of letters received by Hemingway which include fourteen folders from the *Toronto Star* and four folders of letters from Italy, 1918-1919. In the inventory there are notes and transcripts for at least fourteen *Toronto Star* articles. If this much has survived, it is reasonable to surmise that at one time Hemingway probably kept all such notes and typescripts. For the inventory is definitive only for the manuscripts that remained in Mary Hemingway's possession at the end.

One particular *Toronto Star* article, however, is worth reexamining, although Stephens has already demonstrated its significance. In 1922, Hemingway wrote a feature story, "Veteran Visits Old Front," which was the genesis of the opening chapter of *A Farewell to Arms*:

> It was the same road that the battalions marched along
> through the white dust of 1916. They were the Brigata
> Ancona, the Brigata Como, the Brigata Tuscana and
> ten others brought down from the Carco [sic] to check
> the Austrian offensive that was breaking through the
> mountain wall of the Trentino and beginning to spill
> down the valleys that led to the Venetian and
> Lombardy plains. They were good troops in those days
> and they marched through the dust of the early
> summer. . . . It was the same old road that some of the
> same old brigades marched along through the dust in
> June 1918. . . . Their best men were dead on the rocky

---

25 Philip Young and Charles W. Mann, *The Hemingway Manuscripts, An Inventory* (University Park: Penn State University Press, 1969), p. viii.

Carso in the fighting around Goritzia, on Mount San
Gabrielle, on Grappa, and in all the places where men
died that nobody ever heard about. In 1918 they didn't
march with the ardor that they did in 1916.[26]

In the article, Hemingway describes the dusty road from
his vantage point in a hotel at Schio, with the road running
past his window. As Stephens points out, this is the same
sort of vantage point that Frederic uses when he begins to
narrate *A Farewell to Arms*. The dusty road is the same
dusty road that Frederic observed. More important is the
attitude of the narrator in the newspaper feature, for Hemingway in 1922 was already creating the impression that he
had seen all of the Italian war. He was already perfecting
his role as expert, and to do this he must have been finding
out about the Italian fighting during the first three years of
the war. It is interesting to note that he uses the Austrian
spelling of Goritzia rather than the Italian Gorizia. Six years
later, when he began to write *A Farewell to Arms*, Hemingway very likely reread this article just as he must have reviewed most of what he had learned about the Italian war
before beginning the novel. In the manuscript both spellings appear and were not standardized until the typescript
was made. In a 1923 newspaper feature, Hemingway described the Italian king: "Victor Emmanuel of Italy is a
very short, serious little man with a grey, goat-like beard
and tiny hands and feet. . . . His queen is almost a head tall-
er than himself."[27] It is this disparity in height that Frederic
notes in the opening chapter of *A Farewell to Arms*.

On December 1, 1925, Hemingway borrowed the new
two-volume translation of *The Charterhouse of Parma* from
Sylvia Beach's Shakespeare and Company book store in
Paris. Ten days later he returned both volumes, and forever

26 Hemingway, "A Veteran Visits Old Front, Wishes He Had Stayed
Home," *Toronto Daily Star* (July 22, 1922), p. 7.
27 Hemingway, "King Business in Europe," *Toronto Star Weekly*
(Sept. 15, 1923), rpt. *By-Line: Ernest Hemingway*, p. 80.

after the novel appeared on the lists that Hemingway periodically recommended to the attention of young writers.[28] When Hemingway edited *Men at War*, he chose to include Stendhal's account of young Fabrizio at Waterloo. In his introduction Hemingway wrote:

> The best account of actual human beings behaving during a world shaking event is Stendhal's picture of young Fabrizio at the battle of Waterloo. That account is more like war and less like the nonsense written about it than any other writing could possibly be. Once you have read it you will have been at the battle of Waterloo and nothing can ever take that experience from you. *You will have to read Victor Hugo's account of the same battle . . . to find out what you saw there as you rode with the boy; but you will have actually seen the field of Waterloo already whether you understood it or not.* You will have seen a small piece of war as closely and as clearly with Stendhal as any man has ever written of it. *It is the classic account of a routed army. . . . Stendhal served with Napoleon and saw some of the greatest battles of the world. But all he ever wrote about war is the one long passage from "La Chartreuse de Parme"*[29] (my emphasis).

Hemingway also included the retreat from Caporetto in *Men at War*, as if he were inviting comparison. As in *The Charterhouse of Parma*, Book Three of *A Farewell to Arms* presents a limited view of a military disaster, but the action that is seen epitomizes the whole. The reader has taken part

[28] See: "Monologue to the Maestro," *Esquire*, 4 (Oct., 1935), p. 174 A-B; "The Art of Fiction," *Paris Review*, 5 (Spring, 1958), p. 73; *A Moveable Feast* (New York: Scribner's, 1964), pp. 133-134.

[29] *Men at War*, p. xx; for almost identical conclusions on Hemingway's use of Stendhal see Robert O. Stephen's article, "Hemingway and Stendhal: The Matrix of *A Farewell to Arms*," *PMLA*, 88 (March, 1973), pp. 271-280. Stephen's article was published after my chapter had been written.

in the retreat from Caporetto "whether he understood it or not." Frederic's experience, like Fabrizio's, is with a routed army. And, like Stendhal, Hemingway could have written of victories, but he chose to write of defeat; aside from the brief action at Plava, *A Farewell to Arms* presents no immediate military action except the retreat. As in reading Stendhal, the reader of *A Farewell to Arms* must read some overview of the Italian front before he can fully appreciate what he has read.

Hemingway, however, found more in Stendhal's narrative than he indicated in his introduction. A close comparison of the experiences of Fabrizio and Frederic indicates that Hemingway probably supplemented his historical reading with Stendhal's fiction when he came to write of the retreat from Caporetto. Fabrizio, a young Italian, is a truly innocent naïf who fights idealistically with the Napoleonic forces at Waterloo. Although Frederic Henry is older and no innocent, his experiences in Book Three are remarkably similar at times to those of Fabrizio. Both Frederic and Fabrizio are foreigners fighting gratuitously in another country. Both men are involved in a crucial battle that turns into a rout of their forces. Both men become separated from their command and choose to follow side roads because the main roads have become jammed with both soldiers and civilians. Both men eat off the land during their retreat; both are taken for spies; both escape into the neutral ground of Switzerland. When specific passages in *The Charterhouse of Parma* are compared with others in *A Farewell to Arms*, the similarities become even stronger.

For example, there is the matter of accent and speech betraying both Fabrizio and Frederic. Fabrizio speaks French with an Italian accent, which makes his companions suspect him of being a spy. A corporal explains to Fabrizio that the mistake was a natural one, for "in the army one must belong to some corps and wear a uniform, failing which it was quite simple that people should take one for a spy. The enemy sends us any number of them; everybody's a traitor in this war."[30] Frederic Henry speaks Italian with an accent that makes the military police at the Tagliamento suspect him of being a German infiltrator. Such infiltrators were an historical fact, but Hemingway must have been reminded of Fabrizio's difficulties when he wrote Book Three.

There are other passages in Stendhal that bear resemblance to Hemingway's narrative. In the retreat that followed the battle of Waterloo, Fabrizio is caught up in scenes similar to those experienced by Frederic. Like Frederic at Gorizia and Udine, Fabrizio has difficulty making his way through a town because of the congestion: "All these streets were blocked with infantry, cavalry, and, worst of all, by the limbers and wagons of the artillery. The corporal tried three of these streets in turn; after advancing twenty yards he was obliged to halt . . . . finally going through a hedge, they found a huge field of buckwheat. In less than half an hour, guided by the shouts and confused noises, they had regained the high road on the other side of the village."[31] This passage resembles, in some respects, Frederic's passage around Udine, which takes place in the dark and in great confusion.

When Fabrizio regains the high road he finds a scene not unlike the one seen by Frederic between Udine and Codroipo: "The ditches on either side of this road were filled with muskets that had been thrown away; . . . the road, although very broad, was so blocked with stragglers and transport that in the next half hour the corporal and Fabrizio had not advanced more than five hundred yards at the most."[32] Unable to advance on the road, Corporal Aubry leads Fabrizio and three other men across fields, much as Frederic took his men down side roads to make better time. Corporal Aubry stops his group among some trees to divide the food they have in equal portions; Fred-

[30] Stendhal, *The Charterhouse of Parma*, trans. C. K. Scott-Moncrieff (Garden City, N. Y.: Doubleday, 1956), p. 68.
[31] *Ibid.*, pp. 62-63.
[32] *Ibid.*, p. 63.

eric also stopped periodically to care for the feeding of his men. After eating, Fabrizio sleeps until an hour before daylight; the noise from the high road continues, sounding "like a torrent heard from a long way off." Frederic and Piani also slept after they had eaten, and later they too found their way back to the main road by the noise of the retreating army.

Fabrizio is advised by his fellow soldiers to desert: "Get away from this rout of an army; clear out, take the first road with ruts on it that you come to on the right; . . . at the first opportunity, buy some civilian clothes. . . . Never let anyone know you've been in the army, or the police will take you up as a deserter."[33] This is, of course, almost exactly what Frederic Henry does. He too deserts, and he too gets into civilian clothes as quickly as possible. Frederic is almost arrested at Stresa by the police, who know that he was once in the army and believe him to be a deserter. Both Frederic and Fabrizio finally make their way to safety in Switzerland, where they both use cover stories to hide their identities.

Hemingway need not have used the fictional experiences of Fabrizio when he wrote of Frederic Henry, but the parallels seem too strong for coincidence. Hemingway has said that in his early career he thought of himself as writing in competition with great authors of the past. In *A Farewell to Arms*, he seems to have written his Caporetto retreat in direct competition with Stendhal, and in *Men at War* he has invited the comparison by reprinting the two sections in juxtaposition.

In addition to using Stendhal as a source for the retreat, Hemingway also used him as source for Frederic Henry's name. Stendhal had two names: *Henri* Beyle, his real name, and *Frederic* Stendhal, his *nom de plume*. That curious spelling of *Frederic* seems to have come from Stendhal. *Henry* may have also come from the Henry Fleming, the protagonist of *The Red Badge of Courage*. As if asking for

33 *Ibid.*, p. 69.

the comparison, Hemingway placed his own work side by side with Crane and Stendhal and then took a conglomerate name for his own narrator.

Unfortunately for scholars there is one more possibility that has a logic of its own. In 1924 in Paris, Hemingway was introduced to a young Harvard graduate doing a summer in Paris before settling down to the serious business of life. The young man's name was *Barklie* McKee *Henry*. Hemingway remained in loose touch with Henry through the Twenties. After *A Farewell to Arms* was published, Henry wrote Hemingway, joking about names of Frederic *Henry* and Catherine *Barkley*. Hemingway replied in an equally joking tone that he had named all the characters after Henry, and that next time he would work in *McKee*. Henry later said that "Hemingway and I used to kid about the names of the two leading characters in *A Farewell to Arms*. It was my little conceit that if they had had a child they might have given it my middle name."[34]

Hemingway had Stephen Crane before him as the model for writing a researched war novel, and he invited that comparison by reprinting *The Red Badge of Courage* in its entirety in *Men at War*, the only work so honored. Aside from the thematic similarities between Crane's novel and Hemingway's, there is one particular scene in *A Farewell to Arms* in which Hemingway modernizes parts of Crane's Chapter Twelve, in which Henry Fleming receives his head wound.

Fleming, having deserted his position under fire, wandered the back roads behind the front lines until he tried to stop another panicky deserter, who struck Fleming's forehead with his rifle butt. Ironically, this becomes Fleming's "red badge of courage." Because of his head wound, Fleming was accepted by his comrades when he returned to his regiment.

In Chapter Seven of *A Farewell to Arms*, Frederic Henry

[34] Hemingway to Barklie McKee Henry, Dec. 2, 1929; B. McKee Henry to Valerie Danby Smith, March 4, 1966.

discovers a would-be deserter on a dusty road behind the front lines in the Gorizia sector. The soldier, an Italian-American, has aggravated an old rupture in order to get out of the war. Frederic, in sympathy with the soldier, advises him: "You get out and fall down by the road and get a bump on your head and I'll pick you up on our way back and take you to a hospital" (p. 35). But when Frederic returns, the enlisted man's own ambulance has found him and is returning him to duty: "He shook his head at me. His helmet was off and his forehead was bleeding below the hair line. His nose was skinned and there was dust on the bloody patch and dust in his hair" (p. 36). Like Fleming the soldier has his "bloody patch," and like Fleming he returns to his regiment. But whereas Fleming was taken to be a brave man because of his "red badge," the Italian soldier is not mistaken for something he is not. As Hemingway indicates in other parts of the novel, the courage to face the enemy or the lack of it is of no particular value in this war. The very brave are among the first to die. Those who are not brave are killed also, "but there will be no special hurry." Here Hemingway is not so much using Crane as a source as he is paying an oblique kind of homage to a writer whom he admired and from whom he learned something about writing.

II

Biographic Sources

The most immediate biographic sources of information, which are almost impossible to document, are the personal memories of the nurses and soldiers whom Hemingway met in Milan during his recuperation. It was in Milan, for example, that he met a British officer, Eric Dorman-Smith, who had been in the war since 1914, but only recently in Italy. "Chink" Dorman-Smith's stories of the fighting around Mons, France, became the basis for two Heming-

way sketches that appeared in *in our time*. Although Dorman-Smith had not been in Italy during Caporetto, he very
likely had friends with the British artillery unit that had
retreated from the Carso in the debacle. Certainly Hemingway found Dorman-Smith a source of military tactics and
war anecdotes. The two men remained close friends
through the Twenties, and it is not unlikely that Hemingway tested his book knowledge of the Italian war on his
professional military friend.[35]

While Hemingway was at the Red Cross hospital in
Milan, he had the opportunity to speak with other patients
and the nurses stationed there. The patients were Americans who had seen no more of Italy than he had himself, but
some of the Red Cross personnel had been in the country
during the Caporetto disaster. Mary Nolan, a British nurse
at the Milan hospital, had been in Italy since December,
1917, as had Margaret A. Strycker. It is possible that they
were able to provide some information.

In addition to hospital personnel and soldiers at the
Milan clubs, there were numerous chance acquaintances,
any one of whom may have had war stories to tell Hemingway. One such source was Captain Enrico Serena, a veteran
of much of the war who visited Hemingway in the Milan
hospital. Serena told endless war stories complete with
sound effects that Hemingway enjoyed and remembered.[36]
Because he was a good listener, he absorbed from these
sources certain general aspects of the Caporetto retreat and
the war in Italy between 1915-1917. But from such sources
he could not have learned the detailed topography of northern Italy nor the specific timetable of the retreat.

More identifiable sources who contributed to the novel
are the ambulance drivers who served with Hemingway.
Three-quarters of the Red Cross drivers in Italy were former Norton-Harjes drivers from France. Before the United

[35] Baker, *A Life Story*, pp. 85-135.
[36] Mrs. Agnes Stanfield interview with MSR.

5. Seasoned American Red Cross ambulance drivers who drove the emergency units from France to Milan, December, 1917. *Courtesy of Library of Congress.*

6. Hemingway and other patients on the balcony of the Red Cross hospital in Milan, 1918. Three on right are Bill Horne, Ed Alan, and a Mr. Rochfort, who had suffered a severe concussion. *Courtesy of Library of Congress.*

States entered the war, the Norton-Harjes drivers were a free-lance outfit with officer status in the French army. They were accustomed to working hard when there was work to be done, but in the slack periods they did not maintain military discipline unnecessarily. Upon America's entry into the war, the U.S. Army Field Service took over command of the Norton-Harjes group and the drivers were offered enlisted status and continual military discipline. Many of the drivers resented the U.S. Army interference; some of them had already spent two to three years at the front and felt that they deserved better treatment. Large numbers of the Norton-Harjes drivers went into other services—the artillery, the infantry, and the air force. Still other drivers retired to Paris rather than become part of the U.S. Army.

By November 22, 1917, their presence had become something of an embarrassment to the U.S. authorities. The following story ran in the *Kansas City Star* while Hemingway was still a cub reporter there:

ROUND UP AMERICAN DRIVERS
Americans of Military Age in France
Must Join Some Branch of Service
Paris, Nov. 22 — The Paris Herald reports that more
than two hundred young Americans wearing uniforms
of the ambulance drivers have been rounded up
recently by the American military authorities. The
numbers of their passports were taken and they were
told to call at the headquarters and all but five
appeared. They were informed again they must enlist
in some branch of the active service overseas or they
would be sent back to America where they would be
dealt with as the circumstances warranted. The five
who did not appear will meet with harsh treatment
when they are taken it is said.[37]

37 *Kansas City Star* (Nov. 22, 1917), p. 2.

It was in November that Ted Brumback arrived at the *Star* as a former Norton-Harjes driver who must have decided to return home rather than join the army. This attitude is understandable when one considers that some of these men had two to three years' service before America entered the war, and they felt they had first rights on the ambulance driving.

For the Norton-Harjes drivers who remained in France, the Italian disaster at Caporetto presented a reprieve from joining the U.S. Army. The Red Cross had hastily assembled in Paris three sections of ambulances to be ferried over the Alps into Italy. By December the cars were ready, but there were no experienced drivers available. Many of the former Norton-Harjes drivers enlisted with the Red Cross to drive ambulances and thereby avoid the choices offered them by the military authorities. John Dos Passos was among the former Norton-Harjes drivers who signed on with the Red Cross, and he later used his experience in *1919*. A fourth section of drivers was enlisted in the United States, and it was there that Hemingway and Brumback volunteered for service. This fourth section did not reach Italy until early June, 1918.[38]

The importance of this historical background to *A Farewell to Arms* can be measured in the mood of the novel, particularly in Frederic's war weariness. Hemingway himself was at the front something less than a month, during which time he saw little real action. After he was blown up on July 8, 1918, his letters home show no revulsion or weariness with the war, for in fact he had not had time to develop such an attitude. Frederic Henry's attitude toward the war is, on the other hand, both spectatorial and war-weary; he, in fact, is more like the Norton-Harjes drivers in his attitude than he is like the young Hemingway. Frederic's age and experience level is more like that of the

[38] For information on the Norton-Harjes drivers I am indebted to Mr. Clyde Buckingham, Red Cross historian at the American National Red Cross Archives in Washington, D.C.

Norton-Harjes drivers, for they were mostly college gradu-
ates or college sophomores, two to six years older than
Hemingway at the time.

The June, 1918, edition of *Ciao*, the section four newspaper, contained Hemingway's "Alf Letter," but it also contained a lead article entitled "And Yet More Driving":

"We turn away from this Welter of Shock and Gore to
Reflect for a Moment on the Last Peaceful day before Again
We Throw Ourselves into the World Armageddon.

"All ceremonies by Nature are Bores; but Our Farewell
to Milan had one Redeeming Feature: It was brief. We
were reviewed by General Somebody of the Italian Army
in the Piazza Duomo, Milan. Evidently the Gen. did'n Rate
us Very highly: One Look was Enough. The Captains and
the Kings Departed: A few Tears were shed. They were Going to Pour out Their Young and Prominent Lives on the
Mountains of the Trentino. There was a Little Vigorous
Semaphoring . . . on the Part of Certain Fair Ones, But as
the Convoy Weighed Anchor they Turned and looked the
Crowd over for Some New Suckers."[39]

There is nothing idealistic in the *Ciao* writer's attitude
toward the war. Instead, there is a war weariness that has
no use for pomp and ceremony. The writer makes fun of the
standard clichés and the worn-out phrases, perhaps because
he has heard them for too many years and has seen nothing
on the battlefield to match them. The writer has little respect for kings and other dignitaries, and his juxtaposition
of the noble speech with the sign language of the prostitutes
is an ironic touch not unlike some found in *A Farewell to
Arms*. Pictures of the Norton-Harjes volunteers in Milan are
in keeping with this *Ciao* article: dressed in somewhat non-
regulation uniforms with cigarettes dangling from mouths,
they are not your spit-and-polish young soldiers off to make
the world safe for democracy.

Like the writer above, Frederic is unable to listen to
speeches made by dignitaries or heroes. He too looks on

[39] *Ciao* (June, 1918), p. 1.

kings and generals with some disdain. The war weariness
that pervades *A Farewell to Arms* is more a product of
Hemingway's association with the older, more experienced,
and somewhat jaundiced Norton-Harjes drivers, for Hemingway simply was not at the front long enough to wear
down his initial enthusiasm. After the war, as a reporter,
Hemingway became more cynical about European affairs.
When he came to write of Frederic Henry, he was able to
combine his own post-war cynicism with the war weariness
he had seen among his fellow drivers in Section IV even if
he himself had not felt that way at the time.

Count Giuseppe Greppi, a chance acquaintance whom
Hemingway met at Stresa in the fall of 1918, appears un-
changed in the novel as Count Greffi. Throughout the manuscript, his name is spelled *Greppi*; the spelling was not
altered until the *Scribner's Magazine* galleys were being
proofed.

Born in 1819, Count Greppi had long been a prominent
social and diplomatic figure in Milan and Rome. As late as
1915, he was actively involved in the Italian diplomatic
corps. In spite of warnings from the Italian Consul and German authorities, he had personally involved himself in passing letters to members of the Belgian Army. Arrested and
court martialed by the Germans, he was sentenced to two
months imprisonment. The Italian government negotiated
his release, and he returned to Italy.[40]

On his hundredth birthday, March 24, 1919, the *New
York Times* picked up the following story:

DIPLOMAT A CENTENARIAN
_____

Count Greppi of Rome, Contemporary
Of Metternich, Celebrates His Birthday

Rome, March 24,

[40] *NYT*, Feb. 14, 1915, II, 2: 7; I am indebted to Carlos Baker for
pointing me toward the correct Count Greppi. Professor Baker discovered his mistake too late to correct it in the biography (*Life Story*,
pp. 572-573).

7. At age 67, Count Giuseppe Greppi, the prototype for Count
   Greffi; Hemingway met him 32 years after this picture was
   taken. *Courtesy of Carlos Baker.*

. . . notwithstanding his age, [he] is a strong, healthy, alert man, showing great interest in everything going on around him. He can be seen any day at receptions, lectures, or the theatre.

At the age of 102, he collapsed while attending the horse races at the San Siro track in Milan. He died May 8, 1921. His *New York Times'* obituary said:

COUNT GREPPI, OLDEST
DIPLOMAT, DIES AT 102

Italian Statesman, Noted for His
Social Activities, Expires After
Attending the Races

He carried himself like a soldier, and with his distinguished bearing, pure white mustache and immaculate attire, was a notable figure wherever he appeared. It was characteristic of him that he never missed appearing for dinner in evening clothes, even when alone. . . .

[He] began his diplomatic career in Vienna under Metternich, and in 1840 was appointed diplomatic adviser to Marie Louise, ex-Empress of France. He was Italian Ambassador to Paris during the regime of Napoleon III, and served successively in the Italian diplomatic service at London, Stockholm, Munich, and Stuttgart, was Italian Minister at Constantinople and then Ambassador to Russia.

He retained his gallantry to his latest years, and on one occasion, when almost 100 years old, offered a seat to a woman at a theatrical premiere and stood himself throughout the entire performance. . . . [He] has long been one of the most picturesque characters among Italy's distinguished men.

Hemingway's fictional description of Count Greffi is straight from life: Count Greffi was ninety-four years old. He had been a contemporary of Metternich and was an old man with white hair and mustache and beautiful manners. He had been in the diplomatic service of both Austria and Italy and his birthday parties were the great social event of Milan. He was living to be one hundred years old. (p. 254)

In October, 1917, when Frederic played his billiard game with Count Greffi, the real Count Greppi was ninety-eight, not ninety-four. Otherwise, the fictional character's background and manners match those of the life model. Hemingway may have learned of his career firsthand, or he could have read the obituary in the Chicago papers, where he was living in May, 1921.

Although my emphasis has been on Hemingway's use of secondary material in *A Farewell to Arms*, it would be foolish to argue that there was no use of biographic experience. Indeed, Hemingway scholars have already established the main correlations between Hemingway's life and the novel, but these correlations appear rather slender. Both Hemingway and Frederic were blown up by trench mortar shells in Italy during World War One. Both men recuperated in a Milan hospital, where each established a relationship with a nurse. Once in Switzerland, Frederic sticks to terrain that Hemingway knew from experience. As familiar as the Hemingway biography has become, however, there are surprising gaps in the information available. For example, relatively little is known about Hemingway's period of recuperation in the Milan hospital. Eventually, fuller information may appear to flesh out what is essentially an outline of this period, but even now the old biographical information may be profitably re-examined.

On the basis of the Baker biography, it seems reasonable that Hemingway based the experiences of Catherine Barkley on those of three women: Agnes Von Kurowsky, Hadley Richardson, and Pauline Pfeiffer. Agnes, the Red Cross nurse in Milan, seems to dominate Book Two; Hadley Richardson, Hemingway's first wife, contributes heavily to the idyllic winter at Montreux. Pauline Pfeiffer, the second wife, contributed her Caesarean operation, which took place while Hemingway was writing the first draft of the novel. However, Agnes Von Kurowsky did not run off to Switzerland with Hemingway, who, in turn, did not desert the army, having never been in it. Hadley was not pregnant the winter that she and Ernest spent at Montreux, Switzerland, and neither Pauline nor his son died in childbirth. While these points may be obvious, they still bear consideration, for they represent a central point in Hemingway's art of fiction. He never allowed reality to interfere with his fiction, and in the early years he did not allow his personal experience to dictate to his work as an artist. When art and biography were at odds, he would change the remembered experience to fit the needs of his writing.

The most obvious example of Hemingway's use of personal experience can be seen in the wounding of Frederic Henry. Hemingway was blown up while distributing chocolate at a forward listening post along the Piave river. Suffering severe shrapnel wounds in his right leg, he managed to carry a wounded Italian soldier back to the dressing station. While doing so, he was machine-gunned by the Austrians, receiving another wound in his leg. For his action under fire, Hemingway was awarded Italy's second highest decoration, the silver medal. By comparison, Frederic Henry is blown up in the mountains while eating cold spaghetti and cheese. He is not in the front lines, nor does he behave heroically after being wounded. When he recovers consciousness, Frederic is unable to move. Besides suffering stoically, he does nothing that can be called commendable. Hemingway emphasizes this point when Rinaldi visits Frederic at the field hospital:

"You will be decorated. They want to get you the medaglia d'argento but perhaps they can get only the bronze."

"What for?"

"Because you are gravely wounded. They say if you
prove you did any heroic act you can get the silver.
Otherwise it will be the bronze. Tell me exactly what
happened. Did you do any heroic act?"

"No," I said. "I was blown up while we were eating
cheese."

"Be serious. You must have done something heroic
either before or after. Remember carefully."

"I did not."

"Didn't you carry anybody on your back? Gordini says
you carried several people on your back but the
medical officer at the first post declares it is impossible.
He had to sign the proposition for the citation."

"I didn't carry anybody. I couldn't move." (p. 63)

For Frederic to have acted as Hemingway acted under the
same circumstances would clearly be out of character. Here
Hemingway is not just debunking his own silver medal; he
is changing his experience to fit the needs of his fiction. By
having Rinaldi suggest to Frederic that he may have acted
heroically emphasizes the non-heroic nature of Frederic
and draws special attention to the absurdity of being blown
up while eating cheese.

Hemingway's use of his own experiences in this example
is the pattern he follows throughout the novel. Where the
experience is usable in its original form, he brings it whole
into the novel. For example, both Frederic and Hemingway
had Austrian sniper rifles with octagon barrels, and both
men once played billiards with an Italian count at Stresa.
However, Hemingway would always sacrifice his own experience to the needs of his fiction when it was demanded
of him. Agnes Von Kurowsky did not become pregnant by
Hemingway in Milan. But Catherine's pregnancy is necessary to the novel, and Hemingway does not hesitate to in-
vent her dilemma.

Some of the scenes in *A Farewell to Arms* that have their
source in firsthand experience seem to be almost obsessions

with Hemingway, for different versions of them are scattered through his work. One such obsessive image involves flat, low-lying water with either something on the water or crossing it. This image appears twice in *A Farewell to Arms*. The first time it occurs, Frederic and Catherine are walking through Milan at night in the rain on the evening of Frederic's departure. Coming down a dark side street, they reach a canal that is crossed farther down by a bridge across which a street car passes. In Book Three the image reappears when Frederic and his drivers, moving down a side road, come to a river. As they look up the river they see German soldiers crossing on another bridge.

This conjunction of flat water with things either crossing it or hanging over it takes on sinister connotations that can be traced back to Hemingway's own wounding at Fossalta. A later development (1933) of this image appears in "A Way You'll Never Be":

> those were the nights the river ran so much wider and
> stiller than it should and outside of Fossalta there was
> a low house painted yellow with willows all around it
> and a low stable and there was a canal, and he had
> been there a thousand times . . . it frightened him
> especially when the boat lay there quietly in the
> willows on the canal.[41]

This scene is apparently the prelude to Hemingway's bad dream of being blown up at Fossalta, for it reappears in *Across the River and Into the Trees* in Colonel Cantwell's pilgrimage to the site of his first wounding. It is this same conjunction of low-hanging trees over narrow water that informs the end of "Big Two-Hearted River" with its subsurface tension. In *A Farewell to Arms* the image is understated by comparison with "A Way You'll Never Be," but it remains obsessive, culminating in Frederic's leap into the river under the threat of the firing squad.

[41] *Short Stories*, pp. 408-409.

In the Milan section of *A Farewell to Arms*, biography and fiction most nearly overlap. From the moment Frederic left the front for the hospital in Milan, his physical circumstances became those of Ernest Hemingway. Yet, Book Three of the novel is not unadulterated biography as a comparison of fact and fiction will show.

After Frederic is treated at the field hospital, he is told he will be moved back from the front:

> They said I would go to an American hospital in Milan
> that had just been installed. Some American ambulance
> units were to be sent down and this hospital would
> look after them and any other Americans on service in
> Italy. There were many in the Red Cross. The States
> had declared war on Germany but not on
> Austria. (p. 75)

In April, 1917, America had entered the war, but there were no American hospitals in Milan. The hospital to which Frederic is removed is a fictional one based entirely upon the Red Cross hospital in which Hemingway recuperated in 1918. This was the Red Cross hospital at 3 Via Bochetto, which opened on July 11, 1918. The American Red Cross has wondered why Hemingway did not make Frederic Henry a Red Cross driver, and the answer is simple. In 1915-1917 there were no American Red Cross units operating in Italy, just as there was no Red Cross hospital in Milan.

At the hospital in Milan, Mrs. Walker, "an elderly woman wearing glasses," meets Frederic as he gets off the elevator. He is their first patient, and she is unable to tell him which room to take. Finally she breaks into tears (pp. 82-83). This scene is a duplication of Hemingway's own entrance into the Red Cross hospital in Milan in July, 1918. Although there were several elderly nurses at the Red Cross hospital that summer, Miss Anna Scanlan (age 54) may well have been the nurse who admitted Hemingway ar d who became the prototype for Mrs. Walker. Frederic learns that Mrs. Walker is "too old" and of little use to the hospital director (p. 88). Miss Scanlan was also apparently of little use in Milan, for later that summer she was sent back to the States as "no longer fit for foreign service."[42]

There is the tacit assumption among Hemingway critics that Agnes Von Kurowsky, the Red Cross nurse who re- fused Hemingway's proposal of marriage in 1919, was the prototype for Catherine Barkley. The most sensitive specu- lation, of course, is whether Hemingway's sexual experi- ences in Milan matched those of his protagonist. In terms of the novel, the question is, of course, irrelevant. By the time Hemingway wrote *A Farewell to Arms*, he had had ample sexual experience to write of Frederic Henry's in a convincing manner, although when one looks at the specifi- cally sexual scenes in the novel they are few, short and understated.

Agnes Von Kurowsky has herself suggested other sources for Hemingway's characterization of Catherine:

"For a while I was sent to Florence to help with the care of a Red Cross worker who had typhoid in an Italian hospi- tal, and there was an American Red Cross nurse on duty in Florence, who was also on this case. Her name was Elsie Jessup, and I believe she was the pattern for some of Hem- ingway's characterization of Catherine Barkley, as she al- ways carried a cane when in uniform, and had been en- gaged to an English officer who was killed. She was also ill, while I was there, and when I returned to Milan, she went there with me. . . . Miss MacDonald was very fond of Hem- ingway—spoiled him, in fact—but he was always in trouble with Miss DeLong. I remember the big to-do when she found his wardrobe full of empty cognac bottles.

"(The rooms had wardrobes instead of closets.) Mary Hemingway asked me who was the character of "Fergy" taken from, and I couldn't think of any one person. Now I

[42] American National Red Cross, Archives File #954.308, Commis- sion to Italy Personnel Reports and Lists.

believe it could have been a combination of Elsie MacDonald and Loretta Cavanaugh. He always called Miss MacDonald "The Spanish Mackerel," and she was the only Scotch woman among us. Of course, she was old enough to be his mother. Then Loretta Cavanaugh was the kind and helpful type."[43]

The point of age difference is worth noting in more detail, for Frederic Henry is several years older than Hemingway was when he was in Italy. On July 21, 1918, Hemingway turned nineteen. At that time Agnes Von Kurowsky was twenty-six, Loretta Cavanaugh was thirty-four, Elsie MacDonald was forty. It would not seem likely that a nineteen-year-old youth could have seriously engaged the attention of a woman seven years his elder. Yet when Hemingway married Hadley Richardson, she was seven years older than he claimed to be even though he stretched his age by a year. Not only was he attracted to older women, but from the beginning he attempted to appear older than he was. By his early thirties he was already referring to himself as "Papa" Hemingway and using "daughter" as a familiar term for female acquaintances. If Frederic Henry seems more mature than the youthful Hemingway, it is because the author endowed him with the social and political acumen he had acquired in Europe after the war. If Hemingway was accustomed to advancing his own age, it was perhaps because he hoped that it would increase his credibility. Frederic Henry at nineteen would not have been credible, and there is evidence in the Hemingway manuscripts at the Kennedy Library to show that Hemingway tried him out at that age more than once. Hemingway created Frederic Henry in his mid-twenties, partly out of his own psychological needs but primarily out of the needs of his fiction.

Returning to the hospital in Milan, we can see that Hem-

---

[43] American National Red Cross Archives, Hemingway file #954.301: letter from Mrs. William Stanfield to Mr. Clyde E. Buckingham, May 6, 1962.

ingway found there not only prototypes for his fictional nurses but also found the physical circumstances for his fiction. In recreating those circumstances in the novel, Hemingway remembered the arrangement of the hospital with considerable accuracy.

On April 22, 1918, Miss Sara E. Shaw wrote to her superior, Miss Clara D. Noyes, Director of the Bureau of Nursing, advising her of the condition of the newly acquired hospital space in Milan:

"I have secured a pensione, which is now in the throes of being cleaned and remodelled and will soon be in condition for occupation.

"In one separate division we have fifteen private hospital rooms; an operating room, where we can efficiently care for our own American force or meet any special emergency. We have one floor for servants, also linen and supply room, and a wonderful big cellar where food can be stored. One floor can be used for nurses. We have a reception room, lecture hall and library, demonstration room and dining rooms. There are balconies on each floor."[44]

When the hospital officially opened, Miss Shaw wrote another descriptive letter to her superior, giving more specific details about the arrangement of the spaces:

"On the top floor—the hospital floor—are fifteen communicating rooms, the nurses can walk directly through like a ward, yet rooms are private. One half of the rooms each have a small balcony, the other half open with a large terrace. . . . All the rooms are calcimised a soft cherry tint. The old furniture has been varnished and made suitable for hospital use. . . . In the spacious central hall is room for a medicine closet and place for a Nurse to write charts. . . . Separate from hospital and on floor below are eleven rooms for nurses—with bath. . . . I am fearful Miss Scanlan will not hold out—she is difficult to place—all the work seems too

44 ANRC Archives, File #954.11/08.

hard for her . . . Miss Sparrow and Kurowsky have arrived safely."[45]

Comparing the novel with these two descriptions, one notes that Hemingway used the physical layout of the Red Cross hospital when it suited his purpose. In the novel the hospital is multi-storied, with the nurses' quarters below the patients' rooms: "We rode upstairs in the elevator. Catherine got off at the lower level where the nurses lived and I went on up and went down the hall on crutches to my room" (p. 113). This is the same long hallway that Frederic was carried down when he was admitted to the hospital and the same one described by Sara Shaw. Frederic's room smells of "new furniture" or perhaps repainted furniture, and it contains "a bed and a big wardrobe and a mirror" (p. 83). Frederic's room has a balcony like the one described by Miss Shaw, except we do not notice that he shares it with the rooms next to him. Hemingway has changed the communal balcony into a private one for the sake of the love affair. For the same reason he has omitted the interconnecting nature of the rooms. Such an arrangement would have made the liaison between Frederic and Catherine more liable to discovery, and was not necessary to the fiction.

Hemingway has also altered the number of nurses and patients who were present in the hospital. In the novel there are only three other patients with Frederic in the hospital, and they almost never intrude into the private affairs of the lovers. In reality there were at least six other patients with Hemingway in the Red Cross hospital. Accuracy here would again have complicated the love affair and was therefore ignored. Similarly, Hemingway restricted the number of fictional nurses present in the hospital. In the novel Catherine tells Frederic: "They've too many nurses here now. There must be some more patients or they'll send us away.

45 ANRC Archives, File #954.11/08, letter from Sara Shaw to Clara Noyes, July 11, 1918.

8. Red Cross hospital, Milan, 1918. Left to right: Loretta Cavanaugh, Elsie MacDonald, Col. Buckey, Bill Horne, Miss Turini, Catherine DeLong, unknown, Hemingway, Ed Alan, Agnes, Miss Fletcher. *Courtesy of Library of Congress.*

They have four nurses now" (p. 103). In reality this is exactly what happened to Agnes during part of Hemingway's time in the hospital. She was transferred first to Florence to help with an influenza outbreak and later to Treviso. Thus it was Hemingway who saw Agnes off at the train station in Milan as she returned to the medical front. The reason that Agnes could be spared at the Milan hospital was that there were so many nurses and so few patients. The four nurses in the novel do not seem like too many; however, the real number was something between twelve and eighteen. Ten nurses reported to Milan on May 10, 1918. These included Anna Scanlan, May Warner, Meta Markley, Loretta Cavanaugh, Della C. DeGraw, Ruth Fisher, Ruth Brooks, Florence Hill, Annie Larkin, and Elsie MacDonald. About July 11, 1918, Agnes Von Kurowsky and Caroline Sparrow arrived at the hospital. Miss Catherine DeLong had some or all of these nurses under her charge that summer in Milan. Four other nurses—Fletcher, Rittenhouse, Conway, and Jessup—were remembered by Agnes as being in the hospital that summer as well. Hemingway reduced this unwieldy number in order to insure the privacy of his lovers and to keep the novel relatively uncluttered.

Another interesting and meaningful change that Hemingway makes can be seen in the language capabilities of the characters in the novel compared with their prototypes. Frederic Henry, as already noted, speaks Italian fluently and with only a trace of an accent. Catherine Barkley neither speaks nor understands the language. When Dr. Valentini jokes in her presence, there is no recognition (p. 99). Earlier in the novel she told Frederic that she was studying the language (p. 22), but she never shows any signs of comprehension. In reality the language abilities of Hemingway and Agnes Von Kurowsky were almost the opposite of the fictional lovers. Hemingway spoke no Italian when he arrived in Italy and probably very little more when he returned to Milan wounded six weeks later. During his stay in Milan he picked up enough of the language to make his way on the streets and in the cafes, for he apparently had a quick ear for language and the gift to make himself understood with a limited vocabulary. He was, however, by no means as fluent as Frederic Henry.

Agnes Von Kurowsky, on the other hand, was an accomplished linguist, with a far more cosmopolitan background than Hemingway. She grew up in Washington, D.C. She spoke French and German and was quickly picking up Italian during the summer of 1918. Like all Milan-based nurses, Agnes was taking two Italian lessons a day, although she may have had some fluency before she arrived. The effect of allowing Catherine little or no language ability is to put Frederic in the dominant position in their relationship. Frederic's fluency is, of course, necessary if the plot structure is going to work. In order to have Frederic present at Caporetto, he had to be with the Italian army. To be with the Italian army, he had to speak the language fluently. It is his language mastery that makes the role of expert possible, for without the language one is always an amateur in another country.

Although there are several other incidents in the novel that find their source in biographic experience, they follow the pattern established above. That is, Hemingway will use settings and people from his own experience whenever he can, but he never allows his own experience to interfere with his fiction, and he never brings real people into his fiction whole. In this same manner he was able to pick up second-hand stories, newspaper accounts, as well as histories and historical fiction, and use them all to his own purpose.

The Search for Catherine

Miss Barkley was quite tall. She wore what seemed to me to be
a nurse's uniform, was blonde and had a tawny skin and gray
eyes. I thought she was very beautiful. (*AFTA*, p. 18)

There has always been a tacit assumption among Hemingway scholars that for Catherine Barkley there had been a
real life prototype. Insiders knew her name years before the
novel appeared in print. An Irish artillery officer who had
known Hemingway during the war in Italy remembered
her quite clearly in a letter to Carlos Baker, Hemingway's
biographer: "Hem introduced me to his South African
nurse [sic], the girl who figures as the heroine in *A Farewell to Arms* and in an early short story in *in our time*; Ag
of 'A Very Short Story.' She was a gay, charming person of
whom Hem said that it takes a trained nurse to make love
to a man with one leg in a splint."[1]

The nurse's name was Agnes Von Kurowsky. She was not
South African, although her name might lead an Irishman
to make that assumption. But it was probably something
more than her name. Her bearing, her attitude, her sense
of humor would not seem American nor yet quite British to
an Irishman. The point is worth noting, for Hemingway's
fictional Catherine is British.

The name of Agnes Von Kurowsky did not become public
domain until Leicester Hemingway's opportune and somewhat sentimental biography of Ernest appeared in 1961.

[1] Edward Eric Dorman-O'Gowan to Carlos Baker, 1961.

(The funeral meats were barely cold.) Carefully avoiding libelous statements, Leicester wrote that Hemingway was in love with Agnes in Milan and remembered her when he created Catherine Barkley.[2] That seems innocent enough. The *aficionados* would supply the "real" story, for they knew Hemingway wrote about life as he had lived it.

In 1971 Agnes spent a long day's journey into the past, taping memories that were never sentimental. As she approached eighty, she could not afford to indulge herself. Everyone from those days in Milan was dead except her, and she had no illusions about her mortality.

Q: Do you remember your reaction when you first read
    A Farewell to Arms?
A: I wasn't so irritated the first time I read it as I was
    the second time. It was about fifteen years ago
    [1955] that I thought I'd better look at it again.
    That time it irritated me because of the remark I
    heard in the Hemingway museum in Key West. I
    found that a little bit hard to take.

In 1955 Agnes had been working in the public library at Key West, Florida. Hemingway had, of course, left Key West in the forties, and the Hemingway house had become a privately owned museum. It was not long before the museum tour began making references to Agnes as the prototype for Catherine Barkley. In 1972, the museum had her 1918 picture on the wall and still referred to her this way.

A: That's what makes me so mad about Key West.
    Why should anyone in Key West who knew me say
    that's the nurse he wrote about? Wouldn't that
    make you angry? The people in the library knew
    me and knew darn well that wasn't true. This girl at

2 Leicester Hemingway, *My Brother, Ernest Hemingway* (New York: World Publishing Co., 1961), p. 45.

the museum had been told it and she was repeating it to everyone.

In the National Archives of the American Red Cross, her file folder begins:

AMERICAN RED CROSS SERVICE ENROLLMENT APPLICATION

Date: *May 11, 1918*
Name: *Agnes Hannah Von Kurowsky*
Born: *January 5, 1892*
Place: *Germantown, Pennsylvania*
Father: *Paul Moritz Julius Von Kurowsky*
Born: *Königsburg, Germany*
Mother: *Agnes Theodosia Holabird*
Born: *New York*
Maternal Grandfather: *Samuel Aeckley Holabird*

A: My father was of Polish descent and his father gambled and lost every penny that they owned and all the family estates. The Germans had rich regiments and poor regiments at that time. My father wouldn't go from a rich regiment to a poor one, so he came to America instead, emigrated to America. He was teaching in the Berlitz school when he met my mother.
Q: In Philadelphia?
A: No, in Washington. She was going to Germany for a trip and he was teaching German. They fell in love and when she left, he followed her over and they were married in Germany. Oh, it was very romantic at the time. She was quite a belle in her time.
A: My mother was spoiled but my father was a very nice, gentle soul. He could look fierce but he wasn't. I think the war would have just killed him.

It would have broken his heart. He died of typhoid
before the war came along.

Q: After they were married, did he continue teaching?

A: He went into civil service. His commanding officer,
Major Bingham, was ordered to Alaska, to Saint
Michaels, and asked father to go with him. So we
all went. It was in the 1890s and I was about five or
six. It must have been 1898. There was an army
post up there; I went out in dog sleds and took
rides. The Laplanders came over and made a visit.

Q: When you came back from Alaska—

A: We went to Vancouver. . . . My sister died there
when I was eleven. I was so young there wasn't
much effect. She was a year and half older and
smaller than I. She died of scarlet fever. I went to
a convent school at that time, and I picked up
diphtheria that same year. My mother and father
were scared to death that I was going to die. . . . It
seems that every year they had diphtheria at the
convent. So I wasn't allowed to go any more. After
that I had a private teacher for a while with the
grand-daughter of the commanding officer of the
post.

Q: You have such clear pictures in your mind—

A: They are very clear. When I was a girl I always
liked this particular color of blue. When my sister
was alive, she always had pink and I had blue. In
Alaska they had Christmas trees for all the children
around. And they had dolls for us. Mine had a red
dress on and hers had blue. I kept saying, "That's
mine! Give it to me!"

From the closet shelves and the backs of desk drawers
she finds pictures of the past. They come out as jumbled as
memories; there is no chronological order here. Many of the
faces are forgotten. Sometimes she is not sure where the
picture was taken. But many of the images she has not for-

gotten in eighty years. Most of them are snapshots, but there are a few pictures of Agnes as a young girl that are almost professional. When several of them are lined up, you begin to realize that each is carefully posed.

Q: That's a fantastic picture.
A: My mother took it. She was always taking pictures of us. There are pictures of us at all ages. My mother was quite a camera buff. She did her own developing and her own plates. She took hundreds of pictures of me, but I can't find one of her.

Very early Agnes was taught how to pose in a picture: the wistful look so popular at the turn of the century. Bold eyes, head slightly turned, hands holding a prop. Her mother knew about lighting and how to use it. She taught Agnes well. In that whole afternoon of pictures, I rarely saw her eyes staring at the camera—no amateur pictures of the sort that fill most scrapbooks.

RED CROSS APPLICATION
May 11, 1918

Education: *Two Years Fairmont Seminary, Washington, D.C.*
Six months, Public Library, Washington, D.C.
Occupation before entering training school: *Librarian*

A: My grandfather was a Brigadier General who was about to retire. So we went back to Washington and had a house a few blocks from where my grandfather lived. He was a great reader; he had built a great library on to his house, and he had something like seven thousand volumes in it. He was the one that made me start French. The daughter of a classmate of his was hard up and she

spoke French fluently. She hated me like poison,
but she taught me French verbs which was a great
help. Later on I found I was well grounded in
French in spite of her. Then I went to Fairmont
Seminary. I went into third year French even
though I couldn't keep up with the others. I went
out and cried. The teacher—Miss Steel—yanked
me right back in there. That was a help, too.

Q: You spent some time in the Washington Public
Library?

A: I was there about four years in the cataloguing
department. After my father died, my mother and
I moved into an apartment. . . . You know, I have
a little trust fund from my grandfather, and the
last time I went to the bank in Washington, I asked
them if they knew about my cousins because if I
die, I have no issue. I have no children of my own.

In 1914 Agnes left the Washington Public Library. She
was twenty-two years old, very pretty, and somewhat
caught up in the social gospel of the time. The war had begun in Europe, and a way of life was about to disappear.

A: I got tired of the library. I said this isn't active
enough; I want something busier. I wrote to
Bellevue and to Massachusetts General, the two big
ones that I knew of. I had no idea that Bellevue was
the city hospital. I didn't know until I got there. I
looked over and saw all these men running around
in the same kind of bathrobes on the balcony across
the street. Everything I learned at Bellevue was
valuable, and I never met anything in the war that
wasn't there at Bellevue. There was a psychopathic
ward and an alcoholic ward, and I had all those
things to do which you don't get in an ordinary
hospital.

On July 17, 1917, Agnes graduated from the Bellevue Nurses Training School. From that time forward she always thought of herself as a *Bellevue* nurse. It was something very special in 1917. In Italy she was assigned to a Bellevue contingent in Milan. Her close friends had gone through training with her. She was not just a nurse; she was a Bellevue nurse, and that meant a great deal to her. Fifty years later she still took great pride in Bellevue, although the nursing school had since gone out of existence.

A: Now they've turned it over to Hunter College. They don't have any more Bellevue Nursing. Last year they wanted to vote whether or not the Hunter College girls could wear the Bellevue cap. I don't know how it came out. I'm not sure they should use the Bellevue cap because it's so well known.

Agnes voted against the proposal.

Frederic: *"Aren't you a nurse?"*
Catherine: *"Oh, no. I'm something called a V.A.D. We work very hard but no one trusts us."*
Frederic: *"What's the difference?"*
Catherine: *"A nurse is like a doctor. It takes a long time to be. A V.A.D. is a short cut."*
                                            AFTA, p. 25

Q: V.A.D.s—do you remember what a VAD was?
A: An aide—a nurse's aide.
Q: In the novel, Catherine is a British VAD.
A: I don't know where he met a British VAD.
Q: Were there any British nurses with you in Milan?
A: Only the ones we had attached to our place. Peggy Conway, for instance.
Q: Was she a Red Cross nurse?

A: She was a nurse. Not American Red Cross. But a
    nurse attached to our unit. We took nurses in with
    the proper credentials. But we didn't have any
    VADs.
Q: What was Peggy Conway like?
A: I showed you her picture. She was the homely one.

When she finished her training at Bellevue, Agnes took
a job at Long Island College Hospital, where she was responsible for the incoming probationers. There she added
to her training in psychopaths.

A: I ran into a crazy superintendent. I don't mean
    crazy, but she was odd. She was delighted with me
    and we got very buddy-buddy. Once when she got
    ready to go on vacation, I sewed her cap up for her.
    She had ripped it apart. I didn't know what was the
    matter, and then I happened to be at Bellevue and
    ran into Miss Stringer. She asked me how I was
    getting along. And I said, "Well, all right, I guess."
    "What's the matter?" "I don't know." I told her the
    woman seemed strange to me when she came back
    from vacation. She was getting a little odd, you
    know. She had torn her hat all to pieces. I didn't
    think that was very normal. Miss Stringer told me,
    "Get right out of there. I don't want you to stay
    there another minute." That's when she suggested
    the Red Cross.

Miss Clara D. Noyes
Director of Red Cross Nursing Service
Washington, D. C.   Jan. 2, 1918

My dear Miss Noyes,
    I am taking the liberty of writing to you personally to
enquire if I would be accepted as an applicant for mem-
bership in the Red Cross Nursing Service. My father was

German born, and my mother is an American, but my father has been dead for eight years and I have never been in Germany and have no German relatives that I know of.

I have heard that nurses of German parentage have been refused and I am very anxious to volunteer for active service in this country. You may remember me as a Bellevue graduate of the 1917 class.

If I am eligible, will you be kind enough to have the application blanks forwarded to me as soon as possible?

Very sincerely,

Agnes H. Von Kurowsky

RED CROSS NURSING SERVICE
APPLICATION

January 16, 1918

Did your training include the care of men? *Yes*
Contagious diseases: *Yes*
Obstetrics: *Yes*
Are you a registered nurse? *Yes, State of New York*
Employment Record:

> *July 25, 1917 to October 6, 1917, Assistant Night Supervisor at Bellevue Hospital, N.Y.C. October 7, 1917 to January 15, 1918, Instructor at Long Island College Hospital, N.Y.*

What languages other than English do you speak? *German and French*

AMERICAN RED CROSS NURSING SERVICE
PHYSICAL EXAMINATION

Name: *Agnes Von Kurowsky* Date: *January 13, 1918*
Age: *26*
Height: 5'8"
Weight: 133
General Physic: *Well developed, well nourished*
Chest measurement: *35"*

BELLEVUE HOSPITAL

Recommendation for: *Agnes Hannah Von Kurowsky*
Date: *Jan. 22, 1918*
Did training include obstetrics: *Yes*
The care of children? *Yes*
What position or responsibility did applicant hold
during her training? *Pupil's Head Nurse*
What can you say of her personality? *Pleasing*
Is she neat? *Yes*
Refined? *Yes*
Initiative? *Average*
Executive Ability? *Possesses a fair amount*

Q: About the time you went up to Bellevue, World
   War One started. Did that have anything to do
   with your going into nursing?
A: No, I don't think so, I didn't go to war until 1918.
   The group that I went with, a great many of them
   were Bellevue nurses. I had two classmates with
   me, Ruth Brooks and Loretta Cavanaugh.
Q: Catherine DeLong was at Bellevue also?
A: She was in charge of the nurses' home. I grew up
   under her, so to speak. She kept the nurses in good
   order. Miss MacDonald was in charge of the
   nurses' infirmary at Bellevue.
Q: Then it was a regular Bellevue contingent?
A: Oh yes, we knew so many of each other when we
   went over.

Frederic: *"Have you done nursing long?"*
Catherine: *"Since the end of 'fifteen."*

AFTA, p. 20

RED CROSS TELEGRAM
MARCH 14, 1918
TO: MISS AGNES VON KUROWSKY
BE READY TO SAIL AS SOON AS POSSIBLE

WITH MISS DELONG IF INSTRUCTION CAN
BE SENT THEN STOP WIRE REPLY STOP
CLARA B. NOYES

On April 5, 1918, Agnes wired back that she was ready
to sail, but when the DeLong unit left New York on April
20, Agnes was not on board. Her passport, which had been
issued in good order on April 12, had become snarled in red
tape at the Italian Consulate. Because of Agnes' German
name, the Italian Consul held up her visa until May 22.
Agnes left her job at Long Island College, and she was living on money she had saved for traveling expenses and
emergencies. The Red Cross came to her assistance:

April 6, 1918

You are allowed $3 a day hotel bill while in New York
and salary at $2 a day from date of leaving home to
date of sailing. The salary paid is $60 a month and you
are able to make whatever allotment you desire of this
salary before leaving this country. You should carry
with you a reserve fund of at least $100, half of which
should be in cash money for greater convenience.

AMERICAN RED CROSS
NEW YORK CITY

June 15, 1918

Dear Mr. Pucker,
    We have investigated Miss Von Kurowsky's case and
find that owing to the difficulty in obtaining consular
visas, she was not able to take of same until May 29.
She then reported to this office saying she was ready to
sail. Mr. Holland advised her to remain over until
the steamer *La Lorraine* sailed June 15, because there
were no ladies traveling on any of the English steamers.

Yours very truly
A. E. Chiapeari

Out·of old manila folders pictures emerge from the *La Lorraine*. Agnes is posed against the rope railing, or leaning against the rigging up forward on the ship. Her head is frequently cocked to one side. The camera never did surprise her; there are no truly candid pictures of her here. Many of the pictures are filled with uniformed soldiers, crowding about her, joking, smiling. Wherever she moved she collected a following. In group pictures of the Red Cross nurses her face stands out. She would have been remarkable anywhere, but in the war she was almost too pretty, too much the myth of the war nurse, the dream of beauty that all men take to war with them. Caroline Sparrow sailed with Agnes on the *La Lorraine*, but she is noticeably missing from most of the pictures. She was a plain girl who attracted no attention.

Q: During the twenties, moving back and forth between New York City and Europe and Haiti, you were young and very attractive—

A: And unattached.

Q: And unattached. You must have had more than one marriage proposal during that time. Were you not marrying—were you staying unattached because you wanted to?

A: I didn't meet anyone I cared enough about. When I went overseas the first time, I was supposed to be engaged to a doctor, but I forgot him as soon as the boat sailed.—I'm not used to this. I'm not made romantically. And when I came back another girl had got him. She came to me and said, "Don't think you're going to get him back." I said that I hadn't the faintest idea. I hadn't the slightest desire to see him again.

Q: If you were going to characterize yourself in the Twenties, how would you see yourself? What were you like?

A: I was always looking for something. I was always

looking for adventure. I was never ambitious, not the slightest.

Q: You were tall—tall for a girl at that time.

A: I never noticed it. I never had any trouble there. It seems to me that short men always go for tall girls. I don't know that I ever liked them, but they did that. There was one in Rumania—a nice boy, a nice person, very nice to me. But I just couldn't stand them. They were—I don't know—not interesting.

AMERICAN RED CROSS
La Croce Rossa Americana
Via Manzoni, 10
MILANO   July 11, 1918

My Dear Miss Noyes,
. . . Miss Sparrow and Hornowsky [sic] have arrived safely.

Sara E. Shaw

On July 8, 1918, Hemingway was blown up by a trench mortar shell on the bank of the Piave River at Fossalta. On July 17, he was moved to the Red Cross hospital at Milan.

THE AMERICAN RED CROSS
Plainfield and North Plainfield Chapter
Plainfield, New Jersey
Nov. 11, 1952

Dear Mr. Durfee:
   I was one of the nurses who cared for Hemingway in our American Red Cross Hospital, 3 Via Bochetto, Milan, Italy in 1918.
   The story which Hemingway tells in his book "A Farewell to Arms," part II, Chapters XIII, XIV and XV gives a fairly accurate picture of the hospital upon his arrival, and some word pictures of a few nurses. I

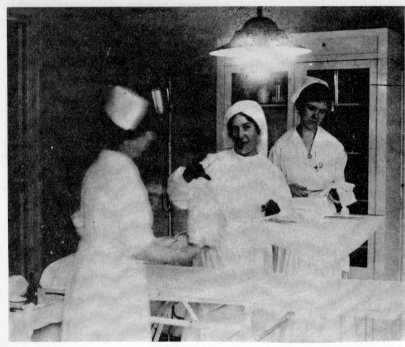

9. Loretta Cavanaugh, Elsie MacDonald, and Agnes Von Kurowsky in the operating room of the Red Cross hospital, Milan, 1918. *Courtesy of Library of Congress.*

10. (*above*) Agnes and Elsie MacDonald going to Milan race track, 1918. *Courtesy of Mrs. Agnes Stanfield.*

11. (*right*) Passport photo of Agnes taken in 1918 before sailing for Europe. *Courtesy of Mrs. Agnes Stanfield.*

assume that you know that he himself was the
wounded man. He was serving with the Italian
Ambulance Corps. [Sic. He wasn't but he led others to
believe he was.]

Shortly after the book received public recognition, I
had a talk with Agnes Von Kurowsky, a member of our
staff in Milan. We could recognize many of the
incidents and could identify most of the personnel. For
example "Miss Van Campen" was Miss Catherine
DeLong, a small, dignified, capable Johns Hopkins
graduate (who was Supt. of Nurses at Bellevue after
the return from Italy). We were quite sure that "Miss
Gage" was none other than myself, as we recalled the
thermometer incident, the making of the bed which he
mentions, and my talking to him like a big sister when
he was "naughty." Miss Barkley appears to be fictitious.

Hemingway was young (about 20), impulsive, very
rude, "smarty," and uncooperative. He gave the
impression of having been badly spoiled. He always
seemed to have plenty of money which he spent freely
for Italian wine and tips to the porter who brought it.

Sincerely yours,
Charlotte M. Heilman

It must have been when Agnes returned from Haiti in
1930 that the proper Miss Heilman asked her about the
novel. There is a strong temptation to believe art even when
you know the reality. Miss Heilman must have had some
gnawing doubts that she had missed an incredible scandal
taking place in her very presence. But Miss Heilman is Red
Cross to the core. "Miss Barkley appears to be fictitious."
She does not mention the flirtatious Ruth Brooks or Elsie
Jessup, nor does she admit the possibility that Agnes may
have contributed anything to the character of Catherine. It
is this sort of denial which confirms the suspicions of wandering scholars, for obviously Agnes' beauty and her physical presence contribute greatly. To claim Catherine to be

fictitious in order to keep the service unsullied is really an
injustice to Agnes. To deny that a relationship existed between Agnes and Hemingway is absurd, and once that absurdity is exposed, there is the temptation to believe that art
is reality.

Q: The uniform Hemingway had made?
A: Oh, that was a fancy one.
Q: But it wasn't an official Red Cross uniform?
A: No, no. But they all did that. It was so easy to get
    tailors there to do things.
Q: Why?
A: They were better looking uniforms. I told you how
    dumpy we looked when we got there. We got our
    shirts shortened and tightened and our coats fitted
    in and all. We had both summer and winter
    uniforms when we went over. The summer uniform
    was the grey thing which was very ugly. They let
    us wear the white one later on. It was human. We
    hardly ever wore the winter uniforms except when
    traveling.
Q: The cape, did you wear it a lot?
A: Yes, I wore it over my uniform.

*I saw Catherine and knocked on the window. She
looked, saw me and smiled, and I went out to meet her.
She was wearing a dark blue cape and a soft felt hat.*
                                            AFTA, p. 147

Catherine Barkley has long blonde hair; Agnes had
brown hair. In the fall of 1971 it was grey, but her eyes were
still blue with that peculiar honesty that does not turn
away from a question.

Q: Elsie Jessup's hair was blonde. Was it long?
A: I don't remember. She had it done up in a knob.
Q: But everyone wore her hair long then?

A: Oh, yes. I never had too long hair, but it came down to my shoulders.

Q: What was Elsie Jessup like?

A: She was very different from the other nurses. She had her own style.

Q: You once said that she brought out the wild streak in you?

A: She was very different. She had her own style— with this cane business and all. She was always carrying a stick. And she smoked a lot which none of the rest of us did in those days.

Q: Did Hemingway pay any attention to any of the other nurses?

A: I don't think so.—Well, he knew them all and joked with them all. He was very—he didn't work that way. I don't think he flirted with everybody. I think he was sort of one at a time.

The problem, of course, is: does Agnes remember what happened, or has she remembered it so many times that now she is only remembering memories? What was it really like that summer in Milan? There are pictures, but pictures always lie. Remember those frightening pictures of the Fitzgeralds on the beach at Cannes? Everyone smiles in pictures, and that is not truth. There are the historical documents, but that is only one kind of truth. An old woman's memories are another kind.

On August 10, 1918, Hemingway underwent the second operation on his badly wounded leg. There was still some question in his mind about losing the leg. It was that same evening that Agnes went out to supper with Captain Enrico Serena, a handsome Italian who frequently visited Hemingway's hospital room.

A: Captain Serena was a fascinating person. He spoke English. I didn't have to worry about my Italian. He was very witty and good company. He

kept saying he'd take me out to dinner, and I said
I wasn't supposed to go—out alone, you know.

Red Cross nurses almost always traveled in pairs or
threes. When Agnes went to the racetrack with Henry Villard, another patient at the hospital, she was accompanied
by Elsie MacDonald. When Agnes vacationed at Lake
Como, Ruth Brooks and Loretta Cavanaugh went with her.

A: Serena kept at me and kept at me. Hemingway said,
    "Oh, go out to dinner with the Captain, Ag." (He
    was the only person in the world that ever called
    me Ag. I never allowed anyone else to do that, but
    you couldn't stop him.) So I went down to Miss
    DeLong and said, "Can I go out to supper tonight?"
    She said, "Oh, yes, sure." She never asked where,
    when, who. If it had been Ruth Brooks she would
    have put her through the third degree. So I dressed
    —we were allowed to take one civilian dress
    along—and I had a dark blue chiffon dress with
    cut-steel beading around here and here [collar and
    neck]. So I was in mufti. We went to a very famous
    restaurant—I found out afterward—Lorenzo and
    Lucia. He had ordered a very nice dinner. He tried
    to get me to drink wine but I don't drink much
    wine. And there was a piano and couch in the
    private room. That intrigued me. I thought this is
    some sort of place for seduction. I kept saying that
    I had to go home because I was on duty at twelve
    o'clock. So I got out of there. That was the day that
    Hemingway was operated on in the afternoon. He
    was the one that kept telling me to go and then he
    was mad when I was out during the evening that
    he was post-operative. "You weren't here!"
    It was the only time in my life that I was taken to
    dinner in a private room with a couch. Serena

didn't have too much money and I expect he spent a ton on that. Serves him right, thinking Americans are easy. They're easier now than they ever were in those days.

She saw herself in one of the mirrors and put her hands to her hair. I saw her in three other mirrors. She did not look happy. She let her cape fall on the bed.
"What's the matter, darling?"
"I never felt like a whore before," she said.
. . .   .
We were very hungry and the meal was good and we drank a bottle of Capri and a bottle of St. Estephe. I drank most of it but Catherine drank some and it made her feel splendid. For dinner we had a woodcock with soufflé potatoes and purée de marron, a salad, and zabaione for dessert.

AFTA, pp. 152–153

During the August heat of 1918 in Milan, Hemingway wrote Agnes letters while she was working the night shift, which was most of the time. The letters were delivered to Agnes during the day, even though he would see her that night. Agnes did not keep any of those letters, nor, apparently, did she answer them.

Henry Villard, an American Red Cross driver from Section One, was admitted to the Milan hospital on August 1, 1918. He was put in the room adjoining Hemingway's. There was a doorway between the two rooms, as all the rooms on their floor interconnected. As soon as Villard's jaundice and malaria permitted, he spent many hours beside Hemingway's bed, talking and listening to the young man whose leg wounds made all others in the hospital seem insignificant. Villard's diary notes that throughout the month of August Hemingway was too bedridden to enjoy the balcony overlooking the Via Manzoni. It was not until September 11 that Hemingway was able to get about on crutches. Villard wrote Carlos Baker in 1962:

"As I realized when I read *A Farewell to Arms*, Ernie must have dreamed a good part of the story during his tedious stay at the hospital. Of course, I recognized Agnes in Catherine Barkley. I remember her as a tall girl, doubly attractive so far from home, cheerful, quick, sympathetic, with an almost mischievous sense of humor—an ideal personality for a nurse. It used to be a standing joke among the patients to get well quickly so we could take 'Aggie' out, and I was properly thrilled when I achieved this goal by inviting her for a cab drive and dinner at the hotel Manin. Miss MacDonald also was a good friend of the patients and devoted to their welfare. It was not easy to arrange a date alone with 'Aggie,' for she and 'Mac' used to stick together, but they made the hospital as cheerful a spot as any American expatriate could wish. Ernie's incipient romance with Agnes had not developed to an extent that called for comment before I left."[3]

If pictures are true, Villard had forgotten that Elsie MacDonald accompanied him and Agnes on the day of that cab drive, for there is a set of pictures of them in the cab in the Library of Congress collection of Red Cross photography.

Hemingway was in love with Agnes, but so were most of the patients. When she showed me her address book from the Twenties, it was filled with names and addresses long unused. The ink had faded brown on the small lined pages and the brown leather binding was frayed from years. The names were predominately male from Europe as well as the States. One of the names was that of Domenico Caracciolo, an Italian nobleman with whom Agnes began a romance after Hemingway had returned to Oak Park. Hemingway's name did not appear in the address book.

By September when Hemingway was up on crutches, the Red Cross hospital was almost completely filled. With its

[3] Henry S. Villard to Carlos Baker, Feb. 1, 1962.

interconnecting rooms and common balcony, it afforded a minimum of privacy to the patients. During the last week of September Hemingway took convalescent leave to Stresa on Lake Maggiore with another ambulance driver. Agnes remained in Milan.

It was the jaundice. I was sick for two weeks with it. For that reason we did not spend a convalescent leave together. We had planned to go to Pallanza on Lago Maggiore. . . . It would have been better than Stresa. . . . Stresa is so easy to get to from Milan that there are always people you know.

AFTA, p. 142

Hemingway returned from Stresa at the end of September. By mid-October Agnes had volunteered for temporary duty in Florence.

A: I remember the first night in Florence. They put me
    in a room in the palace there. It must have been the
    ballroom. It was really gorgeous with great big
    gold angels flying all around and there was this one
    bed stuck in there. And me looking at all this space.

From Florence, Agnes wrote fond letters to Hemingway that she signed with an affection that sounds more intimate today than it probably was then:

October   16: "all my love and double, as ever *your*
                   Agnes"
October   17: "I love you still—ever—Agnes"
October   22: "Your faithful Mrs. Kid"
October   24: "Yours only—Aggie"
November   2: "I miss you dear, and love you so
                   much."
November   3: "Good night sweetheart, your Mrs.
                   Kid"

A: I think Hemingway and I were very innocent at
that time—very innocent—both of us. In those days
we were all pretty innocent. As a nurse I didn't
know that much. I didn't know half the stuff they
know now days.

Agnes returned to Milan November 11, 1918. She had
been gone a month, during which time the Italian Army
had routed the Austro-Germans at the battle of Vittorio
Veneto. The armistice in Italy took effect on November 4;
on November 11, the armistice was signed on the western
front. The war was over.

Q: Do you remember being disillusioned about the
war?
A: I've never been that way in my life. I'm not that
type. I don't have depressions.
Q: In the novel, Frederic and Catherine are very war
weary.
A: I don't think I was up against it enough. I had nice
patients and nice places. Even though I put up with
a good deal of handicaps—with the way of doing
things. You had to make do, but it wasn't hard.

Although the army could celebrate, the war was not over
for the Red Cross nurses. On November 20, Agnes was re-
assigned to an Army hospital at Treviso, outside Padova
(Padua). She does not remember volunteering for the duty.

A: Treviso was outside of Padova. I was there quite
a while. Hemingway came to see me there. I should
have told you that before. And the men all laughed
their heads off at him.
Q: Why?
A: They thought he was the biggest joke. He came in
with his cane and all his medals and those Amer-

ican doughboys, they just roared. I had a 40 bed
ward and before we came there the corpsman only
had time to give shots of strychnine and take their
temperatures. He never made the beds; he couldn't.
He didn't have time. When I got there I started
making beds and changing sheets. One man was
sleeping on three blankets and no sheets.

Agnes to Hemingway, December 16, 1918

"Your news was somewhat startling—about going
home, I mean. And I do hope I'll get to Milan for Xmas
or it will be a miserable day, . . . I tried to find out
when it will be but as yet nothing can be decided. They
are expecting to send all the sick ones to Genoa in a
hospital train and now I've only 10 patients—5 bed
patients and 5 up—So you can see I'm not overworked.
Anyhow, one day I hear we won't be needed after the
end of the week and then I hear they'll never get all
the patients out before Xmas. Besides I think the
officers want us to stay to make things a little more
cheerful—homelike for them."

Agnes to Hemingway, December 20, 1918

"If this hits you about Xmas time, just make believe
you're getting a gift from me (as you will someday).
And let me tell you I love you and wish we could be
together for our first Christmas. May you be cheerful
and contented anyhow.
So long sweetheart. I'm praying I'll see you before
you go."

Hemingway visited Treviso on December 9. Agnes wrote
him a letter on December 10, indicating that his visit was
overnight at most. On December 11, Captain Jim Gamble
wrote Hemingway from Taormina describing the delights

of his rented "little house and garden belonging to an English artist. . . . Now the only thing lacking is company and I only hope that you will take care of that."

Q: Jim Gamble, was he older?
A: Yes. A captain, a Red Cross captain. That was the man that wanted Hemingway to go traveling with him after the war. I sent him home. He hated me for that. I told him he'd never be anything but a bum if he started traveling around with somebody else paying all the expenses. He was so furious when I wrote him that I was too old for him and that he ought to look around. . . . He would have accepted that invitation. I don't think that would have worked out. It wasn't the place for a young fellow. He really would have gotten to be a bum. He had all the ear marks. Leaving Europe wasn't easy to do because Gamble liked him very much and had money. He wouldn't have had to worry about a thing. I think I felt—more or less an obligation to look after him a bit. I don't think I was ever crazy mad about him. He was a very attractive person. He had wit and you could enjoy his company. But I don't think I—I had the feeling that if I shoved him out then he would start off on that European tour.

Between Christmas and New Year's, 1918, Hemingway took the train south to visit Gamble at Taormina. Although he reached Gamble's rented house, he never admitted having done so. When he returned to Milan about the first of January, he told his British artillery officer friend a wild tale about his trip:

He returned to say that he'd seen nothing of Sicily except a bedroom window because his hostess in the first small hotel he stopped in had hidden his clothes and kept him to herself for a week. The food she brought him was excellent and she was affectionate; Hem had no complaints except that he saw very little of the country. I don't know what Hem told Ag![4]

He told her nothing.

> *"You're dirty,"* he [Rinaldi] *said. "You ought to wash. Where did you go and what did you do? Tell me everything at once."*
> *"I went everywhere. Milan, Florence, Rome, Naples, Villa San Giovanni, Messina, Taormina—"*
>
> AFTA, p. 11

Hemingway was discharged from the Red Cross on January 4, 1919. On January 5, 1919 Agnes returned to Milan, where she went to the reception for President Wilson and his wife at the Palazzo Reale. On that same day Agnes wrote Hemingway a letter addressed to Oak Park. They apparently did not see each other in Milan; Hemingway had already left the town to board the *Giuseppe Verdi* at Genoa. He arrived in New York City on January 21, 1919. It seems curious that they should come that close to a final parting and still miss seeing each other. It may have been chance, or it may have been Agnes' desire not to prolong a relationship that had already peaked out for her.

The last time Hemingway saw Agnes was December 9, 1918 in Treviso. For the rest of his life their paths were to cross but they would never meet. When Agnes returned from Italy in July, 1919, Hemingway and friends were fishing in northern Michigan. When Agnes returned to Red Cross work in Paris in 1920, Hemingway was in Toronto. When Agnes returned from Europe the second time on November 9, 1921, Hemingway and his wife, Hadley, were

[4] Dorman-Smith to Baker, 1961.

preparing to sail for Europe. Agnes must have docked in New York almost at the same time the Hemingways were boarding the *Leopoldina*. In 1922, when Hemingway was covering the Greco-Turkish war, Agnes was in New York City applying for Red Cross work in Greece. The job did not come through. When Hemingway returned to Toronto in 1923, Agnes was doing private nursing in New York City. Hemingway made at least two trips there to cover stories for his Toronto paper, but Agnes insists that they did not see each other at that time.

Although they were not to meet again, their correspondence continued. Hemingway returned to Oak Park and his family; Agnes was sent to the devastated region of Torre di Mosto in the company of Loretta Cavanaugh and Peggy Conway.

Agnes to Hemingway, February 3, 1919

"The future is a puzzle to me and I'm sure I don't know how to solve it. Whether to go home, or apply for more foreign service is the question just now. Of course you understand this is all merely for the near future, as you will help me plan the next period I guess. Cavie has been very cruel to me lately, accusing me of being a flirt, which is putting me in Ruth Brooks's class. You know I don't do anything like that, don't you?"

February 5, 1919

"I'm getting fonder every day of life in furrin parts. Every time Miss Conway tells my fortune, she tells me I'm going to travel a lot. How do you like the idea? Goodnight, old dear, your weary but cheerful Aggie."

According to Agnes, Hemingway left Europe thinking that she would soon follow and that they would be married.

She insists that she had no firm intention of marrying him but had wanted to get him out of Europe, which she felt would corrupt him. Such an explanation seems almost too self-sacrificing; perhaps their relationship had become more demanding than she cared for. Certainly during the last month he was in Italy, she seems to have avoided seeing him. We shall never be certain. However, while Agnes was writing these letters to Hemingway, she was also beginning a new relationship with Domenico Caracciolo, the heir of an Italian dukedom.

Agnes to Hemingway, March 1, 1919

"Oh, I'm going to the dogs rapidly, and getting more spoiled every day. I know one thing. I'm not the perfect being you think I am. But as I am, I always was, only it's just beginning to creep out. I'm feeling very *cattiva* tonight. So goodnight, Kid, and don't do anything rash but have a good time. Afft. Aggie"

Soon after this letter, Agnes told Hemingway that their relationship was over. She was too old for him. He should look around for someone his own age.

Q: About your romance with the Italian Duke?
A: That never got any farther than Torre di Mosto. He had to go—his orders were changed. And Rita Ruffo, this little Italian girl who helped in the clinic there—she had one bad eye, wall-eye, you know—she was a dear, followed me all over the place—she was so determined that I was to become an Italian that she wrote to Caracci [sic] in Naples, that was where he was from. And his mother answered the letter. I recognized the handwriting and the paper. Rita had written her that she would love to meet this American girl her son had fallen in love with. His mother said it was just a war experience.

13. (*above*) Agnes in 1920, age 28.

14. (*bottom left*) Captain Enrico Serena, 1918, who may have contributed to Hemingway's characterization of Rinaldi.

15. (*bottom right*) Domenico Caracciolo (1919), the Italian nobleman with whom Agnes was briefly engaged, breaking off her relationship with the young Hemingway.
All photos on this page, courtesy of Mrs. Agnes Stanfield.

12. Agnes Von Kurowsky at age 10.

But the war experience lasted through May, 1919; it was not so short lived as Agnes remembered it.

Q: She was not going to let her son marry an American?

A: Oh, an unknown American! The funny thing was that I saw him twice after that. Once I saw him and next time he saw me and I did too, but I pretended I didn't. Loretta Cavanaugh and I went to southern Italy—Naples, Sicily—we were in Naples, walking down the street, wearing civvies. On the train we had picked up these two Englishmen—very jolly— they attached themselves to us. And along comes this carriage and Cavvie says, "Oh, look who's here." He stood up and gazed all the way back. He was with his mother I think. I pretended that I didn't see him. But he was really a nice person— gentle and kind. But very insistent that I give him all his letters. He burned them.

A: He was very gentle, a gentle, nice soul—much more interesting to me than a nineteen-year-old Hemingway.

Q: Yes, that's the part that—

A: I was very fickle in those days anyhow. I wasn't too interested to tell the truth—not like my friend, Ruth Brooks.

Q: Did she get into trouble in Milan?

A: Oh, yes, everywhere, she—no, I'd better not tell you that either. She was a flirt. All through training at Bellevue she was in trouble. I never broke any of the rules. I was a goody-goody in those days, but I got over that. But when Ruth Brooks went over-seas, Miss DeLong knew her quite well.

On July 9, 1919 Agnes landed in New York City. The fol-lowing day she received her discharge from the Red Cross and returned to professional nursing. Less than a year later, she applied once more for overseas duty with the Red Cross.

AMERICAN RED CROSS
APPLICATION FORM

Name: *Agnes H. Von Kurowsky*
Address: *426 East 26th Street, New York, New York*
Marital status: *Single*
Do you speak French: *Conversational knowledge*
What other foreign languages do you speak? *Italian, fluent; German, slight*
Preferred service: *Nursery*
Would you enter foreign service? *Yes*
In any country or countries required? *Yes*
Earliest date you could take up work? *At once*

Miss Forence Johnson
Director of Nursing   February 19, 1920
Atlantic Division
American Red Cross
My dear Miss Johnson,
    I take great pleasure in recommending Miss Agnes Von Kurowsky for foreign service. She was with me in Italy for one year, during the war, and I found her most satisfactory as a nurse. She has a pleasing personality.
                    Yours sincerely,

                    Catherine C. DeLong
                    Superintendent of Residence
                    Bellevue Hospital

Red Cross to Agnes, March 21, 1920

"Your application for foreign service has been received in this office. The Bureau of Personnel will send you definite instructions concerning your date of sailing; may I request that you do not make any

definite preparations until you receive these
instructions.

. . .   .

You are allowed salary which is $70 per month from
date to sail.

AMERICAN RED CROSS
FOREIGN SERVICE

Efficiency Report on: *Agnes Von Kurowsky*
Beginning: *March 30, 1920*

March 29, 1920   Reported in Paris
April 3, 1920   Assigned permission to Rumania
May 7, 1920   Left for Rumania

Q: I would like to take the dates from your 1920
   day-book and read them on to the tape—the little
   green book.
A: I never knew why I kept all this. I always
   thought I might want those addresses.

Day Book of Agnes Von Kurowsky, 1920

March 29   Arrived Paris
April   9 *Riggoletto* at the Opera
April 11   Visited Chartres with Major Mills and
           party
           (There is a picture of Agnes with Mills
           and his secretary standing beside a Ford
           tri-motor airplane. Everyone has on
           overcoats.)

April 18   Reservations for symphony cancelled on
           account of strikes
May   7   Left Paris with Miss Thompson and
           Miss LeGros
May 11   Arrive Bucharest
May 12   Dance at Tylers

May 22   Dance
May 23   Went to Maxime's for the first time
May 25   Maxime's, at 26 Maxima Street
May 27   Dance at the American Legation
May 29   Maxime's
May 30   ARC dance, Maxime's
May 31   Maxime's
June 18   Invitation to meet the Queen
July 23   Miss LeGros left for Bressau
Sept 14   Left Bucharest
Sept 17   Arrived Constantia

A: Oh, I've forgotten my Rumanian. I can still
speak one or two words. But then I was able to
get along with it pretty well, because I was with
people who couldn't speak English or French
or Italian. So I had to learn the language. It
was useful. Right away the Red Cross sent me
to a camp for T.B., bone and gland cases for
children, and I was the Red Cross worker who
taught them games and played with them. The
director of the place and his sister-in-law and her
two children were there that year and we had
very formal meals Rumanian style. We used
to go back and forth to Constantia to pick up
things to eat like black olives—Turkish olives—I
use to pick them up by the kilo. And the flour and
the sugar candy.

Efficiency Report (cont.)
September 16, 1920   Released from Rumanian
                      Commission; left for Paris;
                      vacation
October 11, 1920   Arrived Paris

Agnes boarded a ship at Constantia and sailed down the
Black Sea to Constantinople and Athens. Cutting through

the Corinth Canal, she continued on ship to Naples, where
Caracciolo lived although she apparently did not see him.
From Naples she took a train to Rome, Florence, and Milan
—revisiting her war memories just as Hemingway was to
do less than two years later. From Milan she took the train
through Switzerland and on to Paris.

Efficiency Report (cont.)
    Retained in Paris for further assignment

December 20, 1920	Assigned to sanitary train to go to Poland
January 21, 1921	Transferred to reserve list, European Comm.
January 28, 1921	Appointed to Junior Red Cross in Rumania
February 4, 1921	Left Paris enroute to Bucharest, Rumania
March 10, 1921	Assigned Brezia, Commission of Health
June 28, 1921	Left Brezia for Tekir Ghiol Sanatorium for child health work and class instruction

Sanitorium
Tekir Ghiol, Constantia
July 29, 1921

Dear Miss Hay,
    The Sanatorium . . . is on the coast of the Black Sea,
an ideal place for making over under-nourished, sickly
children into fat and brown imps. . . . while the
summer colonies are here we have about 300 and I
believe more are expected. . . . I stay on the beach with
them all of the forenoon, while they are taking
sunbaths, and teaching them American games, stunts
and tricks . . . during the late afternoon I try to amuse
the children on the veranda . . . a long low-roofed

building facing the sea and quite open on that side. . . .
I am known familiarly as "Domiseara Von" (Miss Von,
in English) . . . I rather like it.

I am very contented and have absolutely nothing to
complain of in the way I am being treated. The
Rumanian food problem is merely a question of being
polite and eating what is set before you until in time you
really begin to like it. Garlic and sour cream are about
the only things I cannot force down. My room looks out
over the sea, and is big and cool with its stone floors.
I have become very much tanned, even freckled, and
think I am getting fat. My daily swim is making me
very fit after my run down condition when I left
Brezia.

Yours very sincerely,
Agnes Von Kurowsky

Efficiency Report (cont.)

October 8, 1921   Released from service with Junior
Red Cross in Rumania and left
for Paris taking vacation enroute;
three weeks plus travel time
allowed.

October 30   Arrived Paris
November 9   Sailed for United States on *New
Amsterdam* from Boulogne

"Miss Von Kurowsky's service has been especially
satisfactory. She possesses unusual ability and
devotion and a merry heart that makes her acceptable
everywhere with all classes. She is warmly recommended for service anywhere."

On September 3, 1921, while Agnes was caring for hundreds of children on the Black Sea, Hemingway was marrying his first wife, Hadley Richardson. Hadley, like Agnes,
was seven years older than Hemingway, and, like Agnes,

she had a small trust fund. When Agnes returned to nursing in New York, Hemingway and Hadley sailed for Paris, Gertrude Stein, and history.

Sometime in the fall of 1922, Hemingway wrote what appears to be his last letter to Agnes. Like all of his letters to her, it has disappeared. Ironically, he seems to have kept all of her letters while she kept none of his. We cannot be sure what Hemingway said in the letter; from Agnes' reply it is obvious that he told her about Hadley and about his prospective writing career. His letter appears to have been written after he had returned from covering the Greco-Turkish disaster. Her reply reached him during the Christmas season.

December 22, 1922

"After I recovered from my surprise, I never was more pleased over anything in my life. You know there has always been a little bitterness over the way our comradeship ended, especially since I got back and Mac [Elsie MacDonald] read me the very biting letter you wrote her about me. . . . Anyhow I always knew that it would turn out right in the end and that you would realize it was the best way, as I'm positive you must believe, now that you have Hadley. Think of what an antique I am at the present writing, and my ghost should simply burst on the spot, leaving only a little smoke that will evaporate."

Agnes went on to describe in detail her experiences in the intervening four years, telling of her travels and her nursing duties. She had returned to Bellevue as Night Supervisor in January, 1922, but had recently returned to private nursing. She still had a great longing to return to Paris: the smell of roasting chestnuts on a grey, damp fall day; twilight at the Place de la Concorde; Prunier's; the Savoia; and Bernard's, where there was creme chocolate every night. Europe, she said, would always draw her back.

"It is nice to feel I have an old friend back because we were good friends once, weren't we? And how sorry I am I didn't meet and know your wife. Were you in Paris when I was there a year ago this November? How proud I will be some day in the not-very-distant future to say, 'Oh, yes. Ernest Hemingway. Used to know him well during the war.' I've always known you would stand out some day from the background, and it is always a pleasure to have one's judgement confirmed."

A few months after Hemingway received this letter from Agnes, he wrote the rather bitter account of their affair in Milan, calling it, "A Very Short Story." In it the nurse's name was "Ag" in the first printing; he changed it to "Luz" later to avoid libel, he said. Fourteen years later he wrote another story, "The Snows of Kilimanjaro," in which he embedded a fictionalized account of their correspondence.

He had written her, the first one, the one who left him, a letter telling her how he had never been able to kill it. . . . How when he thought he saw her outside the Regence one time it made him go all faint and sick inside, and that he would follow a woman who looked like her in some way, along the Boulevard, afraid to see it was not she, afraid to lose the feeling it gave him. How every one he had slept with had only made him miss her more. How what she had done could never matter since he knew he could not cure himself of loving her. He wrote this letter at the Club, cold sober, and mailed it to New York asking her to write him at the office in Paris. That seemed safe. . . . The office sent his mail up to the flat. So then the letter in answer to the one he'd written came in on a platter one morning and when he saw the handwriting he went cold all over and tried to slip the letter underneath another.

But his wife said, "Who is that letter from, dear?" and
that was the end of the beginning of that.[5]

There is nothing in Agnes' reply to indicate that Hemingway ever wrote this fictionalized letter. Considering that
"Snows of Kilimanjaro" was written when Hemingway's second marriage with Pauline Pfeiffer was coming apart, it is
more likely that the author is using his feelings for Hadley,
his first wife, in this passage. He uses the circumstances of
his relationship with Agnes in 1922 but the emotions involved with Hadley. Hemingway was too professional a
writer to make his art a mirror image of reality.

Agnes never saw Paris or Italy again after 1921. In 1926,
she once again applied for duty with the Red Cross after
four years of private nursing. She was sent almost immediately to Haiti, which at that time was under the governance
of the American occupation forces. Her duties were to assist
in the training of native Haitian nurses, whom she taught
in French, for they spoke little English. On May 15, 1927,
she was promoted to Directress of the training facility at
the Haitian General Hospital in Port au Prince. Her efficiency report submitted by Clara B. Noyes said:

> As Director of Nursing she has conducted the school
> in a very efficient manner. Under her direction the
> standards of nurse education and care of the sick has
> steadily improved. The highest commendations have
> been given her by the administrator, Lucius W.
> Johnson, M. C.

> A: There were no such things as screens at that time in
>   Haiti. Everyone slept under nets. There was very
>   little ice. We kept our food in a cabinet with
>   screening to keep the bugs out. That was the ice
>   box. The nurses had a very nice home there. One

5 *Short Stories*, pp. 64-66.

of the nurses had a horse and when she left the next
fall, she gave me her horse. I love to ride. And I
learned to drive down there. I had my first
Model-T Ford. A doctor was teaching me how to
drive. The first day we ran out of gas. We had to
walk to the rum factory to buy some gas.

In Haiti, Agnes met Howard Preston Garner, an auditor
in the Office of Financial Advisor. A photograph shows
them on the beach with a backdrop of trees. It is one of the
few pictures of Agnes looking directly at the camera.
Garner is a stout, round-faced man with black hair and a
black mustache (not unlike the one Hemingway grew). The
two were married on November 23, 1928. The service was
performed by the Bishop of Haiti in the Episcopal Cathedral at Port au Prince. Her mother placed a one paragraph
announcement in the *Washington Post* twelve days later.

Ten years had passed since Agnes had last seen Hemingway in Italy. Approaching 37, she was still incredibly attractive. It had taken Hemingway those same ten years to
metamorphize the experience of 1918 into *A Farewell to
Arms*. While Agnes was marrying Garner, Hemingway was
in and out of New York City, having just completed the first
draft of the novel. By the time it was published in the fall
of 1929, the Garner marriage had already begun to dissolve.
In 1930 Agnes returned to the States alone; in 1931 she took
her Red Cross savings to Reno to pay for her divorce. She
never asked for any support from Garner.

That is all we know about her: dates, memories, letters,
pictures, reports—none of them any truer than history is
ever true. But there is enough to draw some conclusions.

Agnes Von Kurowsky was a self-sustained, tough, un-
sentimental woman in 1918. She had survived the death of
an older sister at the age of eleven. She was able to sustain
herself in another country in whatever language they chose
to speak. She was surrounded by men—men whose company she enjoyed but with whom she was never madly in

love. For 1918 she was a well-traveled woman: Alaska, Vancouver, Washington D.C., New York City. She was a professional nurse from Bellevue and took great pride in her credentials. She was more sophisticated than most Red Cross nurses and a better linguist. She was older than Hemingway, and it was she who broke off their relationship. She was never devoted to anyone, nor was she ever war weary. It is difficult imagining Agnes ever being "a little crazy" because of the death of a fiance. She valued witty, clever, but gentle men; she was always looking for new experience and further travel.

In short, Agnes Von Kurowsky contributes little to Catherine Barkley other than her presence and her physical beauty. Catherine is not a professional; she is not a linguist; she is not sophisticated; she is not well-traveled; she is sentimental; she is less experienced than Frederic. Catherine makes Frederic the object of her sexual devotion until he becomes her religion. Agnes may or may not have had a sexual relationship with Hemingway. She emphatically denies it. Ultimately it does not matter, for, whatever their relationship, it must be obvious that it could never have been that of Catherine and Frederic.

Q: I think he wrote a lot of things he never experienced.

A: Well, that one in Spain—I know that doesn't sound like anything he would do. Some of the books are fine. *The Old Man and the Sea*—that one stands out in my mind more than anything he wrote. It's so to the point. Nothing comes in to interfere.

Q: Of course the experience never happened to Hemingway.

A: Of course not! He would have put the skeleton of the fish up on the wall if it had.

SECTION THREE
Critical Response: Technique and Structure

"A Farewell to Arms" as Travel Literature

> Milan, the sprawling, new-old, yellow-brown city of the north, tight frozen in the December cold. Foxes, deer, pheasants, rabbits, hanging before the butcher shops. Cold troops wandering down the streets, from the Christmas leave trains. All the world drinking hot rum punches inside the cafes. Officers of every nationality, rank and degree of sobriety crowded into the Cova cafe across from the Scala theatre, wishing they were home for Christmas.—"A North of Italy Christmas" (*The Toronto Star Weekly*, December 22, 1923)

Much of the detail that makes up the historical and topographic fabric of *A Farewell to Arms* has been neglected by critical readers who have been more concerned with the pattern of action or the biographical analysis of the novel. However, the wealth of specific references is not merely window dressing left over from the nineteenth century; they serve Hemingway's art in a vital, if unobtrusive, way. The minute accuracy of these references is not too surprising in an author who specialized in travel journalism. Throughout the Twenties Hemingway had assiduously created for himself the role of expert European traveler.

However, just because Hemingway knew Milan, Stresa, Montreux, and Lausanne from his own experience, it is not necessarily valid to assume that he wrote of them six to ten years later only on the basis of what he remembered. When the treatment of such places is examined, one finds that every street, bar, cafe, and hotel are exactly where the author said they were; every geographic feature is precise.

Hemingway may have had a fantastic memory; he may have been able to live the experience, remember it, and write it. Such an explanation is certainly valid in part, but to accept it completely prevents the reader from looking in other directions. For example, in a 1925 letter giving travel advice to Ernest Walsh, Hemingway recommends the town of Bellagio on Lake Como, but admits that he cannot remember the names of the pubs.[1] Years later Hemingway told his biographer, Carlos Baker, that he did not have a good memory for dates and he always had to check them for accuracy.[2]

Robert O. Stephens has established some useful categories in *Hemingway's Nonfiction* that describe Hemingway's travel writing. Stephens notes that Hemingway's travel essays in the Twenties were not resplendent with "views" and customs; instead "he reported the travel adventures as they provided insights for social analysis."[3] Similarly, *A Farewell to Arms* uses the landscape of Italy at war as a crucible containing both action and commentary. A typical example of Hemingway's travel-writing mode can be seen at the opening of Chapter Thirty-Five:

> The army had not stood at the Tagliamento. They were
> falling back to the Piave. I remembered the Piave. The
> railroad crossed it near San Dona going up to the front.
> It was deep and slow there and quite narrow. Down
> below there were mosquito marshes and canals. There
> were some lovely villas. Once, before the war, going up
> to Cortina D'Ampezzo I had gone along it for several
> hours in the hills. . . . I wondered how the army that
> was up there would come down. (p. 253)

[1] An undated letter in the Hemingway file at Scribner's, probably 1925.

[2] Ernest Hemingway to Carlos Baker, March 10, 1951.

[3] Robert O. Stephens, *Hemingway's Nonfiction* (Chapel Hill: University of North Carolina Press, 1968), p. 65.

The biographic approach would note that Hemingway had been blown up on the Piave in 1918 and that he and his first wife, Hadley Richardson, had wintered in Cortina in 1922. This approach, however, ignores the purpose of the description of the Piave valley, which is used as a backdrop for the final question: *how would the army that was up there get down?* The question poses a problem in military necessity, and it is also an indication that Frederic has not left the war behind as easily as he thought he would when he came out of the river. The paragraph is travel literature but with a purpose beyond the view.

Stephens notes the characteristic of Hemingway's travel writing that most obviously carries over into *A Farewell to Arms*: "Moving about Spain as an *aficionado*, he learned about good cafes, pleasant hotels, breath-taking landscapes, famous paintings, eccentricities of people from diverse provinces, the places to get the best paella and to see the most handsome women."[4] *A Farewell to Arms* abounds with information in most of these categories. Moreover, the information is accurate enough to be used for a travel guide to northern Italy, or to have come from such a guide.

There is a good deal of information about specific hotels in *A Farewell to Arms* as well as general information on how to conduct oneself in a continental hotel. When Frederic and Catherine seek out a hotel in Milan, he knows just the hotel that will allow them to register without luggage and will not question their relationship. When he tells Catherine that he had imagined them once going to the Hotel Cavour (p. 153), he adds that the Cavour would not have let them in under such circumstances. Hotel Cavour was, at that time, one of the most luxurious hotels in Milan, located opposite the Giardini Pubblici.[5] At Stresa, Frederic goes unerringly to the Grand-Hôtel & des Isles Borromées, which Baedeker lists as one of the two first-class hotels, with

4 Stephens, p. 68.
5 Karl Baedeker, *Northern Italy* (New York: Scribner's, 1913), p. 152.

Map 5
Small-scale map of Stresa, including the islands where Frederic
went fishing.

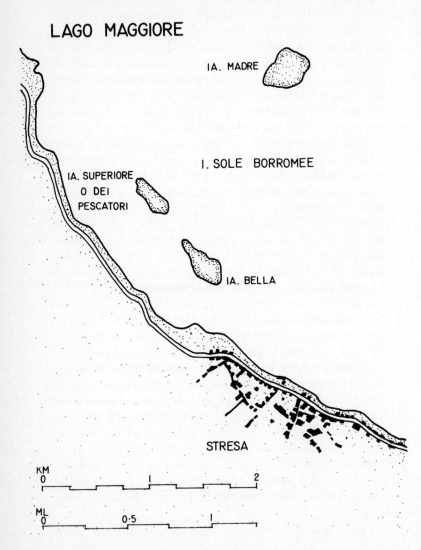

LAGO MAGGIORE

IA. MADRE

I. SOLE BORROMEE

IA. SUPERIORE
O DEI
PESCATORI

IA. BELLA

STRESA

KM
0   1   2

ML
0   0·5   1

240 beds and parks and gardens on the lake.[6] Hemingway
did not stay at this hotel when he visited Stresa as a
wounded ambulance driver in 1918. A letter to him at
Stresa from a nurse in Milan is addressed to the Hotel
Stresa.[7] In Lucarno, Frederic and Catherine stay at the
Hotel Metropole, which is recommended to them by one of
the customs guards. When the two lovers later take up
quarters in Lausanne, he chooses a medium-size hotel
(p. 308), which he describes almost as if he were writing
a travel guide: carriage entrance, elevator, carpets on the
floors, white wash bowls, shining fixtures, brass bed, outside
garden.

In the role of experienced continental traveler, Hemingway also wrote about how to deport oneself in hotels as well
as how to choose them. In *A Farewell to Arms* Frederic has
the same kind of inside knowledge. He knows how to speak
to desk clerks; he knows what to order and how to order it.
In the Milan hotel across from the train station, he orders
a dinner of "woodcock with soufflé potatoes and purée de
marron, a salad, and zabaione for dessert" (pp. 152-153).
He chooses a bottle of St. Estephe to accompany the meal.
To the American reader who had never seen Europe, much
less a bottle of St. Estephe, the meal must have appeared
very authentic. The total effect emphasizes Frederic's
knowledge in these matters, and marks him as an insider.

Much has been made of the drinking capacity of the
Hemingway hero; however, it is more interesting to note
that Frederic drinks with style and the sure knowledge that
he is drinking the best, whether it be a regional wine, a
liquor, or a brandy. When Miss Van Campen discovers the
empty bottles in Frederic's armoire, she is outraged at the
brandy and kummel bottles, but there are also vermouth,
marsala, capri, and cognac bottles (p. 143). Even when he
and Catherine order the strawberry wine that disappoints

[6] *Ibid.*, p. 237.
[7] Agnes Von Kurowsky to Ernest Hemingway, September 26, 1918.

them, they know in advance that it probably will not taste like strawberries.

Frederic is also experienced in the best cafes of Milan:

> We went to dinner at Biffi's or the Gran Italia and sat at the tables outside on the floor of the galleria. . . . we decided that we liked the Gran Italia best, . . . We drank dry white capri iced in a bucket; although we tried many of the other wines, fresa, barbera, and the sweet white wines. (p. 112)

Both Biffi's and the Gran Italia are listed in the period Baedeker as being good cafes. Biffi's has the higher rating of the two; both are located in the Galleria Vittorio Emanuele just off of the cathedral square.[8]

Earlier in the novel Frederic had daydreamed about eating at the Cafe Cova, which is the only cafe with a better listing than Biffi's in Milan. Later in Milan Frederic does go to the Cova to buy Catherine a gift: "I went down the steps carefully and walked up the Via Manzoni. . . . I wanted to buy something at the Cova to take to Catherine. Inside, at the Cova, I bought a box of chocolate" (pp. 118-119). At first it seems curious that Frederic would buy chocolate at a cafe-restaurant, but once again the period Baedeker confirms the point. It locates the Cova on the Via Giuseppe Verdi 2, which is just off the Via Manzoni. The Cova is listed as "a smart establishment with a confectionery department and a pretty garden."[9]

When Nathan Asch called the first draft of *The Sun Also Rises* a travel book,[10] he could have been talking about *A Farewell to Arms* as well. Not only is the novel an accurate guide to places, hotels, food, wine, taxis, railway stations, cafes, and gun shops, but it has the added advantage of being told from the inside. This aspect of *A Farewell to Arms*

---

[8] Karl Baedeker, *Guide to Italy* (New York: Scribner's, 1928), p. 25.
[9] *Ibid.*, p. 25.
[10] Quoted in Carlos Baker, *Hemingway and His Critics* (New York: Hill and Wang, 1961), p. 31.

is another carryover from the travel writing mode that Hemingway developed in his non-fiction travel pieces, for fundamental to his travel writing was the assumed role of expert upon which his credibility as lion hunter or fisherman rested. He portrayed himself as having behind-the-scenes information and the ability to extract full pleasure from any situation within his scope.[11] These travel-writing characteristics carry over into Frederic's character in the novel, for Frederic always has expert knowledge, even though he may have amateur status. His Italian is not quite perfect enough to pass for native, but he is an insider who is recognized by other insiders. The Major who operates on him recognizes the quality immediately. George, the head waiter at the Gran Italia, responds to him as one cognoscente to another; George saves him tables, gives him inside advice on wines, and loans him money when he is short (pp. 112-113). To non-expert readers who have received nothing but snubs from head waiters, this treatment helps establish Frederic's credentials as an expert.

One of the advantages of being an insider is that you belong to a kind of secret society; other insiders do you favors because they recognize you as a member. Emilio, the barman at Stresa, recognizes Frederic as a drinking man who also fishes well. Because of this recognition, Emilio saves the lovers from being arrested at Stresa. It is Emilio's boat that takes Frederic and Catherine to safety. He gives up the boat gratuitously, knowing that eventually he will get back the boat or its value. Emilio knew Frederic from other visits to Stresa, just as Count Greffi knew him and his skill at the billiard table from other times. Playing billiards well is an insider's skill, and Count Greffi is professional in his ability. Frederic loses to the old man after starting with a fifteen-ball handicap, but for the amateur expert to lose to the professional is no defeat. The very fact that the old Count would ask him to play billiards lends further support to Frederic's role as expert.

[11] Stephens, *Hemingway's Nonfiction*, pp. 45-46.

At no time in the novel does he appear as a novice. The reader never sees him learning how to do anything; he already knows. He has served in the war from the beginning; he understands military tactics well enough to criticize blunders with the accuracy of a military historian. The Italian terrain is all familiar territory. In both Milan and Stresa he has prior knowledge of the towns. He knows where to go and where to eat, indicating that he has been there several times previously. "Stresa," he says, "is so easy to get to from Milan that there are always people you know" (p. 142). This is true, of course, only if you first know people in Milan.

This insider's view saves Hemingway a lot of explaining; it allows him to make use of his accumulated knowledge of Italy without accounting for Frederic's knowledge. He does not have to explain how Frederic gained his expertise. For the reader, the insider's view produces a kind of credibility. Our belief in Frederic is established early in the book when we realize that he knows more about the setting and the situation than we do. However, Frederic does not exaggerate his knowledge; frequently he understates or assumes it. But the very fact that he knows which are the best bars and that the barmen there know him enhances his opinions in other areas. The reader is willing to accept much of Frederic's knowledge because he has been presented as the insider who understands the territory. This role is one that Hemingway has effectively carried over from his travel writing of the Twenties.

A further aspect of Hemingway's travel writing, as pointed out by Stephens, was his sampling the sports available in the local area.[12] There is a good deal of sports sampling in *A Farewell to Arms*, some of which carried over almost intact from Hemingway's non-fiction of the Twenties. For example in 1922 he wrote a feature for the *Toronto Star Weekly* describing the sport of luge-ing in Switzer-

12 *Ibid.*, p. 75.

land.[13] Stephens points out: "It was this general background he used as the basis for the Swiss officials touting of Montreux winter sports in the novel. When Frederic and Catherine first land in Switzerland, they divert attention from themselves by asking the customs officials about winter sports in Montreux. . . . Hemingway's comparison of lugeing and tobogganing in the article becomes a matter of dispute for the officials in the novel."[14] Frederic and Catherine also take in the racing at San Siro outside Milan. There, too, he is armed with inside information on how the races are fixed although he feels better when he does not take advantage of it. At Stresa, he trolls the lake briefly with Emilio but fails to catch any fish. In Montreux he and Catherine hike along the iron-hard roads. In Lausanne, Frederic goes to the gymnasium to box while he waits for Catherine's labor pains to begin. Horse racing, hiking, luge-ing, fishing, and boxing all play a minor part in the novel, but Hemingway felt it was important to include them, for they were part of "the way it was." They were also a carryover from his non-fiction travel writing.

When certain narrative passages in the novel are compared with their corresponding street maps, *A Farewell to Arms* takes on further resemblance to a sophisticated travel book instructing the reader on which street to take to see a particular building or reach a particular shop. There are passages in Books Two, Four, and Five that correspond with remarkable accuracy to the map terrain of Milan, Lake Maggiore, and Montreux.

There is, for example, the rather detailed description of the route taken by Frederic and Catherine from the Red Cross hospital to the hotel across from the train station. Frederic narrates their passage with the precision of a tour guide.

[13] Ernest Hemingway, "Flivver, Canoe, Pram, and Taxi Combined Is the Luge," *Toronto Star Weekly* (March 18, 1922), p. 15.
[14] Stephens, pp. 257-258.

I went down to the corner where there was a wine
shop and waited inside. . . . We walked along together,
along the sidewalk past the wine shops, then across the
market square and up the street and through the arch-
way to the cathedral square. There were streetcar
tracks and beyond them was the cathedral. It was
white and wet in the mist. We crossed the tram tracks.
On our left were the shops, their windows lighted, and
the entrance to the galleria. . . . We crossed the far end
of the square and looked back at the cathedral. . . . We
. . . turned down a side street. . . . "This is the way I go
to the hospital," I said. It was a narrow street and we
kept on the righthand side. . . . We turned down a side
street where there were no lights. . . . We walked along
the street until it came out onto a wider street that was
beside a canal. . . . Ahead, down the street, I saw a
streetcar cross a bridge. . . . We stood on the bridge in
the fog waiting for a carriage. . . . It was a long ride to
the station up side streets in the rain. . . . "Go to the Via
Manzoni and up that." (pp. 146-151)

This narrative sequence is remarkable for its guide-book
detail. Following the path of the lovers on a Milan street
map of 1917, one can find every street and every turn. If the
writer constructed this passage from memory six to ten
years after the fact, then it is testimony to Hemingway's
power of recall. Knowing, however, Hemingway to be the
competent journalist concerned with accurate reporting,
one may suspect that he used just such a street map to re-
fresh his memory.

It is important that he thought such accuracy was necessary to his art. This passage could have been written in a
generalized way that would have given the reader only the
impression of Milan by night, or Hemingway could have
used even more specific references—shop names, street
names—overpowering the reader with tour-guide details.
He goes to neither extreme, and the result is "the way it

was." At least part of Hemingway's technique for achieving this dimension is to use the natural terrain accurately but without distracting his reader through over-emphasis.

Another passage that can be traced with map accuracy occurs when Frederic and Emilio, the barman at Stresa, troll for fish on Lake Maggiore:

> We rowed along the shore. . . . I rowed across to Isola Bella and went close to the walls, where the water deepened sharply, and you saw the rock wall slanting down in the clear water, and then up and along to the fisherman's island. . . . I rowed up opposite the fisherman's island where there were boats drawn up . . . I brought the boat up to the stone pier. . . . We went into a little café. (p. 255)

Baedeker's Guide to Northern Italy lists Isola Bella as one of the local attractions on Lake Maggiore in the vicinity of Stresa. Baedeker says the island is a rock rising out of the lake, just as Frederic sees it.[15] The fisherman's island is a literal translation of Isola dei Pescatori, which Baedeker says is "almost entirely occupied by a fishing village." The guide book notes there are two cafes on the island—Ristorante Belvedere and Ristorante del Verbano—"both plain but good."[16] It is of little significance that Frederic and Emilio should stop at the fisherman's island as opposed to Isola Bella. However, Isola Bella was a tourist attraction with gardens, a chateau, and a picture gallery. Isola dei Pescatori was no tourist attraction; Baedeker offers no possible reason for stopping there. It is in keeping with Frederic's mood that he would choose the unfrequented and less commercial of the two islands to stop for a vermouth, and, of course, there Frederic would be in less danger of running into inquisitive people who might question his military status.

15 Baedeker, *Northern Italy*, p. 236.
16 *Ibid.*, p. 236.

Map 6
The escape route of Frederic and Catherine up Lake Maggiore
into Switzerland. (Letters keyed to text)

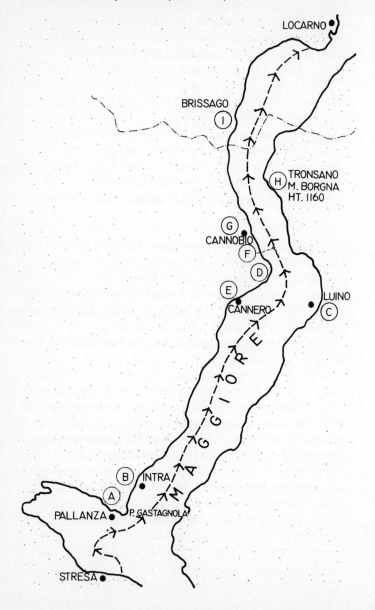

More interesting and equally accurate in time, distance, and topography is the escape route of the lovers up Lake Maggiore to refuge in Switzerland. A map of the lake shows not only the towns mentioned in their proper sequence, but it also shows the geographical features as Hemingway described them. First, Emilio gives Frederic directions for navigating the lake in the dark:

> Past Luino, Cannero, Cannobio, Tranzano. You aren't
> in Switzerland until you come to Brissago. You have to
> pass Monte Tamara. . . . [First] Row to Isola Bella.
> Then on the other side of Isola Madre go with the
> wind. The wind will take you to Pallanza. You will see
> the lights. Then go up the shore. (pp. 268-269)

Emilio's advice is accurate, as the map shows, for the Swiss border lies just below Brissago. The journey, however, does not go as planned:

> We never saw Pallanza [A]. The wind was blowing up
> the lake and we passed the point that hides Pallanza
> [Point Castagnola] in the dark and never saw the
> lights. When we finally saw some lights much further
> up the lake and close to the shore it was Intra [B]. . . .
> I rowed all night . . . looking back I could see the long
> dark point of Castagnola. . . . The lake widened and
> across it on the shore at the foot of the mountains on
> the other side we saw a few lights that should be Luino
> [C]. I saw a wedgelike gap between the mountains on
> the other shore and I thought that must be Luino. . . .
> There seemed to be another point going out a long way
> ahead into the lake [D]. . . . We were closer to the long
> point. There were lights in the bay ahead [E]. . . .
> What looked like a point ahead was a long high head-
> land. I went further out in the lake to pass it. . . . "I
> don't think we have more than about eight miles more."
> [F] . . . We went on up the lake. There was a break in

the mountains on the right bank, a flattening-out with
a low shore line that I thought must be Cannobio [G].
. . . There was a high dome-capped mountain on the
other shore a way ahead [H]. . . . I knew I had to pass
that mountain and go up the lake at least five miles
further before we would be in Swiss water. . . . I was
sure we were in Switzerland now. . . . "I'm pretty sure
it's Brissago [I]." (pp. 270-277)

Frederic's knowledge of the lake is once more expert beyond what one might have expected. When he knows that
the Swiss border lies five miles beyond a certain mountain,
he indicates that he has been up the lake before. The same
inference may be drawn from his recognition of the various
towns in sequence. It is one thing to be told the names of
the towns by Emilio, but the barman did not say on which
side of the lake the various towns would appear. Frederic,
with unfailing accuracy, recognizes each town. It is possible
that Hemingway made a trip up Lake Maggiore in the fall
of 1918 while he was recuperating at Stresa,[17] but even if
he had made such a trip, it seems unlikely that he should
have remembered the details with such accuracy ten years
later. This is merely to suggest that when Hemingway
wrote this narrative passage, he may have checked a map
to see on which side of the lake certain towns were situated
and what the terrain looked like. He could hardly take a
chance on misplacing a town or jumbling the sequence. And
of course this passage adds to the image of Frederic as
expert: he is not only able to row the lake, which is a physical trial, but he is also able to navigate it in the dark, which
is a trial of skill.

Although Hemingway made fun of Baedeker tourists in
Across the River and Into the Trees, there is more than a
touch of Baedeker in his fiction. His short stories set in upper Michigan and his satirical novel, *The Torrents of*

---

[17] Carlos Baker, *Hemingway: A Life Story* (New York: Scribner's,
1969), p. 51.

Spring, are accurate guides to that part of the country. Constance Montgomery has demonstrated their geographical and topographical accuracy in her book, *Hemingway in Michigan*.[18] *The Sun Also Rises* could serve as a contemporary's guide to Paris and northern Spain. Although the Spanish names have been altered, the novel still provides accurate information on bars, hotels, bull fights, food, and fishing. *Death in the Afternoon* is an even more detailed guide book to the bull ring. *The Green Hills of Africa* provides how-to-do-it information on African safaris, while *For Whom the Bell Tolls* gives accurate historical and geographical information on the Spanish civil war. Later, we are told by his biographer, Hemingway took great pleasure in finding the terrain of the country corresponding to that which he described in the novel.[19] In *Across the River and Into the Trees* Colonel Cantwell sometimes sounds like a tour guide of Venice.[20] Years later when he came to writing *A Moveable Feast*, Hemingway was still concerned with accurate distances, specific street names, correct spellings, and the various hotels, cafes, and bars that fill that reminiscence.[21] Clearly part of the Hemingway technique is based on this kind of expert, insider, tour guide accuracy, and the lessons he learned in his non-fiction travel writing he carried over into his fiction.

[18] Constance Montgomery, *Hemingway in Michigan* (New York: Fleet, 1966).

[19] Baker, *A Life Story*, p. 312.

[20] Stephens, p. 82.

[21] Philip Young, *Hemingway: A Reconsideration* (New York: Harcourt Brace, 1966), p. 290.

Technique

I still believe though that it is very bad for a writer to talk about how he writes. He writes to be read by the eye and no explanations or dissertations should be necessary. You can be sure that there is much more there than will be read at any first reading and having made this it is not the writer's province to explain it or to run guided tours through the more difficult country of his work.—"An Interview with Ernest Hemingway" (*The Paris Review*, Spring, 1958)

Critics have noted in passing that *A Farewell to Arms* is carefully planned in an orderly, logical method that is exceptional in the American novel.[1] But critics have not been eager to work out the techniques whereby Hemingway achieves the ordered tightness that they admire. Besides his characteristic prose style, there are three effective techniques that he employs throughout the novel and that deserve some delineation. First, there is the simple technique of foreshadowing; there is no major piece of action in the novel that has not been properly foreshadowed. Second, there is the device of the echo scene. Finally, there is the technique of reversing roles between characters.

In *A Farewell to Arms*, the reader is never taken by surprise, for all the major pieces of action are economically foreshadowed. For example, from the beginning of the spring offensive at Plava in 1917, the reader is led to antici-

[1] Leo Gurko, *Ernest Hemingway* (New York: Thomas Y. Crowell Co., 1968), p. 92; R. B. West and R. W. Stallman, "Ernest Hemingway: *A Farewell to Arms*," *The Art of Modern Fiction* (N.Y.: Rinehart, 1949), p. 622.

pate Frederic's wounding. There are too many references
to the exposed position of the Italian attack and the expected heavy casualties to think otherwise. As a final touch,
Catherine gives Frederic a Saint Anthony medal as he
leaves for the front. As a patron of lost causes, Saint Anthony becomes an ironic foreshadowing of Frederic's incipient wounding.

In a similar manner Catherine's pregnancy and death are
strongly foreshadowed. When Dr. Valentini first sees Catherine, it is the morning after she has spent her first night
with Frederic. The Doctor says:

> "What a lovely girl. I could teach her. I will be a
> patient here myself. No, but I will do all your
> maternity work free. Does she understand that? She
> will make you a fine boy. A fine blonde like she is."
> (p. 99)

This sense of things to come is, like much of the foreshadowing in the novel, ironic. Catherine does not produce
fine children, nor does she receive free maternity care. The
boy she bears is neither blond nor healthy, and the price is
exorbitant.

If there were any doubt that Catherine will become pregnant, it should disappear just a few pages later when Ferguson warns Frederic that he had better not get Catherine in
trouble, i.e., pregnant (p. 108). In the next chapter Frederic worries about their relationship: "I wanted us to be
married really because I worried about having a child if I
thought about it" (p. 115). And on that same page Frederic
expresses his fear to Catherine: "Couldn't we be married
privately some way? Then if anything happened to me or
if you had a child" (p. 115). It comes as no great surprise,
then, when Catherine tells Frederic that she is pregnant.
Once the predictions of her pregnancy are fulfilled, there
can be little doubt that Catherine's prophecy that she sees
herself dead in the rain will also be fulfilled. There is noth-

ing logical in these predictions of death; there is no apparent cause and effect at work. However, both her pregnancy and her death seem inevitable by the time they are achieved. Hemingway is able to create this sense of inevitability in the reader through the steady use of foreshadowing.

While Catherine's pregnancy is the crisis in the world of the lovers, there is a counterpart in the war cycle. The Austro-German breakthrough at Caporetto was the result of Italian military errors that could have been avoided just as Catherine's pregnancy was the result of avoidable errors. Caporetto is just as much a logical result of the Italian strategy on the Isonzo as Catherine's conception is a logical result of her nights with Frederic. Both the war cycle and the love cycle will produce defeat, although the enormity of defeat is not immediately apparent at the crisis. Like Catherine's pregnancy, the Austro-German breakthrough is heavily foreshadowed.

On their first meeting, Frederic and Catherine make small talk about the war. One side must crack, they say, for the war to reach a conclusion. Frederic thinks that the Italian line will not crack. Catherine replies:

"You think not?"
"No. They did very well last summer."
"They may crack," she said. "Anybody may crack."
"The Germans too."
"No," she said. "I think not."   (p. 20)

Later while Frederic recuperates in Milan, he has time to analyze the fighting on the Italian front during the summer of 1917:

The Italians were using up an awful amount of men.
I did not see how it could go on. Even if they took all
the Bainsizza and Monte San Gabriele there were

plenty of mountains beyond for the Austrians. . . .
Napoleon would have whipped the Austrians on the
plains. He never would have fought them in the
mountains. He would have let them come down and
whipped them around Verona. (p. 118)

This seemingly casual reference to the Napoleonic Wars
is actually a complex evaluation on Frederic's part, as well
as an accurate foreshadowing of the Caporetto breakthrough. Twice between 1796-1800, Napoleon thoroughly
defeated the Austrian army on the Venetian Plains.[2] The
key phrase, however, is: "He never would have fought them
in the mountains." When Napoleon once again faced the
Austrians in 1809, his forces in Italy, under the command
of Prince Eugene, were defending a mountain frontier that
was almost exactly the same as that defended by the Italians
before the Caporetto breakthrough. Napoleon recognized
the problems of a mountain war, and he particularly saw
the significance of Caporetto. In a letter to Prince Eugene,
Napoleon warned his field commander that Caporetto was
the key to the Natisone valley. Should the Austrians break
through at Caporetto, the next defensible line was the Piave
river. Just as Napoleon had warned, the Austrian forces attacked at Caporetto on April 10, 1809, and broke through
the Natisone on to the plains. The forces of Prince Eugene,
which were scattered all along the line of defense, were
forced to retreat hastily and gave up all of the Venetian
Plains.[3] It was probably no accident that the Austro-German force chose Caporetto again in 1917.

Clearly, Frederic is referring to the situation of 1809, and
if the reader responds to the reference, he has an idea of

[2] Henry Lachoque, *Napoleon's Battles* (London: George Allen and
Unwin Ltd., 1966), pp. 33-91.

[3] Georges Lefebvre, *Napoleon: From Tilsit to Waterloo*, translated by
J. E. Anderson (New York: Columbia University Press, 1969), p. 63;
Bakewell, p. 19.

what is to come. Hemingway makes another effort to prepare the reader when Frederic discusses the war with the
British major in Milan:

> Did he think they would attack this fall? Of course they
> would. The Italians were cooked. Everybody knew
> they were cooked. The old Hun would come down
> through the Trentino and cut the railway at Vincenza
> and then where would the Italians be? (p. 134)

This piece of foreshadowing comes under the category of
prediction, of which there are several in the novel. The
priest makes an accurate prediction about Frederic's love
life. Catherine makes an accurate prediction about her
death. The British major's prediction is not completely accurate, but in essence it is what the Austro-German forces
do.

The most elaborate foreshadowing in the novel, however,
is that which precedes Frederic's participation in the
Caporetto retreat. During the night in Milan when Frederic
is leaving Catherine to return to the front, he experiences
in miniature what will happen on a larger scale during the
retreat. In Milan Frederic leaves the Red Cross hospital to
return to the front under less than ideal conditions: limp-
ing, jaundiced, and with a pregnant mistress. A few days
later he will leave Gorizia in the midst of the retreating Second Army under less than ideal conditions. In Milan, Frederic begins his journey to the train station with Catherine
by his side. Moving down side streets in the rain, they make
their way to a hotel where they have a last supper before
Frederic's train leaves. On the train Frederic is separated
from Catherine, and he is surrounded by unknown and
somewhat hostile soldiers. In the military retreat from
Caporetto, Frederic begins with companions going down
side roads in the rain. At night he stops at a farmhouse with
Piani where they eat their last supper together. At the

bridge he is separated from Piani by the hostile battle police.

The mood and weather of these two pieces of narrative show similarities. There is a furtive mood about Frederic and Catherine as they make their way through the Milan night, for they are outcasts whose relationship prevents them from going to the best hotels. Catherine particularly cannot afford to be discovered by the authorities. In search of a refuge, they pass the Milan cathedral but do not enter. The hotel replaces the church as a haven in bad weather. During the retreat, Frederic will again be looking for a refuge against the world; instead of a hotel, he finds its rural counterpart, the barn. During the night in Milan, as during most of the Caporetto retreat, there is rain, mist, and fog. The two lovers begin their night trek in mist; the cathedral is shrouded in mist. By the time they reach the bridge, "the fog was turning to rain" (p. 150). It is raining when they reach the hotel; it is raining when they leave. Frederic steps from the cab at the station into the rain. As Catherine pulls away in the carriage her last gesture is to point to the protection of the station. Frederic realizes "she meant for me to get in out of the rain" (p. 158). This rain in Milan is very like the rain that permeates Frederic's retreat from Gorizia to the Tagliamento river.

In Milan, Frederic steers a course down unlighted side streets; leaving Gorizia he will choose the unmarked side streets to make his way to the river. When Frederic reaches the "wider street," he is faced with a canal and farther down a bridge. This is similar to the topography confronting Frederic outside Udine during the retreat; there too he is faced with a canal and a bridge. In Milan he looks up to see a streetcar cross the bridge. Outside Udine he will look up to see a German staff car cross the bridge.

Thus the mood, weather, terrain, and circumstances of Frederic's retreat to the Tagliamento have been foreshadowed in the piece of narrative action that immediately pre-

cedes it. At the end of Book Two, Frederic leaves Catherine
on the train to return to the front; at the end of Book Three
Frederic leaves the front on the train to return to Catherine. In between, Hemingway has placed the structural
crisis of the novel.

While the novelist economically foreshadows the crucial
action of the novel, he is frequently able to achieve irony as
well as foreshadowing. This happens when the expected
event does not turn out as the reader or Frederic has foreseen it. When discrepancy arises between the expected and
the actual, Hemingway produces an ironic effect without
belaboring the point. A clear example of this technique can
be seen in the "prayer" sequences in the novel. When Catherine prepares Frederic for his operation, she tells him to
say his prayers as he goes under the gas so he will not speak
of their relationship while under the anesthetic. Later at
Stresa, Count Greffi enjoins Frederic to pray for him if
Frederic is ever able to pray. Frederic replies, "I might become very devout. . . . Anyway, I will pray for you"
(p. 263). To this point in the book the reader has not heard
Frederic pray. However, the reader is prepared to accept
Frederic's eventual praying. The ironic effect is achieved
when Frederic does pray; it is not for himself or for Count
Greffi, but for the dying Catherine:

> I knew she was going to die and I prayed that she
> would not. Don't let her die. Oh, God, please don't let
> her die. I'll do anything for you if you won't let her die.
> Please, please, please, dear God, don't let her die.
> (p. 330)

When Frederic is finally forced back on the necessity for
prayer it is in a hopeless circumstance. His prayers have the
same hysterical note of Passini's dying prayers in Book One:

> "Dio te salve, Maria. Dio te salve, Maria. Oh Jesus
> shoot me Christ shoot me mama mia mama Mia oh

purest lovely Mary shoot me. Stop it. Stop it. Stop it.
Oh Jesus lovely Mary stop it." (p. 55)

Frederic's prayers are in keeping with his other religious
experiences. The Saint Anthony medal for hopeless circumstances was stolen from him at the dressing station. By his
own admission, Frederic's only feeling for God is a fear of
Him in the night. When he finally comes to pray, Frederic
is faced with a hopeless circumstance, and his prayers are
of no avail.

A more complex type of foreshadowing is the echo scene,
in which Hemingway will run the same scene past the reader twice. However, on the second run the emphasis of the
scene will have shifted slightly so that the reader is invited
to make a comparison between the two scenes. The result
of such a comparison is frequently irony.

The most obvious use of echo scenes occurs early in the
novel. Frederic first daydreams about his relationship with
Catherine, and then the daydream is fulfilled. In the daydream Frederic tantalizes himself with the sensual pleasures he might enjoy with Catherine Barkley in a Milan
hotel:

> I wished I were in Milan with her. I would like to eat
> at the Cova and then walk down the Via Manzoni in
> the hot evening and cross over and turn off along the
> canal and go to the hotel with Catherine Barkley. . . .
> we would go in the front door and the porter would
> take off his cap and I would stop at the concierge's desk
> and ask for the key and she would stand by the
> elevator and then we would get in the elevator and it
> would go up very slowly clicking at all the floors and
> then our floor and the boy would open the door and
> stand there and she would step out and I would step
> out and we would walk down the hall and I would put
> the key in the door and open it and go in and then take
> down the telephone and ask them to send a bottle of

capri bianca in a silver bucket full of ice and you
would hear the ice against the pail coming down the
corridor and the boy would knock and I would say
leave it outside the door please. Because we would not
wear any clothes because it was so hot and the window
open and the swallows flying over the roofs of the
houses and when it was dark afterward and you went
to the window very small bats hunting over the houses
and close down over the trees and we would drink the
capri and the door locked and it hot and only a sheet
and the whole night and we would both love each
other all night in the hot night in Milan. That was how
it ought to be. (pp. 37-38)[4]

This sensual dream vision is fulfilled for Frederic, but the
fulfillment carries with it a heavy irony. The sexual rendezvous takes place not in a hotel, but in a hospital. It is
through Frederic's hospital room that the small bat comes
hunting. When Frederic does keep this hotel rendezvous
with Catherine, it is under circumstances unimaginable in
the earlier daydream. Instead of arriving in Milan, Frederic
is leaving Milan for the front when he and Catherine seek
a hotel to spend their last evening together. The October
rains have chilled the city; it is not hot as in the daydream.
The lovers on their way to the hotel are not beginning a
love affair; instead Catherine is pregnant and Frederic feels
"trapped biologically."

As in the daydream, Frederic and Catherine traverse the
Via Manzoni on their way to the hotel and they "turn off
along the canal." At the hotel the sequence of events dupli-
cates the daydream:

The manager bowed us toward the elevator. There was
much red plush and brass. The manager went up in the

---

[4] Richard Hovey has called Frederic's daydream a "sophomoric
fantasy," which it may well be. However, to dismiss it as such is to
misunderstand the needs and psychology of men at war as well as to
misunderstand Hemingway's technique. Richard Hovey, *The Inward
Terrain* (Seattle: University of Washington Press, 1968), p. 75.

elevator with us. . . . The elevator passed three floors
with a click each time, then clicked and stopped.
(p. 151)

Once inside the hotel room Frederic finds it nothing like
the daydream. He goes to the windows as in the dream vision, but they remain shut, for it is cold and wet outside.
There are no swallows and no bats. In the wet streets he
sees the lights of the hotel reflected, and across the plaza he
can see the train station from which he must leave. There
is nothing amorous or sensual about the room. Catherine
feels like a whore, she says. There is an ironic twist to her
statement, for in the daydream Frederic conceived of her
as a sort of magnificent whore, a concubine.

As in the daydream, the lovers order up a bottle of capri
bianca, but they also order a complete dinner. In daydreams wine may sustain eager lovers, but in reality they
find food a necessity. Here the food brought to the upstairs
room on the night of a departure has the overtones of a last
supper. But there is no silver bucket for the wine as in the
daydream, and the lovers do not make love all the hot night.
Instead they eat their supper and discuss the future of
Catherine and the fetus growing in her womb. There is no
sexual contact.

Frederic is aware of the similarities between his present
circumstance and his earlier daydream, and he tells Catherine about it:

"Once when I first met you I spent an afternoon
thinking how we would go to the Hotel Cavour
together and how it would be."
"That was awfully cheeky of you. This isn't the Cavour
is it?"
"No. They wouldn't have taken us in there."
(pp. 153-154)

At the end of the daydream, Frederic emphasized that that
was "the way it ought to be." Here, both Frederic and the

reader are aware of the ironic discrepancy between the illusion and the reality.

Hemingway uses another echo scene in the rendezvous sequence on Lake Maggiore. When Frederic first got his leave papers, he had planned to meet Catherine for a short holiday on the lake:

> We had planned to go to Pallanza on Lago Maggiore.
> It is nice there in the fall when the leaves turn. There
> are walks you can take and you can troll for trout in
> the lake. It would have been better than Stresa because
> there are fewer people at Pallanza. Stresa is so easy
> to get to from Milan that there are always people you
> know. There is a nice village at Pallanza and you can
> row out to the islands where the fishermen live and
> there is a restaurant on the biggest island. But we did
> not go. (pp. 142-143)

This description is the "way it ought to be" for the lovers at the lake, but once again there is a discrepancy between the illusion and the reality.

Frederic and Catherine do eventually get to Lake Maggiore, but under circumstances far different from those imagined by Frederic earlier. Instead of being a soldier on leave, Frederic is a deserter whose life is in danger. He and Catherine go not to Pallanza, but to Stresa because it is so accessible. As in the earlier plan, Frederic does troll for trout on the lake, but he catches nothing. He also rows out to the islands where the fishermen live, as in the planned vacation, but he goes without Catherine. As predicted earlier, Frederic does run into people he knows at Stresa: the barman and Count Greffi. He also runs into people who know him: the officials who recognize him as an officer out of uniform and who plan to arrest him.

Frederic had planned earlier to take his leave at Pallanza, and his last comment is that they did not go. Pallanza is the first check point for the two lovers as they begin their night

row up the lake to Switzerland. The guide assures them
that they will be able to see the lights of Pallanza (p. 269).
However, just as their earlier plans for reaching Pallanza
did not work out, so they again miss connections:

> We never saw Pallanza. The wind was blowing up the
> lake and we passed the point that hides Pallanza in the
> dark and never saw the lights. (p. 270)

A more elaborate and complex sequence of echo scenes is
used to make Frederic's desertion at the Tagliamento river
not only foreshadowed but also ironic. Early in the novel
just before Frederic is wounded, Manera and Passini tell
Frederic about some Italian troops who refused to attack.
Manera tells how Carabinieri took every tenth man out of
the line and shot him. Passini tells how "a sergeant shot two
officers who would not get out" of the trenches (p. 49).

During the retreat to the Tagliamento, Frederic is faced
with the opposite circumstances when the two sergeants re-
fuse to help with the ambulances. As they turn away from
Frederic's commands and hurry off toward the advancing
enemy, Frederic calmly shoots one of them down with his
new pistol. When he bought the pistol, he was told that it
was a good weapon and that he would not make any mistakes with it (p. 148). After he wounds the most talkative
sergeant, Frederic hands the pistol to Bonello to finish the
execution. He has to tell the driver to cock the weapon;
Bonello then calmly fires two shots into the sergeant's head
point blank. Frederic has narrated the entire scene with
cool detached emotions. That very evening Bonello deserts
to the advancing Austrians.

All of these previous scenes are brought to bear on Frederic's experience at the Tagliamento. Frederic is pulled
from the struggling ranks at the bridgehead where judg-
ments and executions are being dispatched with the same
curious detachment with which he shot the escaping sergeant. Frederic notes that his would-be executioners "had

that beautiful detachment and devotion to stern justice of men dealing in death without being in any danger of it" (pp. 224-225). Frederic, as narrator, does not make the comparison with his own stint as executioner but the reader cannot fail to. The executioners at the river are Carabinieri just as they were in the anecdote related by Manera and Passini. Following the example of Bonello, Frederic chooses desertion rather than impending death. Without overtly reminding the reader of earlier action, Hemingway invests Frederic's desertion with additional irony through the use of echo scenes.

Either there is disparity between the ideal and the real as in the hotel rendezvous and the Stresa sequence, or there is the execution motif approached from different points of view until Frederic himself is finally faced with the reality of execution. Hemingway is able to understate the crucial scenes at the hotel and at the Tagliamento because the neatly devised echo scenes are making his comment for him. Thus the device is a technical one that achieves both foreshadowing and irony while at the same time serving to bind the action into unity.

An extended set of echo scenes takes place between Rinaldi and the priest in Book One. The priest is the representative of the church and the life of the spirit; Rinaldi is the representative of medical science, reason, and the life of the flesh. The conflict between the spirit and the flesh runs through the novel, and it is clearly delineated in the first book. Both the doctor and the priest are dedicated professionals who take pride in their work. Both men are accustomed to visiting wounded soldiers in hospitals. Both men have distinctive bedside manners. The institutions that both men represent hold out hope to the wounded men: the doctor holds out salvation of life; the priest holds out salvation of the soul. In *A Farewell to Arms* the soul has few advocates, and religious faith offers little consolation. What faith there is is placed in doctors and in the flesh. Frederic has great trust in the skill of Rinaldi, Doctor Valentini, and the doctor in Lausanne, but by his own admission he is unable to pray.

The dominance of the flesh over the spirit is illustrated clearly in Book One when Hemingway reverses the roles between the priest and Rinaldi. This reversal takes place in the field hospital where Frederic is waiting to be sent to Milan for surgery and recuperation. Discomfited by heat and pain, Frederic is visited three times in three successive chapters. First he is visited by Rinaldi; second, by the priest; and, finally, by Rinaldi and the major. The three institutions—science, church, and military—are all represented.

The sequence of visits is keyed by the first one in which Rinaldi complains that he now has no roommate. Frederic replies:

"You can make fun of the priest."
"That priest. It isn't me that makes fun of him. It is the captain. I like him. If you must have a priest have that priest. He's coming to see you. He makes big preparations."
"I like him." (p. 65)

When Rinaldi begins to tease Frederic about his relationship with Catherine, Frederic responds with words chosen to anger Rinaldi. Somewhat piqued, the doctor gives Frederic advice about virgins:

"With a girl it is painful. That's all I know. . . .
And you never know if the girl will really like it."
(p. 66)

Both realistic and cynical, Rinaldi then prescribes that Frederic not make a fool of himself. He offers Frederic a brotherly kiss that Frederic does not accept. As he leaves, Rinaldi places the gift bottle of cognac under Frederic's bed.

On the same night the priest visits Frederic. Instead of cognac, the priest brings vermouth, which he and Frederic share just as Frederic and Rinaldi shared a glass of the cognac earlier. When the priest and Frederic discuss the war, the reader is invited to compare their conversation with the earlier one. Whereas Rinaldi could discuss the war only in terms of the operations he was able to perform, the priest sees the war as an unnatural and morally destructive force.

Just as Rinaldi did earlier, the priest gives Frederic advice about love. Whereas Rinaldi's advice was practical and of the flesh, the priest's advice is more theoretical and contemplative:

> "What you tell me about in the nights. That is not love.
> That is only passion and lust. When you love you wish
> to do things for. You wish to sacrifice for. You wish to
> serve."
> "I don't love."
> "You will. I know you will. Then you will be happy."
> (p. 72)

The advice may be good, but it does not prove very useful to Frederic. In his relationship with Catherine, Frederic is the taker. In no way can his desertion at the river or his escape into Switzerland be seen as a sacrifice for Catherine. His actions are self-centered, although he can be considerate of Catherine when there is nothing else to distract him. It is Catherine who makes the sacrifices, and who wishes to serve. It is Catherine who makes a religion of love.[5] As Frederic admits, he is always able to forget those things which the priest knew.

In these two bedside scenes, the representatives of the flesh and the spirit have had their say. Both bring gifts of wine that they share with Frederic. Both speak of the war,

[5] James F. Light, "The Religion of Death in *A Farewell to Arms*," *MFS*, 7 (Summer, 1961), pp. 169-173.

interpreting it in terms of their profession. Both give advice on love, advice representative of their attitudes toward life. Both of them take their leave. Rinaldi offers a kiss, the touch of the flesh, which Frederic refuses. The priest merely pats Frederic on the shoulder, the laying on of hands. In these two mirror scenes the priest has the stronger lines, but Frederic is more at ease with Rinaldi.

The third visit in the sequence follows the same pattern as the first two. Rinaldi and the major visit Frederic in the night, and once again the conversation is about war. Together the three men become drunk, not on the priest's vermouth but on Rinaldi's gift of brandy. The emphasis of their drunken discussion is once more on the flesh. Frederic learns that Catherine will be in Milan to comfort him. The conversation of the three men centers on war and its counterpart, the sexual encounter. As the two men leave, Frederic accepts Rinaldi's kiss, which he had refused the night before. The major pats Frederic on the shoulder just as the priest had patted him on the shoulder. When they leave, Frederic is drunk.

The third visit is both an exaggeration of the first two and a clear indication of the forces that are to dominate Frederic's life. The major and the doctor sit at Frederic's bedside in drunken camaraderie; they have clearly usurped the priest's role as bedside confessor, and they clearly hold sway over Frederic in a way the priest was never able to. For, despite whatever spiritual values Frederic may discover, *A Farewell to Arms* remains a novel of the flesh. Spiritual values are present only by comparison and omission.

A third and more complex technique used by Hemingway to tighten his action and to make covert commentary on the action is the device of role reversal. This device uses both foreshadowing and echo scenes, but it is more complex than either, for it involves the exchange of roles by Frederic and Catherine. This exchange is worked out slowly over the length of the novel, but, in order to appreciate it, the reader must first understand Frederic Henry.

Frederic's difficulties in the novel are several, not the least of which is his role as narrator. In telling his own story, he is self-effacing; to Catherine he characterizes himself as a mediocre baseball hitter. As a wounded soldier, he is ironically aware of how unheroic it was to be blown up while eating cheese. Frederic Henry is not a hero, and he realizes it.

However, one must remember that Frederic is narrating the story at some remove from the action. Time has elapsed since the death of Catherine in Lausanne, and Frederic's self-effacement is in retrospect. Telling his own story, Frederic is temperamentally incapable of making himself a hero of the action. If the reader accepts Catherine as the heroine of the novel,[6] it is because Frederic is always aware of her sacrifice and her death. Frederic's insights into the nature of bravery do not, ultimately, apply to his own action, but they are significant comments on Catherine Barkley:

> If people bring so much courage to this world the world has to kill them to break them, so of course it kills them. The world breaks everyone and afterward many are strong at the broken places. But those that will not break it kills. It kills the very good and the very gentle and the very brave impartially. If you are none of these you can be sure it will kill you too but there will be no special hurry. (p. 249)

As with all of Frederic's insights, which are imbedded in the novel like polished gems, it is important to remember that this is an insight derived after the fact. More importantly, these insights are based upon the experience contained within the novel. Frederic brings no formal systems of philosophy to bear upon his experience, and because he is self-conscious of his role as narrator, his insights are not meant to enhance his own character. Leo Gurko is mistaken

6 Delbert E. Wylder, *Hemingway's Heroes* (Albuquerque: University of New Mexico Press, 1969), pp. 87-88.

in his belief that both Frederic and Catherine are meant to be the good, gentle, and brave.[7] Frederic is incapable of seeing himself in such a light. Quite naturally he has no difficulty seeing Catherine as good, brave, and gentle, for he is alive and she is dead because of their child. One must remember that it was Frederic who early in the novel made the mistake about bravery:

> "They won't get us," I said. "Because you're too brave. Nothing ever happens to the brave."
> "They die of course." [Catherine]
> "But only once."
> "I don't know. Who said that?"
> "The coward dies a thousand deaths, the brave but one?"
> "Of course. Who said it?"
> "I don't know."
> "He was probably a coward," she said. "He knew a great deal about cowards but nothing about the brave. The brave dies perhaps two thousand deaths if he's intelligent. He simply doesn't mention them."
> (pp. 139-140)

No matter how formally British, stiff-upper-lip Catherine may sound, she does become the brave one in the novel. Frederic, for all his skill at self-preservation, is never quite brave. He is always able to save himself; Catherine is not.

Wylder is quite right, therefore, in seeing Catherine as the "hero" of the novel and in seeing Frederic as the anti-hero.[8] However, Frederic's problem of identity goes beyond his status as hero or anti-hero, for he is identified throughout the novel in terms of negatives. The reader is constantly discovering what Frederic is *not*, or Frederic is continually being mistaken for someone he is not. When Catherine first

---

[7] Leo Gurko, *Ernest Hemingway and the Pursuit of Heroism* (New York: Crowell, 1968), pp. 88-89.

[8] Wylder, *Hemingway's Heroes*, pp. 66-95.

meets him, she identifies him as *not being an Italian*. A little later when she goes a little "off," she mistakes him for her dead fiancé. When Frederic is wounded at Plava, he is mistaken for a hero. Rinaldi asks him at the field hospital:

> "Did you do any heroic act?"
> "No," I said. "I was blown up while we were eating cheese."
> "Be serious. You must have done something heroic either before or after. Remember carefully."
> "I did not."
> "Didn't you carry anybody on your back? . . ."
> "I didn't carry anybody. I couldn't move."   (p. 63)

When Frederic reaches the hospital in Milan, he is mistaken for an Austrian prisoner by the Italian barber because he speaks with a foreign accent. At the bridgehead on the Tagliamento during the retreat, Frederic is first misidentified as an officer who has abandoned his troops. Then he is mistaken for an enemy infiltrator in an Italian uniform because he speaks with an accent (pp. 222-224). Once he deserts, he quickly removes the officer stars from his uniform to repudiate his former identity. He is now *not* an Italian officer, but neither is he a civilian. After he has dressed in the civilian clothes he borrows from Simmons in Milan, Frederic confesses that he feels like a masquerader. In Switzerland, he and Catherine live under false identities; first they pretend to be cousins; then they pretend to be married. During Catherine's pregnancy Frederic grows a beard in an effort to establish some form of identity. However, when he sees himself in the gym mirror as a boxer with a beard, he recognizes it as a false identity. Later in Lausanne, Frederic must put on a white doctor's gown to enter Catherine's hospital room:

> I put it on and pinned it in back at the neck. I looked in the glass and saw myself looking like a fake doctor with a beard.   (p. 319)

atmosphere of the time, as it is felt at the roots of human relations."[7]

As all good children of the "New Critics" know, the text must stand alone. Whatever the author's intentions may have been, the work is self-contained with its own rationale. Productive as this approach has been, it has also been misleading to second-generation critics of Hemingway. All too often they have not mastered the tools that their teachers abandoned because they had grown dull. Emerson could advise the American scholar that he need not read books to study Nature, but only after Emerson had read all the books. Now that the first half of the twentieth century is no longer the "modern age," but an historical period of its own, it is time for critics to relearn the use of old tools. The vein of psychoanalytic exegesis has been overworked. The misleading thesis that Hemingway is always his own protagonist has littered the critical landscape with so much debris that it will take another generation of critics to restore the ecology. Letters, manuscripts, source reading, social milieu, and literary biography must all be brought to bear on the published text. Hemingway's reading is as important to his art as that of Coleridge; his textual revisions are as significant as those of Keats. With Hemingway it is time to question constructively all of the explications we have inherited. We must begin the difficult and frequently tedious search for the hard data that will support, modify, or disprove our inheritance.

[7] Edmund Wilson, "Hemingway: Gauge of Morale," reprinted in *Eight Essays* (Garden City: Doubleday and Co., 1954), p. 113.

Time Table for the Writing of the First Draft

1928

Date	Place	Progress
early March	Paris	begins manuscript
April 7	Key West	"hard at work"
April 21	Key West	"ten to fifteen thousand words"
April 26	Key West	MS-108 (p. 45)
June 7	Piggot, Ark.	MS-279 (p. 138)
June 17	Kansas City, Mo.	MS-311 (p. 159)
July 15	Kansas City	MS-457 (p. 228)
July 22	Piggot, Ark.	MS-477 (p. 243)
July 23	Piggot	MS-486 (p. 248)
July 30	Sheridan, Wyoming	
August 7	Sheridan	MS-543 (p. 279)
August 8	Sheridan	MS-548 (p. 281)
August 9	Sheridan	MS-557 (p. 285)
August 10	Sheridan	MS-563 (p. 291)
August 11	Sheridan	MS-573 (p. 296)
August 12	Sheridan	MS-575 (p. 297)
August 13	Sheridan	MS-581 (p. 300)
August 14	Sheridan	MS-585 (p. 305)
August 15	Sheridan	no progress
August 16	Sheridan	MS-599 (p. 310)
August 17	Sheridan	MS-616 (p. 316)
August 18, 19	Sheridan	no progress
August 20	Sheridan	MS-631 (p. 323)
August 21, 22	Sheridan	MS-650 (p. 331)

Rejected First Drafts, Sample Variant Endings, and Titles

Rejected First Drafts

MSS-168-170

"You love god like that?"

"I love god. I really love him with all my heart."

"More than anything else?"

"More than anything else."

~~He was serious~~

"That's a fine thing."

"You don't love him?"

"No. I guess not."

"You don't love anything?"

"Yes. I love a lot of things."

"What are they?"

"I don't know. Lots of things."

"What?"

I thought a minute.

"The night. The day. Food. Drink. Girls. Italy. Pictures. Places. Swimming. Portofino. Paris. Spring. Summer. Fall. Winter. Heat. Cold. Smells. Sleep. Newspapers. Reading." This all sounds better in Italian. (MS-169)

"You'll lose them all."

"And you'll never lose god."

"No."

"Because you'll never get him."

"How do you mean?"

"I don't want to talk. I don't want to try and shake your faith."

He laughed suddenly and kept on laughing. "That's very funny. Why I laughed was because I felt very bad because I was afraid I shake your faith." He stood up. "You make me remember

In the final account the reader knows Frederic by negatives. He is not an Italian. He is not an Austrian. He is not a hero. He is not a German infiltrator. He abandons his identity as an officer, but he is not yet a civilian. He is neither Catherine's cousin nor her husband. He is not a boxer, and he is not a doctor. Such a piling-up of negative identification must finally produce a non-heroic figure.[9]

Frederic's negative identity, including a lack of a usable past, becomes ironically magnified when he and Catherine reverse roles in the novel. When the book opens it is Frederic who has the potential for heroics; his situation is more likely to produce heroic action than is Catherine's. By the end of the novel, it is Catherine who dominates the action; Frederic has been reduced in stature while Catherine has gained. This shift of focus is emphasized by the role reversal in their parallel hospital scenes: the first in Milan, the second in Lausanne.

When Frederic is first examined in the Milan hospital, he is told that his operation must wait on the natural healing process. When Catherine is first examined in the Lausanne hospital, she must wait until the natural process brings her pregnancy to termination. In both cases, however, the natural process is circumvented. Frederic insists upon an immediate operation; Catherine has no choice in the matter, for without the Caesarean she will die. In both cases there are confident doctors who have no hesitancy about the operations. Dr. Valentini operates on Frederic the morning after he first examines him; more conservative surgeons would have waited six months. In Lausanne, Catherine's doctor does not hesitate to recommend the operation: "I would advise a Caesarean operation. If it were my wife I would do a Caesarean" (p. 321).

Thus Frederic and Catherine are both confined to hospitals to undergo operations at the hands of confident surgeons. It is useful to note, however, that Frederic has come to the hospital via the destructive cycle of war; Catherine

[9] For a similar insight see: Robert W. Lewis, *Hemingway on Love* (Austin, Texas: University of Texas Press, 1965), pp. 40-42.

comes to her delivery bed as a result of the natural cycle. Moreover, her pregnancy is a direct result of the nights she spent in Frederic's hospital bed earlier.

In Milan, Catherine was the nurse and Frederic was the patient. It was Catherine who prepared Frederic for his operation, not wanting anyone else to touch him. She gave him instructions on how to behave under the gas so that he would not reveal their relationship while he was unconscious. Catherine says:

> "Say your prayers then. That ought to create a splendid impression."
> "Maybe I won't talk."
> "That's true. Often people don't talk." (p. 104)

In Lausanne the roles of patient and nurse are reversed. Catherine is in the hospital bed because of her love for Frederic, and Frederic is at her bedside in the role of nurse. In Lausanne, it is Catherine who is taking gas, and it is Frederic who is concerned about the effects of the gas on the patient:

> I turned the dial to three and then four. I wished the doctor would come back. I was afraid of the numbers above two. (p. 323)

When wounded, Frederic showed a low tolerance for pain; in Lausanne Catherine calls her worst pains "good ones." In Milan, Catherine had worried that Frederic would expose their sexual relationship; ironically, it is Catherine who exposes them, not by her words but by her expanding womb. In Milan, Catherine had advised Frederic to say his prayers, but it is not until the hospital room in Lausanne that Frederic is able to pray. His prayers, however, do not create a "splendid impression."

Frederic, who began the novel as the active participant, has become the passive participant by the end of the novel.

Whereas it was Catherine who, early in the novel, submerged her identity in Frederic; at the end of the novel it is Frederic who has lost all positive identity. He has switched roles with Catherine until he is finally left with no role to play.

Structure

> How can anyone think that you can neglect and despise, or
> have contempt for craftsmanship, however feigned the con-
> tempt may be, and then expect it to be at the service of your
> hands and of your brain when the time comes when you
> must have it. There is no substitute for it. . . . It is in your
> heart and in your head and in every part of you. . . . It is
> not just a set of tools that you have learned to work with.—
> *Islands in the Stream*, p. 103

From the earliest reviews of *A Farewell to Arms*, critics
have been searching for patterns in the novel that con-
formed with patterns observed elsewhere in Hemingway's
work. Not too surprisingly, the patterns appeared: the
wounded man, the idealized heroine, grace under pressure,
the clean, well-lighted place, the life code. To recognize
such patterns is obviously useful in analyzing the novel;
however, patterns imposed upon the novel can also limit the
critical analysis. To see, for example, all of Hemingway's
"clean well-lighted places" as essentially the same is to say
that Hemingway is merely repeating himself, a not uncommon criticism toward the end of his career. Such criticism
is not ultimately useful, for it admits a severe limitation on
the reader's ability to approach each work as an indepen-
dent unit.

There is, for example, the argument that the Hemingway
hero is a progressive development of Nick Adams. Philip
Young's engaging psychological analysis of Nick established

a pattern from which all other protagonists had to be cut. Thus one discovers that Jake Barnes, Frederic Henry, Robert Jordan, Colonel Cantwell, Harry Morgan, and Santiago are progressively older versions of Nick Adams, who looks suspiciously like Hemingway by another name. There are, without doubt, certain characteristics that these men share, and these are the characteristics which the critics have been eager to see.

The obvious differences among these characters have, for the most part, gone understated until the publication of Delbert E. Wylder's book, *Hemingway's Heroes*, in which he examines each Hemingway protagonist as an individual. Wylder concludes that: "The progressive hero concept, though continually being modified, is also restrictive at times, especially when the hero is too closely tied to the life of the man Ernest Hemingway and the legend he helped to create. . . . the Hemingway novels are quite different in conception and technique and . . . the protagonists are distinctly different characters. Though they may have their similarities, they are fictional creations that exist within specific contexts."[1] Wylder's conclusions sound obvious but they are necessary. The critical patterns have been so inhibiting that the individual characters have almost been lost. Approaching a Hemingway novel today is like restoring a Renaissance painting that has been clouded by several layers of varnish.

Superimposed patterns are not, however, the only critical construction that obscures the novel. The reader must also overcome the cliché that because Hemingway opposed intellectualism he was himself unintellectual. It is an easy cliché, particularly if one ignores all evidence to the contrary. For example, Clifton P. Fadiman, an early reviewer wrote: "I have rarely read a more 'non-intellectual' book than 'A Farewell to Arms.' This non-intellectuality is not connected with Hemingway's much discussed objectivity.

[1] Delbert E. Wylder, *Hemingway's Heroes*, pp. 223-224.

It is implicit in his temperament. He is that marvelous combination—a highly intelligent naïf."[2] This representative kind of intellectual condescension reinforces the image of Hemingway the uneducated, if natural, writer who perhaps did not fully understand the dimensions of his art.

In view of this trend in Hemingway criticism, it is necessary to repeat some obvious things about the structure of *A Farewell to Arms* in order to see it as a unique novel in the Hemingway canon. Whatever patterns are discovered should be inherent to the novel; they should not be imposed on the basis of earlier or later writing. If we allow that Hemingway knew his craft, whatever artistic construction the novel possesses should be credited to the author and not to the reader.

H. K. Russell has noted, for example, that the five books of *A Farewell to Arms* seem very like the five-act structure of the Elizabethan tragedy.[3] Stallman and West find that "the physical form of *A Farewell to Arms* more nearly resembles the drama than it does the majority of American works of fiction. The novel is composed of five separate books, each composed of a series of scenes, and each scene is broken into sections which might be likened to stage directions and dialogue."[4] Leo Gurko has pushed the analogy even further in his suggestion that there are strong parallels between the novel and Shakespeare's *Romeo and Juliet*: "The feud of the Montagues and Capulets is a form of war, . . . The priest in *A Farewell to Arms* is as important as the priest in Shakespeare's play. The Mercutio figure is Rinaldi, skeptical about the war as Mercutio is about the feud, just as bitterly cynical, and just as steadfast in friendship. Fred-

2 Clifton P. Fadiman, "A Fine American Novel," *Nation*, cxxix (October 30, 1929), p. 498.

3 H. K. Russell, "The Catharsis in *A Farewell to Arms*," *MFS*, 1 (Aug., 1955), pp. 25-30.

4 R. B. West and R. W. Stallman, "Ernest Hemingway: *A Farewell to Arms*," *The Art of Modern Fiction*, p. 622.

eric like Romeo, progresses from sex to love, from surface
attachment to abiding passion."[5]

Such comparisons, which sound very fine in the class-
room, tell us little about the novel. They tempt the reader
into increasingly ingenious parallels, which ultimately avoid
the novel. (If Ferguson "represents" Juliet's maid, then who
is Count Paris and what does the Austrian army represent?) Since we know that Hemingway did not write the
novel with a "five-act structure" in mind and that the divisions were made long after the first draft was complete, any
such analogies exist primarily in the mind of the critic. This
is not to imply that the novel is unstructured, but the structure is simple and direct. Following the classic short story
structure, each "book" stops at the natural culmination of
a piece of action. Not only has each of the five books its own
piece of action, but each book takes place in the season most
appropriate to the action.

In the opening two chapters of the novel, which cover the
first two years of the war in seven pages, Hemingway establishes the rhythmical flow of the seasons that counterpoints
the violent pattern of the war. The opening two paragraphs
juxtapose the natural fertility of the Italian plain with the
destructive nature of the war. The plains, "rich with crops,"
and the "orchards of fruit trees" show the natural progress
of the Italian summer, 1915. But during the summer and
fall, when nature grows and ripens, the war also reaches its
most destructive level of the year. The warm dry season of
late summer and early fall is the time for concentrated military activity. In the winter, when deep snow buries the
mountain front, both military and natural activity lie dormant, waiting to be renewed in the spring. Throughout the
book there will be these two cycles in operation: the seasonal cycle of the land and the seasonal cycle of the war.
The destructiveness of the war cycle is dependent upon the
same seasonal weather changes that regenerate the land.
This pattern is made clear in the opening chapters: the

[5] Leo Gurko, *Ernest Hemingway*, pp. 81-82.

spring offensive is followed by the hard fighting of late summer and early fall; the October rains slow the fighting until the first winter snow stops it completely. Like the seasonal cycle of the plant life, the war waits for the spring to be resurrected. Frederic says in Chapter Two:

> I watched the snow falling, looking out of the window
> of the bawdy house, the house for officers, where I sat
> with a friend and two glasses drinking a bottle of Asti,
> and, looking out at the snow falling slowly and heavily,
> we knew it was all over for that year. Up the river the
> mountains had not been taken; none of the mountains
> beyond the river had been taken. That was all left for
> next year. (p. 6)

Within each cycle—fertile and destructive—Frederic finds a female relationship appropriate to the cycle in which he is involved. The destructive cycle of war has its "love" counterpart in the whorehouses that move as the front moves and that are artificially divided into enlisted and officers' houses. The inevitable product of the whorehouse relationship is venereal disease; the inevitable product of the war cycle is death. Within the fertile, natural cycle, Frederic establishes the natural love relationship with Catherine, who is the counterpart to the brothels. Frederic makes this point clear on their second meeting:

> I did not care what I was getting into. This was better
> than going every evening to the house for officers
> where the girls climbed all over you. (p. 30)

The relationship between Catherine and Frederic has as its natural product, Catherine's pregnancy, just as inevitably as the brothel produced Rinaldi's syphilis. And just as the destructive cycle of war produces death, so does the natural cycle of fertility produce death: the child is born dead and Catherine dies in post-operative hemorrhaging.

The parallel between Catherine's death, the destruction

of the war, and the brothel's syphilis becomes overly ironic only if the reader expected a "happy ending." For the seasonal cycle of the earth is the controlling pattern and the pattern ends each year with the winter death. The natural love cycle of fertility may produce life, but it also must end with death. It is in this sense that *A Farewell to Arms* is neither a war story or a love story, for love and war are but two sides of the same coin and the coin has a death-head on either side. The cycles of love and war both imitate the seasonal cycle, but love is not an alternative to war; neither love nor war is a haven from disaster. If Catherine had not died in Lausanne, she would have died later; the soldier who did not die in the mountains would have died somewhere else. As Frederic reminds the reader, sooner or later "it" or "they" will take everyone. If there is any education of the protagonist in *A Farewell to Arms*, this truism is all he learns.

The rhythm of cyclical flow that Hemingway establishes in the first two chapters of Book One is used throughout the novel to both control and unify the action. Chapter Three begins in the spring of 1917 and the last chapter of the novel takes place in the spring of 1918. Each section of the novel has its appropriate season. For example, when Frederic returns from leave in Chapter Three it is spring, 1917:

> When I came back to the front we still lived in that
> town [Gorizia]. There were many more guns in the
> country around and the spring had come. The fields
> were green and there were small green shoots on the
> vines, the trees along the road had small leaves
> and a breeze came from the sea. (p. 10)[6]

Spring is the appropriate season for Book One, for in it Frederic meets Catherine Barkley. The cycle of seasonal renewal has begun in nature, and the two lovers are

[6] It is interesting to note "some" similarity between this opening paragraph and Chaucer's opening lines to the General Prologue of *The Canterbury Tales*.

brought together as part of the natural fertility cycle. The war cycle of destruction is also renewed in the spring, for the Italian offensive begins with the April attack at Plava, where Frederic is blown up by the trench mortar shell. However, these cycles do not operate independently of each other; each cycle interpenetrates the others. The fighting at the front is dependent upon the weather conditions, which are part of the natural cycle. Frederic's and Catherine's happiness is dependent upon the fortunes of the war. Nature itself can be destroyed by the war; fields and orchards can be demolished. The war cycle has also destroyed the possibility of any "innocent" relationship between Frederic and Catherine. There is no chance of romantic sentiment after Frederic has grown old through two years of hauling dead and dying bodies at the front and "dragging ashes" at the officers' brothel. Nor is Catherine's a springtime innocence; she has seen what an artillery shell can do to a fiancé. The physical wound that Frederic receives at the end of Book One is the war's counterpart of the relationship that has begun between him and Catherine.

Book Two of the novel is set in Milan during the summer of 1917. The spring-planted crops grow and ripen during the hot summer days and nights through no volition of their own. The relationship between Frederic and Catherine also ripens involuntarily:

> God knows I had not wanted to fall in love with her.
> I had not wanted to fall in love with any one. But God
> knows I had and I lay on the bed in the room of the
> hospital in Milan and all sorts of things went through
> my head. (p. 93)

Although Book Two remains in Milan, the destructive cycle of the war continues to impinge upon the lovers' relationship. It is the war that has brought them together; their love is consummated in a war hospital. Ironically, it is on a hospital bed that their child is conceived, a hospital bed intended for the war wounded. Throughout Book Two Frederic is reminded of the war by his incessant newspaper reading, by talkative veterans, by his doctors, and by his uniform. As the summer draws to a close, the war impinges more and more upon the two lovers until it finally separates them. The war, which has reversed all normal patterns of behavior, prevents Frederic and Catherine from marrying, for that would mean separation; yet they become separated anyway.

The cycles of nature, love, and war continue in tight synchronization. Summer was the time for growth and ripening in the seasonal cycle of the crops. Within the love cycle it has been the time of conception and growing pregnancy. In the destructive cycle of war it has been the time of the heaviest fighting and severe losses. When Frederic returns to Gorizia, the Major tells him:

"It has been bad, . . . You couldn't believe how bad it's been. I've often thought you were lucky to be hit when you were." (p. 165)

"It has been a terrible summer," said the priest. . . . "You cannot believe how it has been. Except that you have been there and you know how it can be. Many people have realized the war this summer. Officers whom I thought could never realize it realize it now." (p. 178)

While the life cycle has produced Catherine's pregnancy, the death cycle of the war has produced enormous casualties. The ripening fetus in Catherine's womb finds its destructive counterpart in the ripening syphilis that Rinaldi fears he has contracted:

"What if I have it. Everybody has it. The whole world's got it. First . . . it's a little pimple. Then we notice a

rash between the shoulders. Then we notice nothing at
all. We put our faith in mercury." (p. 175)

In the larger sense, "it" becomes the taint of mortality that
everyone is born with. The whole world does have "it."
Book Three of *A Farewell to Arms* is appropriately set
in the fall season—October, 1917:

> Now in the fall the trees were all bare and the roads
> were muddy. . . . The mulberry trees were bare and the
> fields were brown. There were wet dead leaves on the
> road from the rows of bare trees. (p. 163)

If the fall is the harvest season of the spring planting in the
natural cycle, then the Austro-German breakthrough at
Caporetto is the deadly harvest of the long summer's
fighting.

Separated from the life cycle of love, Frederic is once
more submerged in the destructive cycle of the war; however, the love cycle now impinges upon the war cycle. Book
Three is the counterpart to Book Two; all relationships are
reversed. Frederic's relationship with Catherine is super-
seded by his duties as an officer. While he was in Milan,
Frederic was constantly being reminded of the war.
Throughout Book Three, although he is immersed in the
retreat, Frederic is continually reminded of Catherine. He
dreams of her as he dozes fitfully in his ambulance; later in
the flat-car to Milan he daydreams about her. The natural
cycle of love impinges upon the war cycle. Rinaldi is quick
to diagnose the situation when Frederic returns to Gorizia:
"You act like a married man," he tells Frederic (p. 167). At
the end of Book Three a train returns Frederic to Milan just
as at the end of Book Two a train had taken him away from
Milan; the two books stand as balanced counterparts, each
representative of its own cycle.

In Book Four of *A Farewell to Arms* the regenerative
cycle and the destructive cycle once more vie for control as

STRUCTURE 269

they did in Book One. Although the love relationship, which is a refuge against the war, has been re-established, the threat of the war is always present. There is the constant threat of arrest and execution that finally forces Frederic and Catherine to take flight up the lake to Switzerland, a counterpart to Frederic's escape into the Tagliamento river in Book Three. In Book Four, however, it is Catherine as well as Frederic who has abandoned her duties to escape into neutral territory. It is the first week in November when the two lovers row up Lake Maggiore during the hiatus between fall harvest and winter dormancy in the life cycle; in the war cycle the Italian army makes its stand on the Piave, and the fighting is about to close for the winter.

Book Five is set in the Swiss winter of 1917-1918 and begins in a manner strongly reminiscent of Book One:

> That fall the snow came very late. We lived in a brown wooden house in the pine trees on the side of the mountain and at night there was frost so that there was thin ice over the water in the two pitchers on the dresser in the morning. (p. 289)

The winter is the fallow period for the seasonal cycle, the war cycle and the love cycle. Fields wait, generals plan, and the lovers, though happy, are waiting out the gestation period as the summer-conceived fetus grows between Catherine's too narrow hips. Like the war and the fields, the lovers' sexual relationship is also dormant during the last winter months. Although the lovers are safe in their exile, they spend the winter somewhat restlessly, for the certain feeling of waiting pervades their relationship.

The spring rains begin in March, and Frederic takes Catherine into Lausanne. For three weeks they live in a hotel, waiting for Catherine's labor pains to begin. Catherine goes to the hospital the first week in April, 1918, exactly a year after she first met Frederic. Ironically, Catherine dies in the season of rebirth; as the fields regenerate in the seasonal cycle, the love cycle produces a dead baby and a dead mother. Elsewhere the war cycle resumes its destructive course; on the western front the spring offensive begins. The obvious, but no less bitter, lesson that Frederic learns in the novel is that all cycles end in death.

When Frederic and Catherine spend the day at the San Siro racetrack, Hemingway drives his point home. The races are fixed. The lovers have inside information from Meyers, but when they bet on the fixed winner, they discover that the final odds were so low that they have won very little:

"Then we won't get three thousand lire," Catherine said. "I don't like this crooked racing!"
"We'll get two hundred lire."
"That's nothing. That doesn't do us any good. I thought we were going to get three thousand."
"It's crooked and disgusting," Ferguson said.
"Of course," said Catherine, "if it hadn't been crooked we'd never have backed him at all. But I would have liked the three thousand lire." (p. 129-130)

Rather than bet on the fixed winner, Frederic and Catherine choose to back a horse they know nothing about, one "that Mr. Meyers won't be backing." They lose, of course, but they knew they would. Losing honestly makes Catherine feel cleaner.

Scott Fitzgerald found this chapter meaningless when he read the galley proofs: "Definitely dull.—it is alright [sic] to say it was meant all the time that a novel can't have the finesse of a short story but this has got to go. This scene as it is seems to me to be a shame. It's dull because the war goes further and further out of sight every minute. 'That's the way it was' is no answer. This triumphant truth that races were fixed!"[7]

Fitzgerald has missed the point. The truth that Heming-

[7] Fitzgerald to Hemingway [Spring], 1929.

way epitomizes at the fixed races was pithily stated in the title of his 1927 collection of short stories: *Winner Take Nothing*. Life is a fixed race, the conclusion of which we have always known. No matter how the bet is placed, Frederic and Catherine will lose just as surely as everyone eventually loses. The fixed race is Hemingway's metaphor for existence, and he places it immediately preceding Frederic Henry's recognition: "One always feels trapped biologically."

But the knowledge that Frederic acquires does not make *A Farewell to Arms* an initiation story, as some critics would have it.[8] Neither Frederic nor Catherine is portrayed as an innocent in Europe at the beginning of the book. Neither expresses any ideals that have become besmirched by the war. If either Frederic or Catherine has any ideals, in the sense of American pre-war ideals, they do not show them. Frederic is a cognoscente before he enlists with the Italians; he does not start innocent, and he does not end up more knowledgeable. The only object lesson is contained in the much-quoted passage: "That was what you did. You died" (p. 327).

Fitzgerald, like Perkins and Owen Wister, saw the novel as a story of war and love. Wister had written Perkins that the two major themes were not properly rejoined at the conclusion. This bothered him.[9] Perkins agreed with Wister, misunderstanding Hemingway's major theme.

Rather than being a study in war, love or initiation, *A Farewell to Arms* is more properly a study in isolation. Frederic's progress in the novel is from group participation to total isolation; this progress is the central action of the novel and defines Frederic as the central character even though he is not the "hero." When the novel begins in the fall of 1915, Frederic Henry is an ambulance driver with

---

[8] John McCormick, "Hemingway and History," *Western Review*, 17 (Winter, 1953), p. 89; Robert Penn Warren, "Hemingway," *Kenyon Review*, 9 (Winter, 1947), p. 23.
[9] Wister to Perkins, May 6, 1929.

the Italian Second Army, which was a key link in the defenses of the Italian army. The Italian front, in turn, was an extension of the western front in France; Italy was part of the alliance that placed Frederic at the end of a long chain of command. By the end of the novel Frederic is totally alone and in another country. He owes allegiance to no chain of command; he has no friends; he has no prospects.

Frederic's journey into neutral territory begins in Book One when he is wounded. As a wounded man he is separated psychologically from those soldiers who have not been wounded. Moreover, the wound separates him physically from his friends at the front. In Book Two the psychological separation is widened by his love for Catherine. Their relationship gives them an identity separate from the group identity of the war. As their relationship deepens, the institutions that have supported western civilization become increasingly meaningless to them.

The family, the military, and the church are unable to sustain Frederic and Catherine in the face of the "nada" that surrounds the war. The lovers are essentially without family. At one point (p. 154) Catherine assures Frederic that he will never have to meet her father, who has the gout. Frederic replies that he has only a stepfather, whom Catherine will never have to meet. The military itself has become bankrupt; Frederic is assailed on all sides by criticism of the military. Only Ettore, the super patriot, is a war lover. The discussion of troop mutinies and the references to "a separate peace," combined with the socialists' criticism of the war, become an indictment of the military. Frederic finds only the uniform a comfort, and finally that too becomes hollow and false. Religion has become as bankrupt as the family and the military. For Frederic and Catherine organized religion has no valid function and offers no comfort in time of need. Catherine tells Frederic that he has become her religion. Count Greffi tells Frederic that being in love is a "religious feeling" but is not religion. When Frederic and Catherine wander about Milan in the rain, they are tempted to take shelter in the Cathedral, but Catherine says that the church will not do lovers any good. On her deathbed Catherine rejects Frederic's suggestion of seeing a priest. In spite of the priest's sincere plea for the godly life, Frederic never finds the Abruzzi country, where religion has meaning.

Frederic does not realize the extent of his growing isolation until he returns to the front in Book Three. Whereas his wound had set him apart earlier from his friends, he is further isolated by his relationship with Catherine. His feelings for Catherine no longer allow him to participate with Rinaldi in the pleasures of the Villa Rosa. During the retreat from Caporetto, Frederic is sustained not by his duty as an officer but by his duty to return to Catherine. It is the thought of her that sustains him through the retreat and during the bad times on the train to Milan. During the retreat one sees the movement into isolation acted out in the narrative. When the retreat begins, Frederic is part of the Second Army. After leaving Gorizia he separates his three ambulances from the main body of the retreat. When the ambulances get stuck and the sergeant is shot, Frederic and his remaining drivers make their way on foot toward the bridgehead. One driver is killed; one driver deserts. Finally at the bridge Frederic is separated from his last driver by the military police. At the end of Book Three Frederic is totally alone in the river. Thus in the key structural chapter of the novel, Hemingway has epitomized the movement into isolation that is the central theme of the novel.

In the last two books, the isolation of Frederic is completed. At Stresa he and Catherine leave the last of their friends and acquaintances. Both have deserted their posts, and they are utterly alone against the world. Their retreat into Switzerland moves them into further isolation; it is significant that they are in neutral country, one isolated from the war. When Catherine dies in the Lausanne hospital, doctors fail just as priests failed earlier to sustain the individual in the face of death. Frederic is left totally isolated.

He has no person, no beliefs, no institutions upon which to rely. In another country, he is the truly isolated man, and the novel's central concern has been tracing out his journey into isolation.

Hemingway's theme of growing isolation is significant beyond the narrative level of the novel, and it is well to remember that Hemingway wrote *A Farewell to Arms* in retrospect. He had viewed the ten years between the end of the war and the publication of the novel with the critical eye of a practicing journalist. As Philip Young has astutely pointed out: "Something in the evolution of Frederic Henry from complicity in the war to bitterness and escape has made him seem, though always himself, a little larger than that, too. Complicity, bitterness, escape—a whole country could read its experience, Wilson to Harding, in his. . . . When historians of various kinds epitomize the temper of the American Twenties and a reason for it the adventures of that lieutenant come almost invariably to mind."[10]

In the historical sense, Frederic's experience precedes and anticipates the national experience. His rejection of the war in the fall of 1917 came at a time when the American fervor for the war was at its highest pitch. It was not until the mercenary peace treaty, the ill-fated League of Nations, and the Republican election of 1920 that the American people began to reject their former idealistic views of what the war was about. "It was but a short step to the view that America's participation in the war had been a mistake, hence that special care should be taken to avoid the recurrence of a similar situation."[11] The political course of the Twenties led America into the isolationist policy it continued until the outbreak of World War Two. Thus Frederic's escape into Switzerland, neutral and isolated during the war, becomes an image for the entire national experience of the post-war period.

[10] Philip Young, *Ernest Hemingway: A Reconsideration*, p. 90.
[11] Rene Albrecht-Carrie, *The Meaning of the First World War* (Englewood Cliffs, N.J.: Prentice-Hall, 1965), p. 138.

CONCLUSION

Everything I had written was stolen in Hadley's suitcase that
time at the Gare de Lyon when she was bringing the manuscripts down to me to Lausanne as a surprise, . . . She had
put in the originals, the typescripts and the carbons, all in
manila folders. . . . I was sure she could not have brought
the carbons too and I . . . took the train for Paris. It was
true all right and I remember what I did in the night after
I let myself into the flat and found it was true.—*A Moveable
Feast*

In early March, 1928, Hemingway began to write a story
that he had been trying to get on paper for almost ten years.
Writing was never easy for him. Writing well was the most
difficult work he knew. As Hemingway told Waldo Pierce
during that July when he was writing the novel and the
heat was ruining his head, there are no alibis in writing. No
one is interested in why a writer fails.[1] In addition to personal and financial pressures, there was the supreme pressure of his art. Hemingway was a social member of an elite
literary circle—Pound, Joyce, Stein, Fitzgerald, Ford. Although he had written some short stories that were as well
wrought as any of Joyce's, he had not yet produced a novel
of artistic stature. As he told his editor, Max Perkins, the
next novel had to be good. It would be better for him not
to publish than to publish a poorly written book.[2] Working
under such pressures, Hemingway wrote a good novel in
a very short time. Almost fifty percent of his manuscript
pages went into the final copy without revision. Such ease
is almost unbelievable, but it was not the first time that he

[1] Hemingway to Waldo Peirce, July 23, 1928.
[2] Hemingway to Max Perkins, March 17, 1928.

had attempted the novel; he had been working over the material in various forms since the winter of 1919.

When Hemingway returned from Italy to Oak Park, Illinois, in January, 1919, he had three distinct problems: he was in love with a nurse who had remained in Italy; he had returned to a family that was not ready to accept the changes of his life style; he wanted to write fiction. In the following months these problems resolved themselves in familiar patterns. The nurse wrote that theirs had been an infatuation and that she was engaged to an Italian nobleman. His mother threw him out of the house, albeit a summer house. He was left with his desire to write and a small unearned income. Like all Red Cross ambulance drivers, Hemingway had been covered by a Travelers Insurance Company policy that paid him for the leg wounds he had sustained in the line of duty. Between November, 1918, and October, 1919, Hemingway collected $1,398.76, roughly $116 a month.[3] This money allowed him to spend his first year without visible means of support. During that fall and winter in Petoskey, Michigan, he began to write his first serious fiction. Little remains or is known about these stories. Speculation is, however, possible.

Knowing Hemingway's later habit of using geographic locations that he had experienced, we can make the reasonable assumption that this early novel was set in Italy and based on his experience there, particularly his unhappy love affair with his Red Cross nurse. The war was, in fact, his only adult experience at that point and it would have been surprising if the novel had been about anything else.

One of Hemingway's friends that winter in Petoskey was Edwin G. Pailthorp, to whom Hemingway related wild stories about the toughness of the Italian Arditi, as well as romantic stories about his military and sexual adventures in Italy. When *A Farewell to Arms* was published in 1929, Hemingway autographed a presentation copy.

[3] American Red Cross Archives, Hemingway File.

For Dutch Pailthorp to whom I told this story in the
winter of 1919-1920 in Petoskey, Michigan.
                              from his old friend
                              Ernie Hemingway[4]

"This story" was probably the same one that Hemingway
was turning into a novel—the novel that traveled with him
to Paris via Toronto. In 1922 Hadley lost the manuscript in
the Paris train station when a thief stole her suitcase. This
manuscript was the *Ur-Farewell*.

Years later Mrs. Hadley Richardson Mowrer admitted
that she had never read the manuscripts. Hemingway
worked on them in a separate rented room and did not discuss them with her. "I saw nothing or very little of it," she
said. "It was sacred to himself—consequently the loss,
through my misadventure, was deadly to him." In retrospect, Mrs. Mowrer did not think there had been a novel in
the lost suitcase, but the manuscript would not have been
of novel length at that time. As she remembered it, most of
the stories were concerned with the early adventures of
Nick Adams. When asked if she thought that Hemingway
ever tried to reconstruct any of the lost material, she replied: "He did strive to dig parts of it out of the back of his
mind. How successfully I do not know as I never saw a
completed work about this young man Nick Adams. I continue to feel that it was not to be a novel—autobiography
rather."[5]

One of those attempts at reconstruction was begun
June 15, 1925. The twenty-six-page fragment was called
"Along with Youth a Novel," which Hemingway never pub-
lished. As in the lost manuscript, the central character is
Nick Adams and, as Mrs. Mowrer suspected, the story is
highly autobiographical. Nick follows Hemingway's earlier

[4] Constance Montgomery, *Hemingway in Michigan* (New York:
Fleet, 1966), photograph, n.p.
[5] Mrs. Paul Scott Mowrer to MSR, May 14, 1970.

path to the European war on board the *Chicago*. His companions are taken directly from life: two Polish officers, Leon Chocianowicz, Anton Galinski; and The Carper, the nickname for Howell Jenkins, a Red Cross driver who served with Hemingway in Section Four. The fragment begins late in the war; The Carper has already served two years, returned to the States, and is now going back for a second tour. Nick has not been to the war, and he is not sure how he will react. As he and Chocianowicz sip wine in a davited lifeboat, Nick worries about fear:

> "I wonder if I'll be scared," he [Nick] said.
> "No," Leon said. "I don't think so."
> "It will be fun to see all the planes and that stuff."
> "Yes," said Leon. "I am going to fly as soon as I can transfer."
> "I couldn't do that."
> "Why not?"
> "I don't know."
> "You mustn't think about being scared."
> "I don't. Really I don't. I never worry about it. I just thought because it made me feel funny coming out onto the boat just now."
> Leon lay on his side, the bottle straight up beside his head.
> "We don't have to think about being scared," he said. "We're not that kind."
> "The Carper's scared," Nick said.
> "Yes. Galinsky told me."
> "That's what he was sent back for. That's why he's drunk all the time."
> "He's not like us," Leon said. "Listen, Nick. You and me, we've got something in us."
> "I know. I feel that way. Other people can get killed but not me. I feel that absolutely."[6]

---

[6] Ernest Hemingway, "Night Before Landing," edited by Philip Young in *The Nick Adams Stories*, pp. 141-142.

Superficially, these fears sound similar to those of Frederic Henry before his wounding:

> I wish I was with the British. It would have been much
> simpler. Still I would probably have been killed. Not in
> this ambulance business. Yes, even in the ambulance
> business. British ambulance drivers were killed
> sometimes. Well, I knew I would not be killed. Not in
> this war. It did not have anything to do with me. (p. 37)

There is a significant difference between the fears of Nick Adams and Frederic Henry. Nick has no experience in the war; his are the fears of the unknown. Frederic has been at the Italian front for two years; he has seen what war can do.

Ten days after Hemingway began the fragment, he and Hadley packed their bags for the trip to Pamplona that would provide the background for *The Sun Also Rises*. He never returned to the *Chicago* and Nick's voyage to the war. Although he wrote other Nick Adams stories about the war, Nick's experiences there do not overlap significantly with Frederic's except that both are wounded and both had an affair with a nurse in Italy.

Set in 1918, the "Ur-Farewell" would not have used the Caporetto retreat (1917), which is the structural and thematic key to *A Farewell to Arms*. Moreover, Nick Adams could never have been Frederic Henry. He would have been younger, less experienced, and certainly less cosmopolitan than Frederic. The action of the "Ur-Farewell" would also have been different. The present Books One and Three of *A Farewell to Arms*, treating the early war years and the Caporetto disaster, would not have been in the lost novel, for they took place historically before 1918. Books Four and Five, treating the escape to Switzerland and Catherine's pregnancy, could have been in the lost novel, but it is unlikely that they would have been there in their present form. The lost fragment was written before Hemingway had any firsthand experience with the psychology of pregnant women.

As late as the summer of 1925, Hemingway was still trying to write *A Farewell to Arms* with a 1918 setting. Yet, he indicated that the published version of *A Farewell to Arms* was the same story that he told Pailthorp in the winter of 1919-1920, when he was contemplating the "Ur-Farewell." There can be only one section of *A Farewell to Arms* that overlapped with the "Ur-Farewell" and that is Book Two— the love affair between Frederic and Catherine, including Frederic's wounding. The "Ur-Farewell" probably followed Hemingway's own experiences rather closely, including his relationship with Agnes Von Kurowsky. This would put the "Ur-Farewell" closer to "A Very Short Story," which was published in 1924 and which might be seen as another attempt by Hemingway to retrieve some of the lost material. In that short story, the relationship between the wounded soldier and the friendly nurse ends sardonically, indicating the residual bitterness Hemingway felt for Agnes and their aborted relationship.

When Hemingway returned to the plot of *A Farewell to Arms* three years later in 1928, his attitude toward his material had changed considerably from the period of the "Ur-Farewell." The bitterness toward Agnes had disappeared, for it does not touch the characterization of Catherine Barkley. Frederic Henry bears little or no resemblance to Nick Adams. During the three-year break, Hemingway wrote a lightweight satire and his *roman à clef, The Sun Also Rises*. When he returned to his war novel, he chose purposely not to repeat himself, although he could have continued to write satirical exposé, as evidenced in *A Moveable Feast*. At some point between 1925-1928, he came to realize that Caporetto was the key to the war in Italy and that he must take that disaster into account if his novel was going to last. By the time he came to plan the novel, he knew of the precedent set by Stephen Crane in *Red Badge of Courage* of inventing seemingly firsthand experience, and he realized the potential of the reading he had begun years before on the Italian war.

Hemingway's historical reading in the early Twenties was motivated by his desire to understand the war and his own experience there. Once he realized what he would do with his historical knowledge, he either made notes or found copies of the books that he had possibly read earlier. He then located accurate topographic maps of northern Italy and the other aids that we know he must have used in writing the novel. All of this he must have done before March of 1928, when he actually began writing *A Farewell to Arms*.

In a larger sense, Hemingway the artist was always chasing yesterdays, as he did with Hadley that summer at Fossalta, when he searched in vain for the war he had known. Unlike Colonel Cantwell, Hemingway was unable to fix the exact location of his wounding. Fossalta had lost the dignity of its ravagement, and the battlefield itself had gone soft and green. Trenches had disappeared; wire had been removed. Throughout his feature article "Veteran Returns to Old Front," there is a kind of anger that is more than frustrated nostalgia, for one feels that his ritualistic return was his attempt to make sense out of the trauma of his wounding.

Eventually his search for meaning took Hemingway beyond his own experience in the war. From Stendahl's *Charterhouse* and Crane's *Red Badge*, he learned the fictional importance of disaster. Through his historical reading he discovered that the key to the war in Italy was the disaster at Caporetto. At the military level, Caporetto was the obvious conclusion to the two bloody years of Cadorna's mountain campaign. Moreover, Caporetto influenced or motivated everything that came after it on the battlefield. It defined the battle lines of 1918, and it colored the entire Italian war effort. Vittorio Veneto was a smashing victory for Italy. It was as if recapturing the land brought back the national honor that had been lost at Caporetto. To write about the war in Italy, Hemingway discovered he could not avoid Caporetto.

He came to realize that the implications of Caporetto went beyond the battlefield and beyond even the national honor, about which the Italians had become so hysterical. Ultimately, Caporetto stood for the entire war experience, and that experience was defeat. Nations may have won or lost at the military and political level, but the individual soldier in the trenches experienced finally a kind of defeat that had little to do with occupied territory or victorious battles. It was a defeat of the spirit epitomized in the French mutinies of 1917, the Russian October revolution of 1917, and the Italian disaster at Caporetto in 1917. On every front soldiers were experiencing what they would finally come to understand—that the war was a defeat, no matter who won.

It is this concept of defeat which informs the action of *A Farewell to Arms*. Frederic Henry's desertion epitomizes the experience of the individual, regardless of nationality. His desertion is the most rational choice he makes, and it becomes a radical political statement indicating the national goals that had failed to sustain the individual. Frederic Henry's desertion is not that of an American deserting on a "joke front"; it is rather the final conclusion drawn by a war generation who finally understood what their experience had meant. Some discovered such a truth in the trenches during the war; others discovered it in war prisons or in front of firing squads. Hemingway did not finally understand until ten years after the war. At the mercy of deterministic forces, Frederic Henry retreats further and further into isolation in order to survive. But it is a Pyrrhic victory, for he has lost all that he values in this world. In terms of 1929, Frederic's experience is an accurate barometric reading of our political attitudes. As Edmund Wilson said in 1941, Hemingway's "whole work is a criticism of society: he has responded to every pressure of the moral atmosphere of the time, as it is felt at the roots of human relations."[7]

As all good children of the "New Critics" know, the text must stand alone. Whatever the author's intentions may have been, the work is self-contained with its own rationale. Productive as this approach has been, it has also been misleading to second-generation critics of Hemingway. All too often they have not mastered the tools that their teachers abandoned because they had grown dull. Emerson could advise the American scholar that he need not read books to study Nature, but only after Emerson had read all the books. Now that the first half of the twentieth century is no longer the "modern age," but an historical period of its own, it is time for critics to relearn the use of old tools. The vein of psychoanalytic exegesis has been overworked. The misleading thesis that Hemingway is always his own protagonist has littered the critical landscape with so much debris that it will take another generation of critics to restore the ecology. Letters, manuscripts, source reading, social milieu, and literary biography must all be brought to bear on the published text. Hemingway's reading is as important to his art as that of Coleridge; his textual revisions are as significant as those of Keats. With Hemingway it is time to question constructively all of the explications we have inherited. We must begin the difficult and frequently tedious search for the hard data that will support, modify, or disprove our inheritance.

[7] Edmund Wilson, "Hemingway: Gauge of Morale," reprinted in *Eight Essays* (Garden City: Doubleday and Co., 1954), p. 113.

Time Table for the Writing of the First Draft

1928

DATE	PLACE	PROGRESS
early March	Paris	begins manuscript
April 7	Key West	"hard at work"
April 21	Key West	"ten to fifteen thousand words"
April 26	Key West	MS-108 (p. 45)
June 7	Piggot, Ark.	MS-279 (p. 138)
June 17	Kansas City, Mo.	MS-311 (p. 159)
July 15	Kansas City	MS-457 (p. 228)
July 22	Piggot, Ark.	MS-477 (p. 243)
July 23	Piggot	MS-486 (p. 248)
July 30	Sheridan, Wyoming	
August 7	Sheridan	MS-543 (p. 279)
August 8	Sheridan	MS-548 (p. 281)
August 9	Sheridan	MS-557 (p. 285)
August 10	Sheridan	MS-563 (p. 291)
August 11	Sheridan	MS-573 (p. 296)
August 12	Sheridan	MS-575 (p. 297)
August 13	Sheridan	MS-581 (p. 300)
August 14	Sheridan	MS-585 (p. 305)
August 15	Sheridan	no progress
August 16	Sheridan	MS-599 (p. 310)
August 17	Sheridan	MS-616 (p. 316)
August 18, 19	Sheridan	no progress
August 20	Sheridan	MS-631 (p. 323)
August 21, 22	Sheridan	MS-650 (p. 331)

Rejected First Drafts, Sample Variant Endings, and Titles

Rejected First Drafts

MSS-168-170

"You love god like that?"

"I love god. I really love him with all my heart."

"More than anything else?"

"More than anything else."

~~He was serious~~

"That's a fine thing."

"You don't love him?"

"No. I guess not."

"You don't love anything?"

"Yes. I love a lot of things."

"What are they?"

"I don't know. Lots of things."

"What?"

I thought a minute.

"The night. The day. Food. Drink. Girls. Italy. Pictures. Places. Swimming. Portofino. Paris. Spring. Summer. Fall. Winter. Heat. Cold. Smells. Sleep. Newspapers. Reading." This all sounds better in Italian. (MS-169)

"You'll lose them all."

"And you'll never lose god."

"No."

"Because you'll never get him."

"How do you mean?"

"I don't want to talk. I don't want to try and shake your faith."

He laughed suddenly and kept on laughing. "That's very funny. Why I laughed was because I felt very bad because I was afraid I shake your faith." He stood up. "You make me remember

what I believe. I must go. I've stayed too long. You must get well
and come back quickly."

"Do you have to go?"

"Yes I must go." He was shy again but he took my hand.
"Do you want me for anything?"

"No. Just to talk."

He put on his cap and picked the bottle from the floor and
put it on the chair by the/ MS-170/ bed.

"Goodbye. I take your greetings to the mess."

"Thank you for the many fine presents."

"Nothing."

"Ciaou!"

"Ciaou!"

It was dark in the room and the orderly who had sat by the
foot of the bed, got up and went out with him. I liked him very
much and I wondered how he would get back to Gorizia. I had
forgotten to ask. He could ride on a camion or perhaps he had
come on a bicycle. He had a rotten life at the mess. I thought
about the things I had said I loved and added many more. I found
I loved god too, a little. I did not love anything too much.

[These three pages marked "Eliminated" in Hemingway's hand.]
MSS-202-209

Read to here Thursday
Dec. 13, going better
so far

[First Draft]

She came over to the bed.

"Hello Darling," she said. She looked fresh and young and
lovely and beautiful.

"Hello," I said. "Hello Katherine." I couldn't say anything
more. I realized I had forgotten all about her.

She stood there very lovely and beautiful and she looked
toward the door, saw there was no one and stooped over the bed
and kissed me. I put my arms around her and held her to really
feel she was there in my arms and felt her heart beating and
~~smelled her held her so I felt all her~~ kissed her. We had come
together as though we were two pieces of mercury that unite to
make one. ~~We felt like the same person.~~ I felt that way when I felt
her heart beating. We were one person.

"You love," she said.

"Do you feel our heart?" I asked. Her cheek rested on mine and was very soft and cool.

"It's just the same," she said.

"We're all the same thing," I said. "I didn't know it before."

"I did." She straightened up and brought a chair and sat beside the bed. I felt as though/ MS-203/ all of me had gone away. "I'm right here," she said. "Poor darling." She touched me and I held my hand there.

"I didn't know about it before," I said.

~~"You're slower than I am," she said.~~

"Didn't you really?"

"No. I didn't know about anything. Please come back. Come back to the bed."

MS-202 cont.

She touched my arm very lightly. "I can't. I'll do anything. But I can't have them sending me away."

"I'll go with you."

"You can't yet. But maybe we will."

"It's wonderful to have you here," I said. "You were wonderful to get here."

"I must be very good and you must be very careful before other people."

"Please. Come just once."

She smiled, stood up, went to the door and looked down the corridor then came to the bed ~~very softly~~ and was in my arms. When she was gone I knew that there was nothing else that mattered. I had not been in love with her before but I was now. / MS-204/

Before she left she said, "I have to go downstairs now. They may try to send me to another hospital."

"They can't."

"I'll try not to let them but Miss Van Campen doesn't care for me."

"She doesn't like me either."

"I'll have to be very good."

"You might be nice to her. ~~She'll send me away if~~ It wouldn't hurt perhaps."

"I will."

"I have to go."

"Kiss me."

"No. I must practice going. Goodbye Mr. Henry." She smiled and touched me with her hand. "It's very pleasant to see an old friend."

"Come back."

"No. Goodbye Mr. Henry."

"Goodbye Miss Barkley," I said.

She stooped suddenly over the bed and kissed me.

"Dear dear darling," she said. Then she was gone out / MS-205/ the door and I heard her go down the corridor. ~~Then I was alone.~~ When I could not hear her footsteps any longer I was alone and it was the first time I had ever felt really alone. I had not meant to fall in love with Katherine Barkley. ~~I did not want to be with anyone and now that it had come I did not care about anything except to see her again. When you have not known that two people can be one person~~

I had kissed her before and we had made love and it was like people speaking parts in a bad play. I had kissed her and enjoyed it and been excited by it and ~~my mind had~~ thought of other things while it was happening. Then, just now, she had come in the room, come to the bed, and ~~suddenly with nothing happening we had come together like two drops of quicksilver.~~ Suddenly we were the two parts of the same person/ MS-206/ and now she was gone away down the corridor ~~and a big part of me was gone with her~~. I felt as though all of me was gone away with her. The funny thing was I wanted her back. I wanted her in the room. I wanted her to come to the bed so I could feel that she was there and not be alone. It is bad when a woman can leave a room and make you feel that she has taken the whole world with her. I lay there on the bed and wanted her to come back. The world had always been a fine place for me. I saw the things there were to see and felt the things that happened and did not worry ~~very much~~ about the rest./ MS-207/

There were always plenty of things to see and something always happened. You needed a certain amount of money and you did not need the ~~clap~~ gonorrhea but if you had no money and had the gonorrhea life was still quite possible. ~~It was fun~~ I liked to drink and liked to eat and ~~there was an appetite for all things and things for the appetite~~ liked nearly everything. The war was bad but not bad for me because it was not my war but I could see

how bad it would become. That is I was beginning to see how
bad it could become. But it had not ~~touched~~ hit me yet. Although
I found that when it really ~~touched~~ hit people they usually did
not last long, ~~which was perhaps a gift.~~ I suppose that was a gift
to them maybe. But if you can be made/ MS-208/ happy by cavalry along a road in the woods or ~~the water coming out falling
from~~ it raining and the rain coming out of the gargoyles of the
cathedral or by two drinks or by a girl that costs only fifty lire and
loves you all night long ~~and in the morning has no claim after the
fifty lires are paid except, possibly, breakfast.~~ Then if you find
in one day that you ~~need another person~~ are no solider than a
postcard that is torn in two and half of it is another person, that
nothing makes you happy unless the two halves of the postcard
are together, that there is really nothing unless the two halves are
together—that you go along and do not see things anymore. Or if
you do see you do not enjoy them because the other ~~half~~ one/
MS-209/ is not there—then if you have formerly enjoyed ~~things~~
nearly everything by yourself, then you show a certain interest in
keeping the two halves of the postcard together. Anyhow I lay
in the bed in the room of the hospital in Milan and finally Miss
Gage came in.

"The doctor's coming," she said. "He telephoned from Lake
Como."

"When does he get here?"

"He'll be here this afternoon."

New Chapter

Nothing happened that afternoon. The doctor was a little
quiet man who seemed disturbed by the war. He took out a number of small steel splinters from my thigh with ~~a great~~ delicacy
and refined distaste. He used a local anaesthetic called something
or other snow which froze the tissue until the probe, the scalpel
or the forceps got below the frozen portion. The anaesthetized
area was clearly defined by the patient and after a time the
doctor's fragile delicacy was exhausted and he said it would be
better to have an X Ray. Probing was unsatisfactory, he said.

NOTE: If one is determined to find biographical sources for this
scene, I suggest that Hemingway's relationship with Pauline

Pffeifer before he divorced Hadley Richardson is probably more relevant than his relationship with Agnes Von Kurowsky in 1918.

[First Revision]

Bottom of 201

He went out and I heard him laughing in the hall. I heard someone coming down the hallway. I looked down toward the door. It was Katherine Barkley. She came in the room and over to the bed.

"Hello darling," she said. She looked fresh and young and very beautiful.

"Hello," I said. Something had gone on all the time we had not seen each other. It had gone on the same way in both of us. I did not know about it ~~until I saw her~~ while it was happening. She looked toward the door, saw there was no one then she ~~stooped over the bed~~ sat on the side of the bed leaned over and kissed me. I held her and kissed her and felt her heart beating. But I knew about it now.

"You sweet," I said. "You were wonderful to get here."

"It wasn't very hard. It may be hard to stay."

"Feel our heart," I said.

"It's the same." (MS-202)

"We're the same," I said. "Feel. I didn't know about it before."

"I did. I knew about it when we were playing."

She got up from the bed and sat in a chair a little way away.

"Don't go away."

"I'm not."

"I didn't know about it at all," I said. "I'm awfully dumb."

"No you're not."

"Come back," I said. "Come on back to the bed."

MS-471

[deleted passage on false leave papers]

"You must tell me now."

"A Tessera," I [Frederic] said, "and leave papers."

"Write the name."

"Give me a pencil." I wrote the name on the edge of a newspaper. "Someone will call for them."

"Who?"

"I don't know. He will bring a photograph for the Tessera. You will know me by that."

"All right. That will be one hundred and fifty lira."

"Here is fifty."

"Do not worry Tenente."

"What do you say?" (MS-471)

"I say do not worry."

"I do not worry. I am not in trouble."

"You are not in trouble if you stay with me."

Sample Variant Endings

Insert page 641

In a little while the doctor who had been in the room where they had the baby came along the hall. He came over to me.

"What about the baby?" I asked.

"He's all right," he said. "We got him going."

"He's alive?"

"Of course he's alive. Who said he wasn't alive?"

"The nurse."

"She's crazy. Of course he's alive."

"Don't lie to me."

"I'm not lying to you. The baby is alive."

"Christ they shouldn't do things like that to me," I said.

"He's a fine boy," the doctor said.

"Good," I said. I had a son now. I did not know whether to really believe it or not.

(false ending with child)

There are a great many details starting with my first meeting with an undertaker and all the business of burial and continuing on with the rest of my life—which has gone on and will probably go on for a long time. I could tell about the boy. He did not seem of any importance then except as trouble and god knows I was bitter about him. Anyway he does not belong in this story. He starts a new one. It is not fair to start a new story at the end of an old one but that is the way it happens. There is no end except death and birth is the only beginning.

---

p. 323 (pagination from type script ends on 322)

You learn a few things as you go along and one of them is never to go back to places. It is a good thing too not to try too much to remember very fine things because if you do you wear them out and you lose them. A valuable thing too is never to let anyone know how fine you thought anyone else ever was because they know better and no one was ever that splendid. /324/ Also you will bore them and you learn that if you want to keep anything it is best to keep your mouth shut and not talk about it. At the start the nights are the worst times and they seem your worst enemies but in the end the nights are-

———————————

That is all there is to the story. Catherine died and you will die and I will die and that is all I can promise you.

Titles

Along with the manuscript, typescript and galleys of *A Farewell to Arms* at the Kennedy Library, there is a single, undated page of potential titles in Hemingway's handwriting. They are listed below in the order in which they appear on the page. For many of them, I have listed the source, some of which may seem unlikely. There is, however, a pattern. Hemingway seems to have been culling them from the *Oxford Book of English Verse*. It is apparent that he was looking for a title that was right for the novel, regardless of the source. Some of the sources are appropriate; others are irrelevant.

Across the middle of the page, he wrote: "shitty titles," and he asked Max Perkins for reassurance about his final choice as if he had misgivings. In 1957, when the novel was translated into German, it was published under the title *In Einem Andern Land* (*In Another Country*). The entire epigraph from *The Jew of Malta* was included in English as it is found below. This is further evidence that readers should not place undue emphasis on the novel's title, nor rely on the title's source as any sort of thematic key to its content. One must keep in mind that by 1929 the exegetical game had not yet begun in earnest, and Hemingway was not choosing a title with academic critics in mind.

TITLE	SOURCES
Love is one fervent fire Kindlit without Desire	Second stanza of Alexander Scott's "A Rondel of Love"
A World to See	Anon., "A Praise of His Lady" O Lord! it is a world to see How virtue can repair, And deck in her such honesty, Whom Nature made so fair.
Patriot's Progress The Grand Tour *The Italian Journey* The World's Room	Bunyan Anon., "Edward, Edward"

And what will ye leave to your
      bairns and your wife,
  When ye gang owre the sea, O?
'The warld's room: let them beg
      through life

Disorder and Early Sorrow	Thomas Mann
An Italian Chronicle	
The Time Exchanged	
Death Once Dead	? William Drummond, "Spring Bereaved"

Bud doth the rose and daisy,
  winter done;
But we, once dead, no more do
  see the sun.
? Donne's "Death be not proud"

They who get Shot	? *He Who Gets Slapped*
The Italian Experience	

Education of the Flesh	These four titles all play off of
The Carnal Education	Flaubert's *L'Education Senti-*
The Sentimental Education of	*mentale*
Frederick Henry	
The Sentimental Education	

Love in Italy	
Love in War	
I have committed fornication	Marlowe, *The Jew of Malta*
but that was *In Another Country*	
And Besides the wench is dead.	
Sorrow For Pleasure	? Anon., "Icarus"

Blinded they into folly run and
      grief for pleasure take.

A Farewell to Arms	George Peele, "A Farewell to Arms"
Late Wisdom	George Crabbe poem, "Late Wisdom"

The Enchantment	Thomas Otway poem, "The Enchantment"
If You Must Love	Elizabeth Barrett Browning, iv, *Sonnets from the Portuguese* If thou must love me, let it be for naught Except for love's sake only.
World Enough and Time *In Praise of His Mistress*	Both of these from Marvell's "To His Coy Mistress"
Every Day and All	Anon. poem, "A Lyke-Wake Dirge" This ae nighte, this ae nighte, —*Every nighte and alle* Fire and sleet and candle-lighte *And Christe receive thy saule*
Of Wounds and Other Causes *The Retreat From Italy* *As Others Are*	? Earl of Rochester, "Constancy" I cannot change as others do

The italicized titles were underlined by Hemingway.

I. Primary Published Source Material

Hemingway, Ernest M. *A Farewell to Arms*. Scribner Library edition. New York: Scribner's, 1957.
————. *A Moveable Feast*. New York: Scribner's, 1964.
————. *By-Line: Ernest Hemingway*. Ed. William White. New York: Scribner's, 1967.
————. "Homage to Ezra." *This Quarter*, 1 (Spring, 1925), 221-225.
————. "How to Be Popular in Peace." *Toronto Star Weekly*, March 13, 1920, p. 11.
————. "Introduction." *A Farewell to Arms*. Illustrated edition. New York: Scribner's, 1948.
————. "Italy—1927." *New Republic*, 50 (May 8, 1927), 350-353.
————, ed. *Men at War*. New York: Crown Publishers, 1942.
————. "Monologue to the Maestro: A High Seas Letter." *Esquire*, 4 (Oct., 1935), 21, 174a-174b.
————. *The Nick Adams Stories*. Ed. Philip Young. New York: Scribner's, 1972.
————. *The Short Stories of Ernest Hemingway*. New York: Scribner's, 1953.
————. *The Torrents of Spring*. New York: Scribner's, 1926.
————. "A Veteran Visits Old Front." *Toronto Daily Star*, July 22, 1922, p. 7.
————. *The Wild Years*. Ed. Gene Z. Hanrahan. New York: Dell Publishing Co., 1962.

II. Biographical Source Material

Baker, Carlos. *Ernest Hemingway: A Life Story*. New York: Scribner's, 1969.

Baker, Carlos. "Hemingway's Italia." *NYTBR*, January 23, 1966, p. 2.

Brumback, Theodore. "With Hemingway Before *A Fare-well to Arms*." *Kansas City Star*, Dec. 6, 1936, pp. 1C-2C.

Dawson, William Forrest. "Ernest Hemingway: Petoskey Interview." *Michigan Alumnus Quarterly Review*, 64 (Winter, 1958), 114-123.

Fenton, Charles. *The Apprenticeship of Ernest Hemingway*. New York: Farrar, Straus, 1954.

Hemingway, Leicester. *My Brother, Ernest Hemingway*. Cleveland: World Publishing Company, 1962.

Hickok, Guy. "Hemingway First Lives Wild Stories Then He Writes Them." *Brooklyn Daily Eagle*, May 17, 1925, p. 12.

Montgomery, Constance C. *Hemingway in Michigan*. New York: Fleet, 1966.

Moravia, Albert. "The Ghost of Hemingway." *Atlas*, 11 (1966), 337-340.

Plimpton, George. "The Art of Fiction, xxi: Ernest Hemingway." *Paris Review*, 5 (Spring, 1958), 60-89.

Sanford, Marcelline Hemingway. *At the Hemingways: A Family Portrait*. Boston: Little, Brown, 1962.

III. Historical Source Material

Albrecht-Carrie, Rene. *The Meaning of the First World War*. Englewood Cliffs, N.J.: Prentice-Hall, 1965.

Anon. "Enemy Wiles on the Italian Front." *London Times*, Nov. 5, 1917, p. 2.

Anon. "The Great Austro-German Drive Into Italy." *The Sphere*, 71 (Nov. 3, 1917), 100.

Anon. "History of the War." *Fortnightly Review*, 108 (1917), 154.

Anon. "Packed Roads." *London Times*, Nov. 7, 1917, p. 2.

Baedeker, Karl. *Guide to Italy*. New York: Scribner's, 1932.

————. *Guide to Italy*. New York: Scribner's, 1928.

————. *Northern Italy*. New York: Scribner's, 1913.

Bakewell, Charles. *The Story of the American Red Cross in Italy*. New York: Macmillan, 1920.

Dalton, Hugh. *With British Guns in Italy*. London: Methuen, 1919.

Edmonds, Sir James E. *Military Operations Italy 1915-1919*. London: H. M. Stationery Office, 1949.

Falls, Cyril. *The Battle of Caporetto*. Philadelphia: J. B. Lippincott, 1966.

Fenton, Charles. "Ambulance Drivers in France and Italy." *AQ*, 3 (1951), 326-343.

Hereford, William R. "First on the Honor Roll." *Red Cross Magazine*, 13, no. 2 (Nov., 1918), 10-13.

Horne, C. F., and W. F. Austin, eds. *The Great Events of the Great War*. 5 vols. New York: The National Alumni, 1920.

Johnson, D. W. *Battlefields of the World War*. American Geographical Society Research Series No. 3. New York: Oxford University Press, 1921.

Lachouque, Henry. *Napoleon's Battles*. Trans. Roy Monkcom. London: George Allen & Unwin Ltd., 1966.

Lefebvre, Georges. *Napoleon: From Tilsit to Waterloo*. Trans. J. E. Anderson. New York: Columbia University Press, 1969.

McEntee, Gerald L. *Military History of the World War*. New York: Scribner's, 1937.

Oliver, Dame Beryl. *The British Red Cross in Action*. London: Faber, 1966.

Page, Thomas N. *Italy and the Great War*. New York: Scribner's, 1920.

Price, G. Ward. "The Italians at Bay." *Century*, 73 (1917), 635-652.

Report of the Department of Military Affairs. Rome: [N.P.] 1919.

Reports by the Joint War Committee of the British Red Cross Society . . . 1914-1919. London: [N.P.] 1921.

Seth, Ronald. *Caporetto*. London: Macdonald, 1965.

Speranza, Gino. *The Diary of Gino Speranza*. Ed. F. C. Speranza, 2 vols. New York: Columbia University Press, 1941.

Villari, Luigi. *The War on the Italian Front*. London: Cobden-Sanderson, 1932.

Ward, Robert De C. "Weather Controls Over the Fighting in the Italian War Zone." *The Scientific Monthly*, 6 (Feb., 1918), 98-105.

IV. Critical Source Material

Antonini, Giacomo. "*Addio alle Armi* Venticinque Anni Dopo." *La Fiera Letteraria*, 9, no. 1 (March 21, 1954), 1-2.

Baker, Carlos. *Hemingway and His Critics*. New York: Hill and Wang, 1961.

———. *Hemingway: The Writer as Artist*. 4th ed. Princeton, N.J.: Princeton University Press, 1972.

Baker, Sheridan. *Ernest Hemingway*. New York: Holt, Rinehart, 1967.

Benson, Jackson J. *Hemingway: The Writer's Art of Self-Defense*. Minneapolis: University of Minnesota Press, 1969.

Canby, Henry S. "Chronicle and Comment." *Bookman*, 70 (Feb., 1930), 644.

Cowley, Malcolm. "Not Yet Demobilized." *NYHTBR*, Oct. 6, 1929, p. 6.

———, ed. *Viking Portable Hemingway*. New York: Viking Press, 1944.

Fadiman, Clifton. "A Fine American Novel." *Nation*, 129 (Oct. 30, 1929), 498.

Gerstenberger, Donna. "The Waste Land in *A Farewell to Arms*." *MLN*, 76 (Jan., 1961), 24-25.

Grebstein, Sheldon. *Hemingway's Craft*. Carbondale: Southern Illinois University Press, 1973.

Gurko, Leo. *Ernest Hemingway and the Pursuit of Heroism.* New York: Crowell, 1968.

Halliday, E. M. "Hemingway's Ambiguity: Symbolism and Irony." *AL*, 28 (March, 1956), 1-22.

Hanneman, Audre. *Ernest Hemingway: A Comprehensive Bibliography.* Princeton: Princeton University Press, 1967.

Herrick, Robert. "What is Dirt." *Bookman*, 70 (November, 1929), 258-262.

Hovey, Richard B. *Hemingway: The Inward Terrain.* Seattle: University of Washington Press, 1968.

———. "*The Torrents of Spring*: Prefigurations in the Early Hemingway." *CE*, 26 (March, 1965), 460-464.

Hutchinson, Percy. "Love and War in the Pages of Mr. Hemingway." *NYTBR*, Sept. 29, 1929, p. 5.

Keeler, Clinton. "*A Farewell to Arms*: Hemingway and Peele." *MLN*, 76 (Nov., 1961), 622-625.

Lewis, Robert W. *Hemingway on Love.* Austin: University of Texas Press, 1965.

Light, James F. "The Religion of Death in *A Farewell to Arms*." *MFS*, 7 (Summer, 1961), 169-173.

Linat, Carlo. *Scrittori anglo-americani d'oggi.* 2nd ed. Milan: Corticelli, 1944.

McCormick, John. "Hemingway and History." *Western Review*, 17 (Winter, 1953).

Marcus, Fred H. "The Impact of Irony and the Irrational." *EJ*, 51 (Nov., 1962), 527-535.

Marion, Denis. "L'Adieu aux Armes." *Nouvelle Revue Francaise*, 41 (Oct., 1933), 632.

Morra, Umberto. "*A Farewell to Arms* di Ernest Hemingway." *Solaria*, 2 (1930), rpt. in *Antologia di Solaria.* ed. Enzo Siciliano. Milan: Editore Lerici, 1958, pp. 377-380.

Praz, Mario. "Hemingway in Italy." *Partisan Review*, 15 (Oct., 1948), 1086-1100.

Rossi, Alberto. "Ernest Hemingway e la guerra italiana." *Nuova Stampa*, Anno 10, Num. 261 (Nov. 2, 1954), 3.

Rovit, Earl. *Ernest Hemingway.* New Haven: Twayne Publishers, 1963.

Russell, H. K. "The Catharsis in *A Farewell to Arms.*" *MFS*, 1 (Aug., 1955), 25-30.

Sarason, Bertram D. *Hemingway and the Sun Set.* Washington: NCR, 1972.

Stendhal. *The Charterhouse of Parma.* Trans. C. K. Scott Moncrieff. Garden City, N.Y.: Doubleday, 1956.

Stephens, Robert O. *Hemingway's Nonfiction.* Chapel Hill: University of North Carolina Press, 1968.

————. "Hemingway and Stendhal: The Matrix of *A Farewell To Arms.*" *PMLA*, 88 (March, 1973), 271-280.

Warren, Robert Penn. "Hemingway." *Kenyon Review*, 9 (Winter, 1947), 1-28.

West, R. B., and R. W. Stallman. *The Art of Modern Fiction.* New York: Rinehart, 1949.

Wylder, Delbert E. *Hemingway's Heroes.* Albuquerque: University of New Mexico Press, 1969.

Young, Philip. *Ernest Hemingway: A Reconsideration.* revised ed. New York: Harcourt Brace, 1966.

Young, Philip, and Mann, Charles W. "Fitzgerald's *Sun Also Rises*: Notes and Comment." *Fitzgerald/Hemingway Annual.* Washington: NCR, 1970, pp. 1-9.

————. *The Hemingway Manuscripts, An Inventory.* University Park: Pennsylvania State University Press, 1969.

Zumalde, Ignacio. "La novela de guerra." *Nuestro Tiempo.* 36 (June, 1957), 749-753.